Making sense of tyra

Making sense of tyranny
Interpretations of totalitarianism

Simon Tormey

ıchester University Press
ıester and New York

Distributed exclusively in the USA and Canada by St. Martin's Press

Published by Manchester University Press
Oxford Road, Manchester M13 9NR, UK
and Room 400, 175 Fifth Avenue, New York, NY 10010, USA

Distributed exclusively in the USA and Canada
by St. Martin's Press, Inc., 175 Fifth Avenue, New York,
NY 10010, USA

British Library Cataloguing-in-Publication Data
A catalogue record for this book is available from the British Library

Library of Congress Cataloging-in-Publication Data
Tormey, Simon, 1963–
    Making sense of tyranny : interpretations of totalitarianism /
Simon Tormey.
        p. cm.
    Includes bibliographical references.
    ISBN 0-7190-3641-0. — ISBN 0-7190-4594-0 (pbk.)
    1. Totalitarianism.   I. Title.
    HC481.T62   1995
    320.5'3—dc20   94-31958

ISBN 0 7190 3641 0 *hardback*
     0 7190 4594 0 *paperback*

Photoset in Linotron Sabon
by Northern Phototypesetting Co. Ltd, Bolton

Printed in Great Britain
by Bell & Bain Ltd, Glasgow

Contents

Acknowledgements

I would like to thank, first, Neil Harding, Professor of Politics at University College, Swansea, for his help over many years. Although not directly involved in this project, as the supervisor of the thesis upon which much of this work is based his guidance was invaluable. I have also benefited from the advice and comments of David McLellan, Charlie Jeffrey and John McClelland. Thanks also to Richard Purslow, politics editor at Manchester University Press, who provided much positive advice on various aspects of this project as well as 'keeping the faith'. Peter Morriss of Liverpool University also cast a very helpful eye over some of this material, and his comments, suggestions and encouragement were particularly useful at an important stage. Finally, I should express thanks to my wife Véronique for putting up with me and my infernal tapping. I would like to dedicate this work to her in the hope that she will carry on doing so.

Introduction

It is now almost sixty years since the concept of totalitarianism was first used to describe the apparently novel forms of dictatorship that emerged in Europe between the wars. The term was thought by many to convey well the belief that in the twentieth century a new and more horrifying form of tyranny had been born. The regimes of Hitler, Stalin and to a lesser extent Mussolini seemed to mark a radical departure from the dictatorships and tyrannies of an earlier age. To begin with they were all based on movements with a clear ideological goal to achieve. These leaders were motivated not merely by the desire for power or wealth, although they arguably craved that as well, but by the desire to sweep away the sick and decaying old order and replace it with an entirely new form of society. In short, they had 'positive' goals they wished to achieve, going beyond the merely 'negative' goal of retaining power for themselves or a select elite. Furthermore, advances in science and technology appeared to have increased enormously the potential for the control and surveillance of whole populations. The growth of literacy, the development of mass communications and information technology appeared to give regimes a much greater leverage on the thoughts and actions of all those subject to their rule. The image of millions of people participating in torch-lit rallies, parades celebrating victory over some enemy real or imagined and the crowds of people saluting some distant despot, seemed to confirm that a radical leap forward had occurred in the capacity of regimes to manipulate those subject to them. These familiar images showed the enormous increase in the scope and power of the state over the now 'defenceless' individual. The concept of totalitarianism was, and to a large extent still is, an expression of the belief that a new, more virile form of dictatorship has emerged in the twentieth century. It is the expression of fear, a fear of the power of despots to control and co-ordinate the lives of millions of people by brainwashing and indoctrination.

Almost as soon as the concept of totalitarianism had become established in the 1950s and 1960s as a tool for the analysis of modern dictatorship it became, however, the subject of intense criticism. These criticisms tended to take three forms. On the one hand there are those who question the manner in which the concept has been applied. It was at first generally accepted that the regimes of Hitler and Stalin must be considered totalitarian, and they seemed to be the prototypes for this new, more virulent strain of tyranny. Yet many historians of the regimes and periods concerned deny that they can be considered totalitarian at all. An intense and often acrimonious debate within particular area specialisms has arisen about whether the concept of totalitarianism has any application. Historians have typically questioned the amount of power able to be wielded by Hitler and Stalin, the nature of relations within the state apparatus presented by the totalitarian model, and the account of the relationship between such regimes and the people who live under them. Yet many of these disputes remain unresolved, and not only as concerns Nazi Germany and Stalin's Russia, the two most often identified as being totalitarian. It is safe to say that there is not a single regime or system that has been labelled 'totalitarian' without someone challenging the aptness of the description. Wherever the concept has been applied a storm of protest and denial has generally followed.[1]

Side by side with those who question the applicability of the concept to particular systems and regimes are those who question the analytical basis of the 'totalitarian model' itself. The problem as these critics see it is that it is difficult to imagine how the type of society described by those who use the concept could come to exist. For these critics the problem is thus not so much the accuracy of the historical accounts given by theorists using the model as the way in which the relationship between regime and ruled is presented by them. Can it really be true, they ask, that Hitler, Stalin, and the other totalitarian leaders wielded 'total power' or 'total control' over the population? Is it really the case that people living in totalitarian systems are 'atomised' or 'totally dominated' as some theorists claim? This second form of criticism is thus a challenge to the very idea of a totalitarian system. What these critics seem to be claiming is that there is no conceivable use for the term because it describes a dystopia, a society that can only exist in the worst nightmares of an Orwell or a Huxley, rather than a society that has existed or will exist.[2]

In the wake of these apparent difficulties with the concept a number of critics such as Herbert Spiro, Benjamin Barber and Frederic Fleron have, thirdly, come to the conclusion that, far from being a useful term for comparative analysis to be slotted alongside other concepts in the lexicon of political discourse, the concept of totalitarianism is nothing more than a manifestation of the desire to label certain regimes as bad for the purposes of simplifying global politics.[3] In their view the concept of totalitarianism is thus essentially little more than, in Fleron's phrase, a 'boo word' to pin on 'boo regimes'.[4] As these critics point out, it is no coincidence that the term became popular at the height of the Cold War when enmity between the superpowers was at its greatest because it is clear that the values it projects are the values of liberal-capitalism. By bracketing together communist and Nazi regimes, and refusing to acknowledge changes that were taking place in the former, theorists using the term merely confirmed their bias towards systems and cultures that do not match up to liberal expectations about how political, social and economic life should be ordered. The concept of totalitarianism is, it seems, too amenable to ideological manipulation. In the view of these critics it should therefore be pensioned off in the interests of neutral inquiry.

Despite the serious nature of these criticisms, it is evident that the concept of totalitarianism has not been pensioned off. Far from it; it is quite evident that the concept has found a niche in the language. We only have to open a newspaper, listen to the news or consult the list of recently published books on politics to realise that despite the best efforts of its many critics use of the term remains undiminished. The term appears to serve a need and we are therefore faced with the curious situation of a concept without a home to go to. Not only is the application of the term challenged by area specialists in whatever context it appears, but doubts are expressed about whether the type of system described as totalitarian can really exist. In short, we appear to lack some agreement about the core or the essence of totalitarianism, about what the principal characteristics of a totalitarian system are and about the nature of totalitarian ideologies. That common stock of assumptions that we share when we talk about other types of political system, whether it be democracy', 'tyranny' or 'dictatorship' appear to be missing. Totalitarianism is a concept that exists in a limbo of jumbled and often contradictory meanings, offensive to some, useful to others.

The aim of this book is to help resolve some of these questions. It seeks to provide an explanation for why the concept appears so difficult to define, and why when it is defined it appears to create so many problems and antagonise so many people in so many different fields. It is an attempt to find some solutions to the questions raised above, such as: what is totalitarianism? What is a totalitarian system, and how does it differ from other forms of dictatorship or tyranny? Is there a specific totalitarian ideology, or are some ideologies simply more prone to producing totalitarianism than certain others? Furthermore we shall be asking which systems can be considered totalitarian. Was Hitler's Germany totalitarian, or Stalin's Russia? Or is the term applicable as some have claimed to a variety of modern dictatorships? Does totalitarianism have a future, or is it, as Francis Fukuyama has recently claimed, an anachronism, a thing of the past?[5] Have the conditions and character of contemporary life changed so as to make the re-emergence of totalitarianism unlikely if not impossible? These are the core questions that we shall be attempting to resolve in the course of this book and we shall proceed by looking in turn at some of the best-known works on totalitarianism. In each case an account will be given of how the author concerned sees totalitarianism developing, and what the characteristics of a totalitarian system are. We will then assess the strengths and weaknesses of this account in our attempt to judge the overall utility of the term and how best it might be applied.

The first chapter begins with an account of *The Road to Serfdom* by Friedrich von Hayek. Published in 1944, the work was among the first to use the term in a systematic fashion. In Hayek's view the cause of totalitarianism in Nazi Germany and potentially in Britain, the United States and other liberal-democracies was collectivism. Collectivism is the belief that the state should ensure 'social justice', that it should provide a basic level of well-being for the population. In his view the belief in collectivism is replete with danger for in pursuing collective happiness the state inevitably extends control over an ever-enlarging scope of activities. Together with an enormous increase in the power and size of the state goes a diminishing sphere of individual freedom. In his view it is thus the onset of planning, in particular central planning, that must be regarded as the source of modern totalitarianism. In the second chapter we look at what might be regarded as the classic work in the field, *The Origins of Totalitarianism* by the German-American political philosopher Hannah Arendt. As the title of the book implies, the goal of *Origins* is primarily to seek an explanation for how it was that totalitarianism emerged in Germany and Russia. However, the book also contains one of the most penetrating accounts of the actual character of the totalitarian systems that emerged out of the Bolshevik and Nazi movements. In her view the character of totalitarian systems is shaped by the extreme radicalism of the movements that create them. These movements come to power promising to transform the world, yet their failure to do so draws them into a war against their own people. The culmination of this conflict is the concentration camp, the ultimate manifestation of the desire for 'total domination'. In the third chapter we consider what has long been regarded as the standard work on the subject, namely *Totalitarian Dictatorship and Autocracy* by Carl Friedrich and Zbigniew Brzezinski. It was these two who in this work provided the description of totalitarianism in terms of a six-point 'syndrome' of traits and characteristics that went on to become the focus for much of the debate about the concept of totalitarianism in the 1960s and 1970s. Their goal was different to that of either Hayek or Arendt in that what they sought was primarily a definition of totalitarianism rather than an account of its origins. Totalitarianism for them was more than a spectacular 'event' as Arendt argued. It was the modern incarnation of an ancient political form, the autocracy. It was autocracy adapted for the conditions of 'mass society'.

Although as critics have often pointed out most of those writing about totalitarianism have done so from a liberal or conservative perspective (as were the theorists already mentioned), this has by no means been exclusively the case. In the fourth chapter we look at perhaps the most celebrated account of totalitarianism from a theorist of the left, Herbert Marcuse's *One Dimensional Man*. A member of the Frankfurt School of 'critical theory', Marcuse's analysis of totalitarianism is radically different from the theorists just mentioned. In his view totalitarianism is an affliction not of Nazi Germany or Stalin's Russia but of 'advanced industrial civilization' in general, and the United States in particular. In his view the 'openness' and 'pluralism' that are said to characterise liberal-democracies is merely a façade hiding the operation of 'vested interests' and the domination of 'instrumental reason'. If, he argues, totalitarianism represents the most refined form of repression, as indeed many theorists think it is, then it is these so-called democracies, not the brutal dictatorships of Hitler and Stalin, that must be considered totalitarian. In the final chapter we consider one of the most recent contributions to the study of totalitarianism, the essay 'The Power of the Powerless' by the Czech playwright who became the president of his country, Václav Havel. The significance of this work is that Havel attempts to draw a distinction between totalitarian regimes, which he considers to be a 'traditional' form of dictatorship, and what he terms 'post-totalitarian' systems of the sort found in the Eastern Bloc before the 'Velvet Revolutions' of 1991 swept away the communist order in this region. In his view what characterises post-totalitarian systems is the ability of regimes to mask underlying discontent and alientation by confronting each individual with a choice between conformity and safety on the one hand, and dissidence and punishment on the other. The atmosphere of calm and stability that many theorists have noted is a characteristic of the 'mature' totalitarian system does not indicate an end to terror or the development of legitimacy. It represents the sublimation of terror to the point where it is invisible to the untutored eye.

In the Conclusion we then go on to consider the questions outlined above in the light of the work that has been presented. In particular we will attempt to establish what continuities and similarities if any exist between these accounts and whether it is possible to distil some core essence or meaning of the concept of totalitarianism. We will then move to consider the possible application of the concept both to past regimes and systems and to current systems that have been considered totalitarian such as the Islamic republics of the Middle East and the communist regime of Kim Il-Sung in North Korea. In short we will be attempting to see whether the concept of totalitarianism has any utility as a description of a particular political system, past, present or future.

Notes

1 Readers will find references to works critical of the application of the concept of totalitarianism to Nazi Germany and the Soviet Union in the footnotes of the concluding chapter. The bibliography also contains a full list of these works.

2 Analytical difficulties with the totalitarian model are discussed in, for example, Robert Orr, 'Reflections on Totalitarianism, Leading to Reflections on Two Ways of Theorizing', *Political Studies*, 21 (1973); Michael Walzer, 'On "Failed Totalitarianism"', in *1984 Revisited. Totalitarianism in our Century*, edited by Irving Howe, (New York, 1983); and in Frederic J. Fleron, 'Soviet Area Studies and the Social Sciences: Some Methodological Problems in Communist Studies', *Soviet Studies*, 16 (January 1968).

3 The classic critique of the concept of totalitarianism as a weapon of the Cold War is Benjamin Barber and Herbert J. Spiro's article 'Counter-Ideological Uses of "Totalitarianism"', *Politics and Society*, 1 (1970). For other views on the ideological origins of the concept of totalitarianism see especially Les K. Adler and Thomas G. Peterson, 'Red Fascism: The Merger of Nazi Germany and Soviet Russia in the American Image of Totalitarianism, 1930s-1950s', *American Historical Review*, 75 (1970); Abbott Gleason, '"Totalitarianism" in 1984', *Russian Review*, 43 (1984); Pierre Ayçoberry, *The Nazi Question. An Essay on the Interpretations of National Socialism (1922–1975)* (London, 1981); and Daniel Tarschys, 'The Soviet Political System: Three Models', *European Journal of Political Research*, 5 (1977). For an analysis of how the concept was used more recently in the struggle between the superpowers, interesting not least because it appeared in East Germany, see Hans Pirsch, 'Wiederbelebung der Totalitarismusdoktrin', *IPW Berichte*, no. 2 (February 1983), pp. 8–13.

4 'I should guess', Fleron remarks, 'that if we knew enough of the psychology of research we would find that there are those who wish to retain "totalitarianism" in studying communism because of its negative connotations. This may be one of the reasons why the definition of "totalitarianism" is constantly revised so that as the Soviet Union changes (e.g. away from the overt use of terror) the concept can still be used to denote that system. Various acrobatics are performed with the concept (e.g. "mature totalitarianism") so that we can continue to pin a "boo" label on a "boo" system of government', 'Soviet Area Studies', p. 339.

5 This in broad terms is the thesis contained within *The End of History and the Last Man* (London, 1992).

1

Friedrich von Hayek
The Road to Serfdom

Having established why it is important to re-examine the concept of totalitarianism, we can now begin to consider some of the best accounts of the origins and character of totalitarianism. Our aim will be to establish how the works of these theorists differ from each other, and which of them appears to give us the best foundation for understanding what totalitarianism is or was. In this first chapter we will examine the work of a theorist who, along with Karl Popper, did more to popularise use of the term in the immediate post-war period than probably any other person, namely Friedrich von Hayek. The chapter will begin with an account of what Hayek means by totalitarianism concentrating on his best-known work *The Road to Serfdom*. We will then conclude by examining this account to establish whether it gives us a satisfactory description of a totalitarian system.

It may at first seem inappropriate to begin a study of totalitarianism with the work of Hayek. Firstly, it is usually assumed that the systematic study of totalitarian regimes did not really get under way until the publication of Hannah Arendt's *The Burden of Our Times* (later retitled *The Origins of Totalitarianism*) in 1949. Indeed some might argue that it was not until the appearance of the more self-consciously empirical *Totalitarian Dictatorship and Autocracy* by Carl Friedrich and Zbigniew Brzezinski in 1956 that a clear view of what was meant by totalitarianism really emerged. Unlike these works, Hayek's *The Road to Serfdom* published in 1944 is not an attempt at defining what totalitarianism is or might be. There is no explicit description of a totalitarian system of the sort found, for example, in Friedrich and Brzezinski's work, nor does the work attempt to set totalitarian systems into comparative perspective with other forms of dictatorship or tyranny. It is a book primarily about planning. More specifically, it is a book that attempts to show how planning, or, more accurately, central planning, represents very real dangers to liberty. In his view the civilised world was being lulled quite remorselessly into the abyss. The horrors being perpetrated under Nazi and communist rule were palpably the product of planning. Yet in his view not only were people in democratic countries failing to see that this was the case, but they themselves were in the process of being duped into accepting more planning and hence greater state control over their lives. All the Allied powers had introduced planning during the War to facilitate the production and distribution of needed materials. Furthermore, all of them were promising to retain the powers that planning vested in the state to further some nebulous and ultimately damaging conception of 'social justice'. They were all in Hayek's view in danger of surrendering the liberty of the individual to the power of the state. As Hayek argues: 'When it becomes dominated by a collectivist creed, democracy will inevitably destroy itself'.[1] Thus *The Road to Serfdom* is not an academic treatise on the nature and characteristics of tyranny, but a heartfelt plea to the post-War reading public to wake up before it is too late. In this sense it is perhaps closer in spirit to Orwell's *Nineteen Eighty-Four* or Yevgenii Zamyatin's *We* than to the studies we will be considering in later chapters.

Nevertheless, although he remained largely aloof from the intense debates of the 1950s and 1960s about the adequacy of the concept of totalitarianism, Hayek must be considered an important figure in the development of the study of the subject. He was among the first to argue that totalitarianism was the product of the pursuit of a specific ideology, with specific aims and aspirations. He was one of the first to point to the specifically modern character of totalitarianism, and one of the first to attempt to explain the apparent attractiveness of totalitarian ideas for ordinary people. By any measure Hayek's account of totalitarianism must thus be considered a valuable and original contribution to the subject.

*

As Hayek makes clear in *The Road to Serfdom*, the origins of totalitarianism in the twentieth century are to be found in collectivism, in socialist ideology. Socialism, he argues, represents the desire for the construction of a better form of life. The world according to socialists is an appalling place. It is full of people trying to make money by exploiting others and leaving them in penury. The product of this relentless competition between individuals is widespread unhappiness and a feeling of lack of worth in those who have not succeeded in the rat race. For socialists, problems stem from the existence of private property and the free market. The market allows individuals to accumulate vast riches at the expense, so socialists argue, of ordinary people. It therefore follows that to create a decent society in which people can make the most of their talents and abilities, and hence develop a sense of personal worth, a new mechanism for the production and distribution of goods will be needed to replace the market. As Hayek has argued throughout his life, to maintain a competitive market order inequalities, if not class stratification, have to be tolerated and accepted as a part of everyday life. If we want to abolish inequality then we will have to abolish the free market as well. However, this leaves the problem of how the production of goods and services is going to be organised in the new socialist order. If the market is abolished, how are goods and services going to be distributed? Who, in short, is going to get what?

The solution that socialists have put forward for dealing with such matters and for ensuring the maintenance of equality is planning. According to socialists planning is far more rational and far fairer than the free market. The market is a rather chaotic institution. It works by allowing people with something to sell (including their own labour power) to trade with anyone who wants to buy what they have to offer. Since a person can never be sure at any moment precisely what is going to be sold, or what objects others will want to buy, the market has to a socialist an uncontrollable, 'spontaneous' air about it. This naturally offends against the socialists' desire for equity and predictability. Since they are concerned with ensuring that everyone has the same amount of any particular object, i.e. so that all are equal, the practice of buying and selling according to the vagaries of supply and demand has to be stamped out. If the market were allowed to exist then inequalities would necessarily follow, and so the whole business of production and distribution has to be controlled by society. However the question inevitably arises of who will make the day-to-day decisions regarding production and distribution. Who will oversee the operation to make sure that people get their fair share? The simple answer is the state. The state has the authority and the power to enforce the will of the people. It can make sure that no one transgresses the rules and attempts to make more for themselves; and, since the state's role is to ensure that 'social justice' is achieved, exploitation and domination will necessarily wither away. The state has the power, in other words, to take the entire productive process into its own hands. It can plan to cater for what people really need, and it can also organise men and materials to ensure that these needs are met. In a socialist society the state exists to make sure we are happy and fulfilled; that is its *telos* or goal. Hence the notion that the state could become the enemy of society, that it could deny liberty or well-being is one that socialists deny. As far as they are concerned, the more planning the state does the better able it will be to distribute goods in a fair and equitable manner.

Hayek is quite prepared to concede that all of this could look quite attractive to the man on the Clapham omnibus. The prospect of a secure job with a guaranteed standard of living and access to social provision is one that would obviously appeal to many. Hayek is not saying that the dream of equality is necessarily a bad dream: individuals are entitled to their private whimsies and fantasies. The point he wants to make is that what socialists say planning will achieve is almost completely irrelevant; it is not what people say they are going to do, but what they *actually* do that is important. It is actions that must be judged, not intentions. This is crucial for Hayek, because he is not saying socialism is a wicked or immoral ideology. What he is saying is that pursuing socialist ideals will lead to totalitarianism whether the holders of such ideals want to create a tyranny or not. Socialism is a flawed ideology, and because it is flawed it does not produce the results intended by those charged with attaining a socialist society. Instead of chuffing serenely towards Harmony and Bounty, once it reaches a certain point, the socialist train veers off the tracks and into the siding marked 'Gulag'. It is this observation on the disparity between promise and execution that lies behind the missionary zeal of *The Road to Serfdom*. We have, Hayek argues, been blinded by the promises of socialism without being able to see what the necessary consequences of socialist measures are. Hayek is therefore doing us a service by opening our eyes to the logic contained within the socialist project.

Planning is in itself no bad thing: everyone does it, and, indeed, not making plans for the future is tantamount to folly. However, there is a world of difference between individuals, families and businesses making plans and planning by the state. Firstly, to institute the sort of planning that socialists want (i.e. planning that guarantees 'social justice'), the state has to take the entire productive process of the country into its own hands. The state cannot leave certain enterprises outside its control, because if it did so it could not guarantee that the product of that enterprise would be distributed fairly. All of this means taking something that previously belonged to private individuals and giving it to the state in the name of the collective good. This act of expropriating individuals to ensure 'fairness' is fine for those who are set to gain therefrom. What, however, of people who have lost control of their property, their land, their factories? How will they regard this 'rationalisation' of production? It is unlikely, though not impossible, that they will feel quite so happy about matters. Unless they expressly consented to the state taking responsibility for what belongs to them, they will feel coerced and unhappy. They will feel that a great injustice has been done, and not without reason. At the very birth of this new, more just state of affairs injustice will thus already have been perpetrated by the state.

These acts of injustice against select individuals (i.e. the rich) are, however, merely the start. They do not add up to totalitarianism; more like organised theft. The real problems begin when the state attempts to reorganise production and distribution through the mechanism of planning. As Hayek argues, even to begin formulating a plan that is to encompass the entire productive life of the country there must exist a basic consensus about the sort of goods to be produced. Agreement is needed because otherwise the plan will not appear rational or sensible to those who are charged with carrying it out. As Hayek makes clear: 'The effect of the people agreeing that there must be central planning without agreeing on the ends will be rather as if a group of people were to commit themselves to a journey which most of them do not want at all'.[2] A plan stipulates the amount of any product that will be made during a given period. It states, for example, that over the next five years x million tonnes of carrots will be grown, y tonnes of tomatoes, and so forth. This is why socialists say planning is rational: the state works out what society needs first of all, and then organises the people and the means of production to achieve those targets in a given time span.

The question liberals such as Hayek want to ask is how the state arrives at its figures detailing the amount of any product to be made. How does the state arrive, for example, at the figure x tonnes for carrots and the figure y tonnes for tomatoes? Without a market in which people are able to express their choices by spending their money as they wish, how does the state know what people are going to need or want? According to socialists, once the apparatus of production is under social control people will be able to decide for themselves what goods and services they wish to have. Production will reflect their real needs because the initial decision about what to make will be taken by everyone. In a socialist society – so it is promised – planning will involve the entire population. Everyone will be able to voice their opinion about what the priorities of production should be and about how production should be organised. Since the aim of such discussions is to arrive at a plan that will meet with the acceptance of the community, socialists anticipate that people will tend to agree on what goods should be produced. Individuals are after all being asked to think not of themselves but of society and 'social justice', and hence it should be possible to reach a broad consensus about what goods and services the state should supply.

In Hayek's view it is at this point that the socialist dream of equality becomes fantasy. The idea that in an advanced industrial society a given population will be able to arrive at a consensus about what goods to produce in what quantity is simply ludicrous. As Hayek was at constant pains to make clear throughout his life, what socialists always seem in a great hurry to forget is that people are different. They differ in their physical and mental characteristics, and in their talents and capabilities. They differ about what is valuable or beautiful. They differ about what vegetables taste good. People differ about everything. The idea, therefore, that people living in a highly diverse industrialised society accustomed to buying or selling a vast array of products would be able to reach a consensus about what should be made or grown is one that defies every expectation we should have about how real people behave. If a person is an avid tomato eater he will want to be able to buy tomatoes. If the Planning Council for Agricultural Production (or whatever) has decided that tomatoes will no longer be grown because more people like carrots, he is unlikely in Hayek's view to be very pleased. He will see it as an imposition on his liberty to buy what he wants and hence will view the Planning Council's decision as a meddlesome intrusion in affairs it has no right to be involved with. People, in short, are not like socialists imagine them to be. They are happy when their own needs are satisfied, not when some notion of 'social justice' has been achieved.

According to Hayek, even if an incoming socialist government is sincere about introducing 'democratic planning' to run the economy what will happen in practice is that government will become more bureaucratic and more authoritarian. As socialists correctly surmise, planning is only possible when there is a consensus about the ends of the plan. If there is no consensus then opposition will emerge and the regime's legitimacy will be threatened. Yet what they do not seem able or willing to recognise is that for the reasons outlined above people will inevitably disagree about what the priorities of the plan will be. The government will therefore be forced, if it wishes to keep faith with planning, constantly to reduce the amount of people involved in the planning process. Though a socialist government may well attempt to introduce a system of planning by the masses, the practical need to find a consensus forces it to ignore the opinions of what will likely be the majority. Production needs to be organised, crops have to be sown, and products have to be delivered to shops. People soon get dissatisfied if they do not have things to buy. Yet the greater the number of voices allowed to be heard regarding the ends of the plan, the less likely anything will be done because the necessary consensus will inevitably be lacking. If, therefore, a socialist government is serious about planning, it will quickly have to abandon the idea of consulting people about how production is to be organised. On the other hand, if it allows itself to be deluded into thinking that planning can be carried out democratically then very soon production will grind to a halt. With production failing it will then only be a matter of time before the people take to the streets to force the regime out. As Marx himself recognised, revolutions are produced by hunger not by ideas. What he failed to see, however, is that poverty and misery are far more likely to occur in a socialist than in a capitalist society.

By cutting down on the number of people involved in formulating the plan the socialist administration can at last take control over the productive life of the country and make it serve 'the people'. However, problems remain. In cutting down on the number of people involved in the planning process the regime creates further difficulties for itself. If only those whose opinions coincide with the planners are involved in the process of formulating the plan, then that inevitably leaves a large number of others out in the cold. Ignoring or discounting the views of a significant element of the population is a potentially dangerous course of action to take. It involves the risk of provoking widespread disenchantment, the emergence of opposition and perhaps eventually resistance to the regime. In addition, the existence of a large group of people who are not in sympathy with the views of the planners would naturally be taken as evidence of the regime's lack of success in attracting the population to the ideals and values of socialism. According to Hayek, socialists cannot tolerate the idea that some people would be drawn to oppose their policies. Socialism is a universal ideology that claims to have provided a recipe for curing the ills confronting the whole of humanity, not just certain groups or classes. Socialists crave unanimity and thus without the achievement of a genuine consensus their project remains incomplete and imperfect.

No one should be surprised, therefore, when on attaining power socialists oppose and attack those who do not agree with them. Socialists want their plan not merely to work, but to be met with universal approval. They want each individual not only to agree with the policies of the regime, to turn up for work, to do the statutory hours per day, and so forth, but to see in such policies the embodiment of justice and truth. Socialists are not interested in grudging acquiescence. They want people to believe that what they are doing is in the true interests of humanity. They want people out on the streets singing the praises of the planners, not moaning about the lack of bread in the shops. If, therefore, people do not appear to approve of what the regime is doing they must be confronted and made to change their attitudes, values and beliefs to those more suitable for life in a socialist society. It is no use having people around who believe, for example, in free enterprise and private property. Such beliefs are antithetical to the values being fostered by the state. It follows that the people holding such views must be coaxed, per-suaded and, if necessary, forced to give them up. If they will not, then they will become obstacles to the achievement of unanimity and hence potential opponents of the regime.

It is, Hayek argues, because of this 'quest for unanimity' that socialist regimes inevitably become totalitarian in character. If what is required by the regime is herd-like followers who will agree with whatever the regime does, then the state will have to take control of every agency of socialisation from the family and schools to the printing presses and radio stations. People, as Hayek reminds us, have different needs and wants, different interests and values. The only way to make people think the same way and to believe in the same things is therefore to control completely the environment in which they live their lives. All outside influences that may have a bearing on the way people think about themselves and the society in which they live must be controlled. Reading matter must be censored so that negative influences are held at bay. Music and the arts must positively extol the virtues of the community. History and the sciences must conform to the regime's account of reality. In addition, to inspire the loyalty of the masses, Platonic myths must be propagated explaining the origin and destiny of the community. If after all attempts to encourage devotion to the state a person still refuses to submit to the superior wisdom of the planners he or she must be rooted out and eliminated in case his or her poisonous individualism influences the rest of the population. There is room for only one truth in socialist systems and that one truth perpetuating the illusion of rationality upon which the legitimacy of the system depends must be publicly adhered to by all members of the population.

The totalitarian regimes that have appeared in the twentieth century are the product of the attempt to implement socialism. Socialism is an ideology that demands the creation of a society in which the attainment of the collective good is regarded as the goal of the state. The collective good is represented by a global plan that organises and regulates the entire spectrum of human activity to arrive at a just form of society. In so doing the expression of individual needs and desires not in sympathy with those regarded by the planners as legitimate is outlawed. The inevitable consequence of the suppression of individual needs is the crushing of autonomy and liberty and the reduction of each person to a mere moment or cog in the all-embracing edifice of an administered social life. Socialism, in other words, provides the theoretical justification for totalitarianism, it underpins the particular practices and institutions that characterise this form of rule. If it were not for the rise of collectivism totalitarianism would have no rationale.

*

Hayek's account of totalitarianism is a persuasive and highly influential one. It seeks not merely to describe the features of totalitarian rule, but also to lay bare the logic that informs the development and functioning of such systems. Communist and Nazi regimes must be considered members of the same species, not merely because they appear to be similar in form, with similar features and institutions, but because the rulers of such systems agree about what the state is attempting to achieve. They all agree that the task of rule is to secure a form of society in which the individual is subordinated to the collective good. This is why Hayek thinks it is so important to get clear about what totalitarianism really represents. Far from being a return to a form of pre-modern despotism, totalitarianism is the product of the eminently modern concern with establishing 'social justice'. Totalitarianism is what results when institutionalised do-gooding is allowed to determine the aim and content of each indivi-dual's life. If we cannot see that this is where totalitarianism comes from then we are doomed to reproducing the experience of the Germans, the Soviets and everyone else whose liberty has dis-appeared as a result of planning.

In this section we will assess the merit of Hayek's analysis of totalitarianism. However, before determining whether Hayek is right about the connection between planning and totalitarianism we need to address a more immediate difficulty, which is the appli-cability of Hayek's analysis of totalitarianism to Hitler's Germany. On the face of it, the description of communist systems as totalitarian seems perfectly plausible if we are prepared to accept his view that the pursuit of the collective good through central planning inevitably results in a loss of individual liberty. We can say that to challenge Hayek's view of communist states we need to show that he is wrong about the connection between planning and despotism; but the same does not appear to be true in the example Hayek spends most time discussing in *The Road to Serfdom*, that is Nazi Germany. Yet Hayek states quite unequivocally that: 'If we want to form a picture of what society would be like if, according to the ideal which has seduced many socialists, it was organised as a single great factory, we have to look to . . . contemporary Ger-many'.[3] Thus before moving to a more general examination of Hayek's analysis it is interesting to ask, firstly, if the system he himself considers to be the most refined model of a totalitarian state really became totalitarian for the reasons he gives. Was it really central planning that shaped the character of the Third Reich?

As should by now be clear, Hayek believes that totalitarianism is the product of the collectivist quest for a just and egalitarian society. Socialists believe that the market order perpetuates inequality and human suffering and they therefore propose replacing the market with 'democratic planning' in which everyone will be given the opportunity to have his or her say about what goods should be produced. Those goods would then be distributed more or less equally, ensuring that everyone would be able to enjoy a reasonable standard of living along with a degree of control over the most important decisions facing the community. Problems begin because, as Hayek argues, planning can only be made to work where people are not only excluded from the process of decision-making, but are forced to agree with the values and priorities of the planners. This is how Hayek sees totalitarianism developing; but to what extent is this scenario an accurate account of what occurred in Germany under the Nazis?

Hayek is surely justified in assuming that since they called them-selves 'National Socialists' the Nazis must actually have been socialists, albeit of a particular hue. They professed what appeared to be an ideology of the 'common man', in that they were anti everything that invoked fear or loathing in many ordinary Germans. They were anti-Weimar, anti-capitalist, anti-Marxist, and anti many other things besides. In addition, their own programme calling for the construction of a *Volksgemeinschaft* or People's Community appeared on the surface to share the collectivist aim of securing 'social justice', solidarity and harmony. It called for the construction of a system in which unemployment, homelessness and moral decay would be supplanted by order and collective strength. It sought to sweep away all the conflicts and antagonisms that otherwise beset life in modern society, and to build a society in which each person would have and know his or her place. Of course this was not all. The Nazis' distinctive brand of 'socialism' also called for the banishment of all degenerate or 'alien' influences from society, the subjugation of lesser, non-German races to ensure that the needs of the *Volk* were satisfied, and the pursuit of a healthy, Aryan form of life reinforcing the 'natural' division of labour in the home. What national socialism offered was a paternal system in which the needs of the Germans would take absolute priority over the needs, interests or desires of any other race or creed. As Hayek implies, it would therefore be wrong to think that the Nazis had no programme for social recon-struction or that they were driven by purely negative goals such as the destruction of the old order or the killing of Jews. They did possess a vision of society that appeared to call for radical change in the social, political and economic life of the country. National socialism was not merely a 'revolt against reason', but contained, as Hayek asserts, a type of 'collectivist' project. Was it, however, the pursuit of this 'socialist' vision that made the Nazi system totalitarian? It is certainly true that part of the attraction of the Nazis to many ordinary people was that they appeared to be anti-capitalist and hence set against those who appeared to be profiting from Germany's woes. They constantly attacked the power of the major capitalists, regarding them as exploiters, and, worse, as agents of the Jewish 'world conspiracy'. They styled themselves as saviours of the working class, promising jobs, security, and the benefits and services only otherwise available under the more self-evidently socialist administrations of the Popular Front. Yet it is also apparent that this anti-capitalism was less the product of an ideological hostility to wage labour and commodity production than a sign of the Nazis' more general unwillingness to regard any area of social or economic life as autonomous or outside the potential control of the state. To recognise the right of property owners to dispose of their capital as they wished was, for the Nazis, to recognise a limitation to the exercise of power. It would be to acknowledge that individuals have a right to do what they want with their property and hence that their needs should be regarded as more important than the needs of the community or *Volk*. It would be to argue, as many liberals and conservatives do, that the role of the state is not to set goals for the individual, but to maintain a framework of rules in which individuals can set their own goals, pursue their own desires and serve their own interests. The Nazis were quite unprepared to regard any of these considerations as valid or binding on their own behaviour. The Nazis, therefore, were not anti-capitalist because they were pro-socialist or, even less, pro-communist. As well as proclaiming their distaste for the entrenched power of the capitalist elite, they were, it has to be remembered, virulently opposed to the organised labour movement. Indeed, trade unionists and social democrats were amongst the first to be rounded up after the seizure of power. The Nazis did not favour transferring economic or any other sort of power to the people. What they wanted was a system in which the people obeyed and remained loyal to them rather than to other groups or movements. The notion, shared by most socialists, that people should participate in decisions regarding the production and distribution of goods is one that was largely rejected. For this reason, the option of organising the economy through 'democratic planning' was never seriously entertained by the Nazi regime.

For these reasons, that the Nazis were able to count on the support of many industrialists in Germany both before and after the seizure of power should not be so surprising. Unlike the communists, the Nazis were not ideologically committed to ending private ownership of the means of production and to constructing a 'workers' state'. Indeed it was because they were not that they were able to count on support from wealthier elements of the population. As John Hiden and John Farquarson point out: 'Many supporters were expecting from Hitler nothing more than the preservation of their existing status . . . [therefore] they saw in him an insurance against pro-letarianization'.[4] There were certainly Nazis who possessed a vision of a different form of society; but the realisation of this vision did not, it seems, make necessary the wholesale demolition of existing classes and elites. In this sense there was a considerable gap between the rhetoric and reality of Nazi rule. Rather than pursue overtly revolutionary goals involving radical changes to the fabric of German society, they set out in a more pragmatic fashion to achieve certain tangible political ends. They wanted, for example, to get rid of unemployment, the primary source of discontent and instability in Germany at the time. They wanted to increase dramatically the power of the armed forces, and they wanted Germany to become economically self-sufficient, thereby preparing the way for the successful conclusion of the imperial campaigns to come. As soon became apparent, achieving these goals did not necessarily involve dismantling the capitalist basis of the economy or depriving industrialists of their profits. Indeed, certain goals, such as the expansion of Germany, were regarded favourably by the latter who saw that with the incorporation of new lands they would have a ready source of cheap labour and materials, as well as new markets to exploit. In this sense far from being opposed, the Nazi regime and the owners of the major German industries enjoyed something of a symbiotic relationship. The Nazis relied on the industrialists, particularly in the early years, for financial support and political credibility, whilst the industrialists needed the Nazis to stave off the communist threat, to restore discipline in the workplace and in society more generally, and to provide them with the necessary orders to maintain profitability in the hard years of the early 1930s. This is not, however, to say that this relationship was one of equality. This tolerance of private enter-

prise remained highly contingent in the Third Reich. Clearly the
Nazis regarded all aspects of life as potentially subject to control by
the state and no obstacles or barriers were allowed to remain to the
exercise of state power. Indeed, as Hitler's power grew through the
1930s, the ability of industrialists, landowners or any other group to
prevent the Nazis interfering in the economy diminished to such a
point that it is highly doubtful they could have resisted any Soviet-
type plan to nationalise the major industries. Even in the early years
of their reign, it was evident that the Nazis were prepared to intervene in the economy to ensure that particular political goals were
met. For example, the lack of cheap food in the early 1930s was met
by a significant reform of the agricultural system that trampled on
the toes of many landowners and farmers. Similarly, the drive for
rearmament required the creation of a special plan to co-ordinate
and organise the production of men and materials. Targets for the
production of strategically important goods were set, incentives in
the form of tax breaks and credits were offered, together with a
whole series of other inducements. Yet, despite the impressive array
of fiscal and monetary measures employed by the Nazis, the desire to
shape the economic life of the country does not mean they imple-
mented the form of planning described by Hayek. There was planning in Nazi Germany, just as there was planning in every other
industrialised country, including the United States under Roosevelt.
However, as in the majority of these countries, it was planning
designed to improve the performance of particular sectors of the
economy, particularly those connected with the war effort, rather
than planning designed to bring the entire apparatus of production
under state control. As Martin Broszat argues, planning 'merely set
out state production programmes, whilst maintaining the basic
structure of the private market economy'. Thus, as he notes, 'there
was no systematic construction of any comprehensive state
economic administration'.[5]

   If Hayek is really saying that it was planning that was responsible
for the character of Nazi Germany then the conclusion we have to
come to is that his analysis is flawed. It is perfectly true that the Nazis
recognised no limits to the scope of their power in economic affairs,
but this is not the same as saying that they themselves controlled the
economy; they did not. The Nazis presided over a largely capitalist
economy in which most of the productive apparatus was privately
owned. They were able, because of their largely unassailable position

within the German polity, to influence heavily the direction in which
production developed. Yet, even if we were to submit that Hitler was
able to make the industrialists do exactly what he wanted, that he
exercised complete control over their power of decision, this would
still have fallen well short of the type of planning found in the Soviet
Union. Hayek argues that what is novel about totalitarianism, as
opposed to other forms of despotism, is that a system ostensibly
designed as a means of providing for all has become a system in
which all are dominated in every facet of their lives. Although the
Nazis were concerned about providing for all, or, rather, all the
members of their tightly defined constituency, this concern was never
translated into a system of central planning.

   Hayek might want to argue in his defence that although Nazi
Germany had not yet developed a fully blown system of central
planning it had developed all the characteristic features associated
with one. In other words, he might argue that merely by initiating
moves towards the creation of a centrally planned economy the
Nazis had provided the basis for totalitarianism to take root. However, this is essentially quite a different argument from the one we
have so far considered. What it really says is that it is not so much
central planning that causes totalitarianism, but any sort of planning
by government or any sort of significant intervention in the
economy. It is an argument that implies that to embark on any
planning at all is at the same time to diminish liberty.

   Although such a view is not too far removed from Hayek's
thinking, we have to assume that he would not want to go quite as far
as this. Firstly, if Hayek were really saying that *all* forms of state
planning, even those conducted within the context of a capitalist
economy, are inherently despotic he would have difficulty explaining
why it is that democratic systems such as Britain, France and the
United States failed to develop into totalitarian states during the war.
He would also have to explain why it is that the vast majority of
advanced industrial states have managed to remain democratic
despite their emphatic embrace of planning and their uninhibited
attempts not merely to intervene in the market, but to manage it. To
take one example, the British wartime economy was just as heavily
managed as that of the Germans. Yet to argue that Britain became
totalitarian either during or after the war when many of these
controls were retained to aid reconstruction and create a better
environment for the returning troops would surely be wrong. The

extension of planning to all areas of economic activity was not accompanied, as Hayek said it would be, by the forcible inculcation of a state ideology. There was censorship of the press and other media during the war, free expression was curtailed and other controls were imposed. Yet, no matter how far-reaching these powers became they did not amount to the propagation of a distinct, definable set of values and beliefs of the sort possessed by the Nazis or the Soviets. Books were not burned, heretics were not rounded up, and there were no show trials for errant professors. School curricula were not made to toe any party line, and no overall organisation for the indoctrination of 'youth' was created. The government was of course highly self-conscious about maintaining 'morale'. It did attempt to foster a feeling of 'pulling together', of co-operating, and, as it were, 'digging for victory'; but this is all a very long way from what was going on in Germany, Italy and the Soviet Union. Furthermore it is highly significant that normal democratic procedures were restored the moment the war ended. Indeed, what greater symbol is there for showing how Britain had failed to become a totalitarian society than the fact that the administration that had presided over the enormous extension of state power during the war was sent crashing to defeat in the 1945 election?

It is difficult, therefore, to imagine that Hayek really wants to say that all planning leads to tyranny. If he does then he must, by extension, be saying that every advanced industrial nation has been totalitarian since the war. They have all introduced planning to a greater or lesser extent, and they have all intervened in the economy in the hope of securing political goals such as full employment. Indeed some countries like France introduced a much fuller and arguably more successful planning regime than was ever the case in Britain either before or after the war. It is hard to believe that Hayek wants to say that all systems in which there is an element of planning are or are about to become totalitarian. What he really wants to say is surely that planning will not meet the goals that people hope will be achieved by it, and will not, as many hoped, solve the cyclical crises that beset capitalism. It will not ensure growth or full employment, nor will it produce 'social justice'. It will, in his view, do the opposite: it will make everything far worse. However, this is a quite different argument, and whether Hayek is justified in what he says about the efficacy of planning is not an issue that we need to discuss. Nevertheless, to return to the original point, if Hayek wants to say that it is not planning *per se*, but central planning that causes totalitarianism then he has a problem. Like most commentators on totalitarianism, he wants to argue that if any state can be considered totalitarian it is Hitler's Germany, and much of *The Road to Serfdom* is devoted to proving precisely that point. Little mention is ever made within the work of the Soviet Union, or indeed of any other political system. Yet the factor he believes to be behind the rise of totalitarianism in modern states is missing. There was planning in Germany; but it was not in the form described by Hayek, and in any case did not differ significantly from the forms of intervention found in many other palpably non-totalitarian states to oversee the war effort. A market in commodities and labour power continued to exist, major enterprises remained under private control, and land continued to be privately owned. On the other hand, many of the features that Hayek justifiably believes to be a part of totalitarian rule *were* fully developed in the Third Reich: the cult of the 'Leader', the messianic ideology, the terrorisation of wide sections of the population, and so forth. We may well agree with him therefore that Nazi Germany was totalitarian, but we do not have to agree that it was totalitarian for the reasons he gives, and as we have seen there are good reasons why we should not do so.

Although Hayek's account of totalitarianism is not disproved because the example of Nazi Germany cannot easily be fitted into it, it certainly appears to make less sense of his account. Since those who have used the term have generally assumed that if any regime can be described as totalitarian it must be that of the Nazis, any analysis of such systems that cannot incorporate the Third Reich into it will inevitably be regarded as weakened. That Hayek's account does not appear able to do so detracts from its persuasiveness, not to mention its utility. Hayek's analysis appears to be on much firmer ground, however, when it is applied to the Soviet Union and to communist systems more generally. At least in these systems we do see a full-blown centrally planned economy established with the radical transformation in the nature of people's lives that it entails. We also see many of the features that Hayek and, as we shall see, many others associate with totalitarian regimes: the ideology, the cult of the 'Leader', the use of terror, and so on. All have been present at some point in the evolution of such systems. However, what needs to be established is whether it was central planning that led to the establishment of these practices. Was the development of tyranny in the

Soviet Union due to the creation of a planned economy?

Planning was first introduced in the Soviet Union during the period of 'War Communism' which lasted from mid-1918 to 1921. Lenin had promised in the early days of the regime that power would be exercised by the soviets. In *The State and Revolution* Lenin argued that the revolutionary councils that had sprung up in 1905 and then again in 1917 would be able to become the new assemblies governing the life of the community. Membership of the soviets would be open to everyone, and all decisions regarding the production and distribution of goods would be taken within them. However, it very quickly became evident that such a scenario was unrealistic given the situation confronting the country after the revolution in October 1917. Russia was still at war with Germany and, indeed, looked close to collapse as the morale and infrastructure of the Russian army withered. Opposition to the Bolsheviks was also gaining pace in many regions of the country, culminating in the launch of the Civil War in the spring of 1918. Finally, production of badly needed food and materials ground to a halt as communications broke down and capitalists and landowners fled the country. In such circumstances Lenin's faith in popular rule by the soviets was quickly replaced by the less idealistic but more practical vision of a planned economy run by experts and professional bureaucrats supervised by a proletarian vanguard. Thus at the start of 'War Communism' planning was introduced with much of 'the commanding heights of the economy' being nationalised and placed under central control. What democratic pretensions the Bolsheviks might have held were quickly quashed and replaced by a more authoritarian approach. The soviets became mere executors of the state's orders, whilst opposition parties and groups were banned and outlawed. Dissent was clamped down upon. Indeed even the Party soon became dominated by the views of Lenin, albeit without the trappings of leadership to be associated with the later 'cults' of Stalin, Hitler and Mussolini. Terror became an instrument of social control as the Civil War descended into a brutal contest of will between the Reds and the Whites. A state ideology was developed to secure the loyalty of the population and to justify the measures pursued by the Bolshevik regime. In short, many of the features that Hayek associates with totalitarianism were developed and nurtured by the regime during this period. However, there remain difficulties in arguing that the development of these practices can be put down to the introduction of central planning. To begin with, many of the most extreme measures employed by the regime were introduced in direct response to the outbreak of the Civil War rather than being the product of planning. The Red Terror, for example, was largely a case of fighting fire with fire, the Bolsheviks understanding that if they were not prepared to match and surpass the brutality of the Whites the regime was unlikely to last. Many of the other limitations on liberty were, moreover, the same as those used by any regime in time of war, and indeed mirrored measures used under the Tsars and the Provisional Government. This is not to say that the Bolsheviks acted entirely without concern for securing their own pre-eminence. It is simply to note that the tendency for regimes to become more authoritarian during times of war is hardly confined to states engaged in the process of developing a centrally planned economy. What is perhaps of more significance in determining whether totalitarianism was the product of the planning structure introduced during War Communism is that when planning was suddenly and dramatically dropped at the start of the New Economic Policy period very little changed in the character of the regime. Although War Communism had made it possible for the Party to marshal the resources needed to win the Civil War, it was inappropriate for the task of building a sustainable socialist society. Lenin, Bukharin and other senior Party figures therefore proposed that for the sake of maintaining Soviet rule – which of course meant the rule of the Party – the market should be reintroduced in agriculture and industry. As they argued, without the support of the peasants and of the population more generally the system would collapse along with the socialist aspirations of the communists. A peaceful interregnum was thus called for involving the legalisation of property ownership and the operation of private business. Strategically important elements of the economy such as the railways and the banks were kept in the hands of the state, but most other areas of the economy were returned to the private sector to encourage the economy to develop. Only by returning to the market order and to quasi-capitalist forms of ownership, so it was argued, could social peace be secured and the industrial base built up allowing for the eventual transition to a genuinely socialist society. However, whilst the economy was almost fully liberalised, little changed in the character of the polity. Indeed, alarmed by growing opposition to the regime amongst previously loyal elements of the population such as the Kronstadt sailors, a complete ban on factions and groupings within the Party was introduced at the Tenth Party Congress in March 1921 thereby making the regime even more authoritarian than it had been under War Communism. The ban on parties was maintained, as was the control on newspapers, publishing and all other media. Dissidents and opponents were hounded, jailed, exiled and shot, and many other measures were taken to ensure that no challenge could be mounted to the Party leadership. Thus although there was a considerable liberalisation of the economy, the state became if anything yet more dictatorial. It is difficult to see how, therefore, the growing authoritarianism of the state was caused by or even linked to economic factors. It was not developments in the economy that made the state more despotic; on the contrary the economy was subject to fewer controls than at any time since the Bolsheviks assumed power. What caused the development and con-solidation of the dictatorship was surely the Bolsheviks' insistence on maintaining a monopoly on power. They believed that they were able to understand the nature of the historical process and they believed, furthermore, that they were the only ones who could guide Russia to socialism. All the other political parties had effectively shown they were in error by not always supporting the Bolshevik line. It followed, therefore, that no other group or party had the right to exist let alone participate in government. The dictatorial character of the Soviet state thus had less to do in these early days with any economic measures introduced by the Bolsheviks as with their unwillingness to contemplate the possibility that any view or opinion other than their own had any validity.

Hayek's argument that central planning leads to totalitarianism appears more appropriate when applied to the Soviet Union after 1928 when Stalin introduced the first of the Five Year Plans. It is at this point that we see an enormous extension of the power of the state into people's lives, with the establishment of massive planning bureaucracies and the quite unparalleled intrusion of the state into every person's life. It is at this point also that the state develops more fully those characteristics that many have regarded as quintessentially totalitarian. Firstly, the violence that had always been a part of Soviet life escalated into what can only adequately be described as a war against certain sections of the population, prin-cipally the Kulaks or land-owning peasants, the Jews, and the mem-bers of more obdurate nationalities such as the Ukrainians and

White Russians. It is true that as recent studies have pointed out
certain sections of the population such as the skilled working class
benefited from the extension of state powers.[6] It is also undoubtedly
true that there was considerable support for Stalin's 'left turn'; but
this does not in any way detract from the basic point that life in the
Soviet Union became immeasurably harsher, not to say terrifying,
for much of the population. Furthermore, it is after 1928 that Party
rule finally gave way to full-blown tyranny and the consolidation of
Stalin's personal cult. The Party became little more than a rubber
stamp for Stalin's decisions and in any case was rapidly filled by his
own place-men who owed their jobs and in many cases their lives to
Stalin. Adulation and obeisance thus became the order of the day. It
was no longer enough merely to comply with what Stalin ordered;
each person had to show that he believed the leader was right about
everything, that he was infallible. It was Stalin's desire to elevate
himself to the level of omnipotent prophet that gives the era its
unique character: the show trials of those who had strayed from the
path of orthodoxy, the celebratory parades, the endless eulogising of
the wisdom of the *Vozhd*, and the purges. All these images of the
Soviet Union testify to the transformation of the Soviet Union after
1928. They also appear to validate Hayek's argument that central
planning leads to despotism. Stalin was of course an immensely
powerful figure before central planning was brought in, but it was
only with the transformation of the economy that he was able to
cement his own personal tyranny and to set about radically changing
Soviet society. To Hayek this intensification of state power is not of
course accidental. Stalin did not in this sense acquire greater power
simply because he wanted it. For Hayek the concentration of power
is the consequence of central planning, and is an inevitable product
of it. Thus where central planning is established the result is bound in
his view to be a form of Stalinism.

Persuasive though this account may be, it is still not entirely clear
how central planning as opposed to other factors led to the practices
associated with the period. It is certainly true that the establishment
of planning on the scale of the Soviet model resulted in an enormous
increase in the power of the state, and it is also true that there was an
immense increase in the size of the bureaucracy. Any pretension that
the Soviet regime might have had to establishing 'democratic planning' was completely forgotten by the time it came around to setting
up a planned economy at the end of the 1920s. By this time a cult of

the expert had firmly established itself in the Soviet Union. Every-thing was to be solved scientifically, according to the precepts of Marxism-Leninism-Stalinism. Planning was to be conducted along rational grounds, rather than, as Lenin had apparently hoped in the headier days of 1917, through democratic discussion. However, much of the violence that characterised this 'Revolution from Above' was the product of collectivisation rather than planning. Stalin was not content merely with dictating what the peasants could or could not grow and what prices goods could be sold for, which is the form agricultural planning took in Britain and Germany during the war. He demanded the extension of the ownership and control of the land together with the collectivisation of the peasantry into enormous state or co-operatively run farms, the *Kolkhoz* and *Sovkhoz*. It was this wholesale and quite unprecedented revolution in property rela-tions and in agricultural production that lay behind much of the violence of the period. Land was simply confiscated and much of the peasantry was rounded up and herded off to unfamiliar and often inhospitable new lands. There was little attempt at mediation or compromise. No compensation was offered or given to those about to be dispossessed, indeed quite the contrary. Since Stalin considered the process of transfer as part of the class war and as part of the price to be paid for building 'socialism in one country', he was quite prepared to order the deportation or even the killing of those who failed to comply. It was not therefore the extension of planning that was responsible for the violence associated with collectivisation, but the decision to bring agricultural production under state control. Stalin in this sense was not forced to nationalise land because he introduced planning. He did so because he believed that the abolition of private property and the placing of production in the hands of the state were necessary steps in the construction of socialism. Stalin was not alone either in arguing that such steps could only be achieved through force. Trotsky, Preobrazensky and many others had long argued for the same course of action. Nationalisation and col-lectivisation were thus aims of the regime rather than courses of action made necessary by the introduction of planning. Central planning could have been brought in without violence against property owners, as indeed it was in Britain and elsewhere during the war by use of incentives and quotas. The point is that the regime had decided that the existence of private property was no longer compatible with the existence of a socialist state. The tide turned against peaceful co-existence with the peasants and other land owners. Socialism was to be brought in whether they liked it or not. It is also difficult to see why the introduction of planning could be held responsible for many of the other practices associated with the Stalinist period. The move, for example, from Party oligarchy to one-man rule was not surely the product of planning, but of Stalin's desire to achieve a position of omnipotence within the system. It is one thing to say that planning produces a concentration of power in the hands of the state, which is undoubtedly true, yet quite another to say that it makes necessary the creation of tyranny. Nor is it immediately apparent how planning could be said to have led to the pursuit of ideological uniformity. The desire for uniformity is surely a reflection of the fact that the Bolsheviks believed they possessed the truth and thus that other opinions and arguments could not be tolerated. The quest for ideological uniformity is implied in the whole idea of a 'party line', that is a position to which a person has to adhere whether he or she privately believes it to be right or wrong. It was the success of the Bolsheviks in acceding to the disciplines imposed by the line that held them together through 1917 when many of them including Stalin argued against seizing power. It was this discipline that enabled them to come through against all odds the constant crises they faced in the early years of the regime. It was this discipline that justified the banning of opposition and the putting down of the rebellion at Kronstadt, and it was this unity that Stalin ultimately managed to manipulate for his own advantage in the inner Party struggles of the 1920s. The tendency of the Party to seek ideological conformity was not something that grew out of planning; it was part of the culture of the Bolshevik leadership. The grotesque spectacles of adulation that were such a feature of Stalin's rule were merely extensions of this culture of discipline and conformity, a culture and mentality brilliantly explored in Arthur Koestler's *Darkness at Noon*.

It is difficult to see therefore how planning shaped the character of Stalin's regime. There certainly was an increase in the power of the state, but this fact alone does not explain why Stalin's rule developed in the manner it did. It helps to explain how the Soviet Union was able to gather the resources necessary to begin revolutionising the system of production. It helps to explain how the Soviets managed to modernise the system of production and to provide the means for defeating Hitler in the Second World War. It also helps to explain the emergence of what became known as the 'new class', that is, the comparatively privileged sector of bureaucrats and apparatchiks who went on to govern the system until the Soviet Union finally expired. However, it does not appear to help us explain the mass deportations, the war on the peasants, the liquidation of classes, the co-ordination of society, the imposition of a quasi-messianic doctrine, or the elevation of the leader to the status of prophet. In short, it does not help us to explain the particular character of the tyranny that emerged under Stalin.

There is no doubt that Hayek is at least partly right about central planning. His assertion that planning leads to a strengthening of the state and to the development of a large bureaucratic apparatus and an increase in the power of officialdom appears to be sound. In every state where central planning has been introduced the state has of necessity grown to cope with the increased responsibilities that go with planning an economy. We need not, in other words, agree with Hayek that planning is a bad thing, i.e. that it diminishes individual liberty and leads to economic and social stagnation, to recognise that the assumption of such powers makes inevitable a growth in the scope and power of the state and hence in the number of officials, the amount of resources under command, and so forth. Hayek is right to argue that planning inevitably involves taking a certain amount of decision-making power away from individuals, particularly those owning land or factories affected by the introduction of planning, and putting it in the hands of state-appointed officials. This is not in dispute except amongst those who still cling to hopes of 'democratic planning'. What is in dispute is whether that extension of state power requires the introduction of tyrannical methods and practices to make it work. What is still not clear, in other words, is why this growth in the power of the state makes necessary the development of totalitarianism. Why does planning have to lead to despotism, to the enforcement of ideological uniformity, to the Gulag?

The difficulty with Hayek's argument appears to stem from his assumption that planning can only work where there is complete ideological uniformity, or rather where people appear to act in complete ideological uniformity. As we saw earlier, Hayek thinks that planning can only work where everyone thinks and acts in the same way. Successful planning requires the possession of a model of human needs so that production can be aimed at meeting these needs and no others. The state has to develop a consensus about the ends of the plan, for otherwise people will become discontented as their needs are left unfulfilled. Yet in Hayek's view, given that people differ in their opinion about what they need, such a task is necessarily impossible to achieve. People do not agree about what they want and so therefore it is impossible under normal circumstances to arrive at such a consensus. It is partly for this reason that Hayek favours the market as a mechanism for the production and distribution of goods. In the market it is the individual who through exercising his choice as a consumer decides what products and services are provided. The only way to make a plan work, on the other hand, is to manufacture a consensus by imposing a model of needs on the population. It is thus this desire to create uniformity, to make everyone essentially the same, that leads to totalitarianism. So in his view centrally planned systems are terroristic and totalitarian because they attempt to force their reluctant citizens into an ideological straitjacket.

The problem with this account is that it confuses two quite separate issues, the inspiration for central planning and the mechanism by which central planning works. It is perfectly true that central planning is, in a sense, the product of collectivist ideology. Socialists have argued for central planning because they thought that planning was the best way of ensuring economic growth and social justice. Planning has never in this sense been justified (as the market has) because it is 'natural', but because it was thought by those advocating its introduction to be more efficient and fairer. It is also true that most of the systems that have introduced central planning have been communist and that communist regimes legitimate their actions by reference to Marxism-Leninism. Furthermore these regimes have sought to impose an ideology on those subject to their rule. They have attempted to convince or persuade their populations that Marxism-Leninism is true, that it gives us an accurate picture of how the world develops. However, what is not clear is that there is a necessary connection between the *operation* of central planning and the imposition of an ideology. Indeed it is not clear that there is a necessary connection between the introduction of central planning and the use of force or coercion at all. Again the example of Britain is instructive. Here, although planning was extended for the first time to many areas of economic and social life, there was comparatively little complaint amongst those such as the owners of land and factories about the intrusion of the state into their hitherto private concerns. The point is that Britain was fighting a war of national survival and most people understandably felt that sacrifices had to be made and a collective effort fostered to make sure the war was won. The extension of planning thus met with little disapproval because people saw that it was necessary for the sake of *preserving* liberty. Some immediate loss of control over individual powers of disposition was justified therefore because of the far greater advantages that would result from it. Planning as many people saw it was a means to an end, not an end in itself. No real compulsion was therefore needed because most people saw the benefits of intervention. After the war planning was regarded rather differently. Churchill made his notorious remark that in order for planning to continue a 'Gestapo' would be needed to ensure that plans were carried out. In this sense Churchill echoed directly Hayek's concerns; but of course Churchill lost the election by a landslide. It was 'the planners' in the form of the Labour Party who were regarded as being in touch with the needs of the British people, not those who promised a return to more 'libertarian' arrangements. 'Never Again', the great slogan of the immediate post-war period, meant not only an end to war, but an end to poverty, to destitution, to ignorance, and to enforced idleness.[7] To banish these evils more not less planning was advocated and, as the results of the 1945 election show, most people agreed. The state did not need to enforce an ideology, no Gestapo was needed, no uniformity of minds was sought. Planning did not mean despotism. It did not mean a growing uniformity of needs. What it meant to most people was on the contrary the satisfaction of needs, of the need for health, education, work and housing. The introduction of planning appeared to promise these things and indeed to a significant extent it succeeded, and that is of course why many people accepted it.

What appears to be clear in considering these examples is that contrary to Hayek's belief there is no necessary connection between planning and despotism at all. He is quite right to argue that planning involves an extension of the state and that it involves more power for officials over the lives of ordinary people; but the extension of state power is not the same as despotism nor indeed totalitarianism. An 'extended state' can after all remain a democratic state, and as the example of Britain illustrates, it can remain a liberal and largely tolerant state as well. What is crucial is surely the attitude of ordinary people to the extension of power; whether they see the extended scope of the state as justified. If most people think it is

better to live in a state in which taxation is minimal and in which the
individual is as a consequence free to make his or her own arrangements regarding education, health, housing and transport, then
planning designed to order these spheres will be regarded as a gross
denial of liberty. In this situation then of course coercion would be
needed to make the plan work, for without it the state's orders will
not be obeyed. If, on the other hand, there is a strong movement in
favour of providing these services, if people do want the state to play
a major role in the provision of goods and services, then planning
will not be regarded as a hindrance to liberty. It will be regarded as
the means of increasing freedom and happiness. Hayek may or may
not be right about the relative merits of the market and *laissez-faire*
economics as against planning. He may, that is, be entirely correct in
arguing that only the market can provide goods and services at
optimum efficiency. However, what Hayek ignores is that what is
most effective in economic terms does not always coincide with what
people want or perceive themselves to need. Although we have to
assume that Hayek would find such a suggestion extraordinary, it
seems perfectly reasonable to suggest that people might even want to
trade off a degree of economic competitiveness for a degree of 'social
justice' or welfare measures. They may choose, in other words, to
have more planning even if it is less efficient than the market to enjoy
the perceived benefits of public sector provision of 'essential'
services. Indeed the enduring popularity of such provision in the
teeth of New Right and libertarian critiques inspired to a certain
extent by Hayek's analysis gives such a suggestion a degree of
credibility. That Hayek is unwilling to countenance such thoughts
testifies to the problematical nature of his own political philosophy.
He argues that it is the right of individuals to choose for themselves
how to live their lives. Yet Hayek evidently mistrusts individuals
when they choose a course of action with which he is not in sympathy. The choice of people in Britain and in many other countries to
implement planning to win wars and better their own lives is not a
valid choice because it is one made in favour of a system and an ethic
that Hayek abhors. He abhors it because it represents everything he
dislikes and finds offensive. It represents slavishness and
dependency, indolence and safety. He wants risk-taking, adventure,
responsibility and entrepreneurship. He cannot believe that people
could possibly choose to live such an apparently subservient form of
existence and so he insists that it must end in disaster, in a

confrontation between regime and people. However, persuasive though Hayek's account might seem, the truth is that the historical record stands against him. Planning has not led to despotism because it has helped provide many of the things that, Hayek notwithstanding, people living in modern states want.

*

Hayek is no doubt partly right about central planning. His assertion that planning leads to an increase in the power of the state is without doubt true and there are few who would want to dispute the fact. He is also surely right in his central assertion that 'democratic planning' is a pipe dream within the context of a modern highly industrialised state. As he warns, the attempt to regulate and oversee a vast and complicated economy by such methods is bound to end either in economic collapse or dictatorship or both. The history of the Soviet Union surely gives us enough material to find in Hayek's favour on both counts. Even a commentator as sympathetic to the socialist cause as Alec Nove can find no basis for the hope that a centrally planned economy can be run on the direct participatory lines suggested for example by Lenin. As he notes:

> Those who choose to attribute the distortions of the planning system to bureaucracy and lack of democracy put the cart before the horse. Given the aim of substituting planning for the market, administrative resources allocations for trade, the visible for the invisible hand, central control becomes an objective necessity. . . . In no society can an elected assembly decide by 115 votes to 73 where to allocate ten tonnes of leather, or whether to produce another 100 tonnes of sulphuric acid.[8]

However, it is one thing to argue that planning results in an extension of the state and quite another to argue that it results in totalitarianism. As our discussion has shown, although there are many examples of centrally planned systems that have been tyrannical, it is not clear that the tyrannical character of the state is down to or caused by central planning. The Soviet Union was already a dictatorship long before central planning was finally established. It simply made it easier for the regime to control the population and order affairs as it wished. On the other hand there are many examples of systems that have introduced central planning and not become tyrannical in the least. We have mentioned Britain but

we might equally well have discussed the multitude of other welfare
state systems that have been established since the war. In very few of
these cases has anything approaching the nightmare servile state
Hayek describes been established. On the contrary, not only have
welfare measures been popular with the people, they have proved
essential in maintaining the legitimacy of the political order during
periods of difficulty. The availability of welfare benefits and access to
various facilities and services must be counted one of the more
significant factors in the relative stability enjoyed by advanced capitalist systems over the last fifty years. The attack on intervention,
planning and welfare over the last two decades has been more a
response to the problem of continuing to fund extensive services than
to any perceived threat of encroaching totalitarianism. A final sign of
the inadequacy of his account is that the system most often described
as totalitarian, namely Nazi Germany, cannot be fitted into it.
Although the Third Reich displayed all the characteristics Hayek
associated with totalitarianism, it never developed planning beyond
the stage found in many other states such as Britain. Planning in Nazi
Germany remained largely piecemeal and confined to those areas of
the economy directly connected with the building up of military
power. Hayek may be justified in regarding the Third Reich as the
prototype of a totalitarian system; but not for the reasons he gives.

Notes

1 F. A. Hayek, *The Road to Serfdom* (London, 1986), p. 52.
2 *Ibid.*, p. 46.
3 *Ibid.*, p. 95.
4 John Hiden and John Farquarson, *Explaining Hitler's Germany. Historians and the Third Reich* (London, 1983), p. 99.
5 Martin Broszat, *The Hitler State*, translated by J. W. Hiden (London
   1981), p. 300. For a direct comparison between the planning regimes of
   Hitler and Stalin see the article by Paul Dukes and John W. Hiden,
   'Towards an Historical Comparison of Nazi Germany and Soviet Russia
   in the 1930s', *New Zealand Slavonic Journal*, no. 1 (1979), pp. 56ff.
6 A great deal of work is currently being done in this area, much of it
   showing how inadequate it is to regard Stalin's actions during and after
   the 'Revolution from Above' as wholly without support in the Party or the
   country more generally. See in particular the works of Sheila Fitzpatrick
   and Gabor Rittersporn referred to in the bibliography.
7 For an account of the character of the British economy during and

immediately after the Second World War see Peter Hennessy, *Never Again. Britain 1945–1951* (London, 1993). See also Arthur Marwick, *Britain in the Century of Total Wars: War Peace and Social Change, 1900–1967* (London, 1968).

8 Alec Nove, *The Economics of Feasible Socialism* (London, 1983), p. 77.

2

Hannah Arendt
The Origins of Totalitarianism

Although Hayek would have some justification in arguing that he was the first to address the question of what caused the emergence of totalitarianism, *The Road to Serfdom* only treats at a tangent the nature of totalitarian regimes themselves. Hayek's book, as should by now by clear, is not so much addressed to the question of what totalitarianism is, but of how it might be avoided. Hayek's goal was thus prescriptive rather than explanatory. He wanted to challenge what he considered to be the growing menace of 'collectivist' ideas, and to persuade people of the justice and rationality of the *laissez-faire* approach to government. What characterised totalitarian regimes, what gave them their particular character was a question which Hayek dealt with only in passing.

It was not until 1949 and the publication of Hannah Arendt's *The Burden of Our Times* (*The Origins of Totalitarianism*) that the study of totalitarianism was pursued in a really systematic fashion. Hayek, as we have seen, was interested not so much in totalitarianism itself as in the question of how liberal-democratic states could themselves be prevented from declining into totalitarianism. Arendt's approach was quite different. She was interested in the significance and meaning of totalitarianism as a historical event. She wanted to understand what had happened in Germany and the Soviet Union, and what had allowed totalitarianism to emerge in these countries at all. She wanted, as she puts it in *Origins*, to establish 'What happened? Why did it happen? How could it have happened?'[1] Totalitarianism, for Arendt, was not just another new political phenomenon, and totalitarian regimes were not just a novel form of state to be added to the list of possible dictatorships and despotisms. Totalitarianism was a cataclysm in Western life; it was a sign of the decaying if not moribund character of mass society, of the exhaustion of an entire political and social culture. Studying how totalitarianism developed was not therefore of mere historical interest; it was bound up with a process of self-understanding and of coming to terms with what it means to live in a modern society.

Although *Origins* concentrates on attempting to explain or understand the emergence of the regimes of Hitler and Stalin, her work has, nevertheless, been enormously influential for those seeking to define the concept of totalitarianism for comparative purposes. Indeed, it is evident that *Origins* has become the classic text in the field, although it is only in the last third of the book that she discusses what totalitarianism is and what characterises totalitarian regimes. The other two sections contain an archaeology of the ideas and assumptions that she feels are at the root of totalitarianism, principally racism and imperialism. The work was a constant point of reference for the debate that raged throughout the 1950s and 1960s as to the meaning of the term 'totalitarianism'. Later on during the 1980s when the concept of totalitarianism was in the process of being rehabilitated, Arendt's work was cited as an inspiration by a new generation of thinkers trying to understand communism.[2] *Origins* is thus a key text in the study of totalitarianism. Establishing the extent to which her arguments about the character of Nazism and Bolshevism and the systems they erected are convincing will go a long way to showing how useful the concept of totalitarianism is.

*

Like Hayek, Arendt was convinced that totalitarianism is a specifically modern phenomenon. Like him, she was impressed by the fact that ideology and the propagation of a distinct world view seemed to be of such importance to the regimes that emerged from the fascist and communist movements of the early part of the century. Unlike Hayek, however, Arendt did not believe that it was socialist ideology that was the common factor between them, or that it was socialism that was to blame for the rise of totalitarianism. Whilst the Bolsheviks clearly possessed a form of socialist ideology and sincerely believed that class was the essential determinant of social life as well as historical development, the Nazis, as she makes clear, were inspired by a quite different set of assumptions. They may well have donned socialist clothes to broaden their appeal to the working class, but the Nazis' ideal society, the *Volksgemeinschaft*, was above all a community united by relations of blood and race rather than class. If, however, it is not socialist ideas that unite these two otherwise disparate movements then what in her view is it?

According to Arendt the key to understanding how Nazism and Bolshevism resulted in the same form of rule is to look not at the content of their respective ideologies, but at their form. What we should be looking at, she says, is not what Nazis or Bolsheviks say, but the manner in which their arguments are expressed. Look, in other words, at what is implied by belief in an ideology, what changes in outlook and behaviour result from it. An ideology, Arendt explains, is a set of ideas that purports to provide an all-encompassing explanation for social and historical development. Ideologies work by isolating some alleged fact about human life, about nature, or society, and elevating it into the key that determines all other facts about where we have come from and where we are going. Belief in an ideology is therefore tantamount to belief in the power of mankind to solve the riddle of history. It is a belief in our ability to comprehend scientifically the process that makes us who we are. As Arendt puts it, 'An ideology is quite literally what its name indicates: it is the logic of an idea. Its subject matter is history, to which the "idea" is applied; the result of this application is not a body of statements about something that is, but the unfolding of a process which is in constant change.'[3] Bolshevism, for example, being derived from Marxism claims that the whole of human history can be characterised as a struggle between classes. Classes, they believe, rise and fall according to objective forces that are out of the control of any particular individual. History is thus an objective process that can be studied and understood in exactly the same way as processes in the natural world. Nazism, on the other hand, regards the struggle between the races as the motor of history. Nazis see the world as an eternal competition for supremacy between different castes and creeds, seeing all human action as in some sense guided by the interest of the group. As Arendt makes clear, this singling out of one aspect of human existence and making it the key that determines how everything else develops is not, however, the preserve of apparently extreme or radical ideologies like Bolshevism (or communism) and Nazism. Unlike Popper, for example, who wants to distinguish between dangerous 'historicist' ideologies such as these and ideologies such as liberalism that support and sustain the 'open society', Arendt argues that all ideologies share this dogged essentialism. They all, that is, embody the modern faith in our capacity finally to comprehend the workings of mankind. For Arendt this faith is not, however, derived from reason, but from an aggressive and potentially dangerous form of hubris.

The danger lurking within ideologies is very clear to Arendt. An ideology is above all a closed system of thought. Ideologies start with a certain fact, say about human nature, and then explain all other facts about social life by reference to it. Ideological thinking is therefore characterised by its 'stringent logicality'. It assumes that knowledge of fact A will lead to knowledge of facts B, C, D, etc. Knowledge of fact A thus gives a person knowledge of all other facts because all facts are held to derive from the initial one. This means that once fact A has been established debate and discussion about everything else is rendered superfluous. Bolshevism, in Arendt's account of it, starts with the fact that class struggle is the underlying factor determining the character of history. This is taken by Bolsheviks to be fact A. Since fact A has been located, to understand the rest of reality all one has to do is work back to it. If we want to know why a given person acted in a particular way we go back to the original fact. We know that class struggle explains how humans behave, therefore to understand why a person is behaving in a particular way all we have to do is to ask what class he or she belongs to, and what his or her relation is to other classes. The same is true for the explanation of large-scale historical events. Possession of an ideology in this sense does away with the need for reasoning, indeed, with the need for thought. Since all facts are in effect knowable by simple application of the key, all that is left is deduction. The world thus becomes a collection of facts that are comprehensible through the process of logic. Once one knows how the logic works, no further steps are needed. History is determined by fact A. To understand everything within history, to understand all societies, all epochs, all actions, we simply deduce from it. It is, so Arendt believes, this reduction of reality to logical terms that makes ideology so dangerous. Once a person becomes a convinced follower of an ideology he or she has, Arendt thinks, effectively surrendered the freedom and capacity to think. Ideologies are logical and logic cannot be challenged because it is entirely self-referential. Once it is established that $2 + 2 = 4$ then, Big Brother notwithstanding, it is impossible to challenge that statement. Yet, to give up the desire to challenge, to contemplate, to reason is at the same time to give up one's freedom because without thought one is reduced to a mere member of a species. More radically, it is to give up being an individual, a subject. Individuals are people who are able to differentiate themselves from those around them. They are people who have opinions, preferences and needs that are specifically their own, not those of a group. However, they cannot differentiate themselves if they have given up thinking because thought is the basis of all subjective life. All individuals possess self-consciousness and hence the capacity to think for themselves; but by succumbing to belief in an ideology they succumb to the demand for uniformity and sameness. Unwilling and unable to sustain their own distinct views, they lose their sense of self and dissolve into the mass of other believers. Thus, as Arendt argues:

> Ideologies are harmless, uncritical, and arbitrary opinions only as long as they are not believed in seriously. Once their claim to total validity is taken literally they become the nuclei of logical systems in which, as in the systems of paranoiacs, everything follows comprehensibly and even compulsorily once the first premise is accepted. The insanity of such systems lies not only in their first premise but in the very logicality with which they are constructed. The curious logicality of all isms, their simple-minded trust in the salvation value of stubborn devotion without regard for specific, varying factors, already harbours the first germs of totalitarian contempt for reality and factuality.[4]

A further danger inherent to belief in an ideology is that because ideologies are logical 'closed' systems of thought there is always a disparity between the view of reality embodied in the ideology and reality itself. An ideology presents a consistent, uniform view of the world. It says that to understand why things are as they are we need only look at their origins. Since all phenomena in the social world are caused by the same factor (human nature, race, class, or whatever), once that factor has been understood then everything else will become clear. Unfortunately, as Arendt explains, reality is not like that. The world is highly complex, highly diverse and hence difficult to comprehend in the simplistic terms offered by ideologies. This complexity is, Arendt argues, given in the very nature of human life. Part of what distinguishes mankind from other species is the 'fact of natality'.[5] We are born without any predetermined character or programmed habits or attitudes, and as such there is an element of unpredictability in the fact of birth. We do not know what the child will be like, what he or she is and what he or she will become. Thus for Arendt there are no 'facts' about human nature or any other aspect of our existence conspiring to shape society and human evolution behind our backs. There is no 'invisible hand' determining how we must behave or limiting the possibilities open to us. Each person is the author of his or her own actions and thus completely responsible for them. Accordingly, in Arendt's view, ideologies inevitably struggle to contain and explain everything that happens. The world is simply too complex to be able to be grasped in the way ideologists claim. History is a story that is yet to be written, thus the notion that an ideology could explain history or predict where the forces of history are taking us is utterly false. As Arendt argues: 'No ideology which aims at the explanation of all historical events of the past and at mapping out the course of all events of the future can bear the unpredictability which springs from the fact that men are creative, that they can bring forward something so new that nobody ever foresaw it.'[6]

Confronted by the inability of his or her ideology to account for everything that occurs a person holding an ideology therefore has two choices. He or she can capitulate to the world's complexity and thereby recognise that it is more difficult to explain than ideologies would have us believe. Such a capitulation would represent the return to thought, to reason. It would signal that the former believer had given up the nursery blanket of ideological or superstitious belief, and was prepared to recognise that simplicity is not a virtue when it comes to thinking about what is 'out there'. The other choice is to repel reality: to withdraw ever further into the recesses of certainty and dogma. Yet this still leaves the problem of preventing reality from pressing against the thin shell of ideological belief. How can reality be prevented from exploding the myths upon which every ideology is based? The answer is to withdraw ever deeper into the fictitious world shared by the other believers in the same creed. It is to maintain a ruthless vigilance against anything and anybody who might disturb the ideology. It is to protect, cover up, hide away the 'truths' of the ideology so that they are in effect irrefutable. It is for this reason that those who follow an ideology are forced, Arendt thinks, to adopt conspiratorial, 'closed' methods of organisation. They cannot afford emotionally or practically to have their cherished beliefs challenged. For this reason they move underground, out of harm's way. Yet this is, she explains, only a short term solution. The only action that would really guarantee the health and vitality of the ideology is the conquering of reality itself. If the world were mastered, if every thought and every action were completely controlled, then nothing would be able to refute the ideology, nothing would be able to show up its lack of verisimilitude. According to Arendt, implicit to belief in an ideology is thus the desire for 'total domination'. This is the real *telos*, the real goal of ideologies and to ignore it is to ignore the real dangers posed by them. Those possessing ideologies must seek expansion, they must seek to conquer everything that contradicts or clashes with their logical view of the world. Because people are capable of spontaneous action we represent a threat to the consistent universe demanded by ideologies. It follows that all individuals must be dominated in every aspect of their lives. In this sense, as Arendt makes clear, *all* ideologies are totalitarian. They all demand a 'total explanation' of the world and thus they all demand that the world be mastered and subordinated to conform with the ideology itself. This is also the reason totalitarian regimes represent such a threat to global security. As Arendt argues:

> The struggle for total domination of the total population of the earth,
> the elimination of every competing nontotalitarian reality, is inherent
> in the totalitarian regimes themselves; if they do not pursue global rule
> as their ultimate goal, they are only too likely to lose whatever power
> they have already seized. Even a single individual can be absolutely
> and reliably dominated only under global totalitarian conditions.[7]

Yet if it is true that, as Arendt argues, all ideologies contain the seeds of totalitarianism then we are still left with the question of why some ideologies result in totalitarianism and others do not. Why, for example, did Nazism and Bolshevism lead to tyranny if in content they are no worse than any other ideology?

In Arendt's view the reason for the rise of totalitarianism has less to do with the ideological content of Nazism and Bolshevism than with the emergence of certain conditions that lent themselves very favourably to the emergence of totalitarian movements in Germany and Russia. As she makes clear in the first two sections of *Origins*, part of the blame has to lie with the character of modernity. In common with many other social theorists, not least Marx and Weber, Arendt believes that industrialisation and urbanisation led to a profound change in the character of modern life. Modernity for

Arendt means alienation and anomie.[8] It means a greater distancing of people from the decisions that will shape how their life is lived. It means a greater attachment to the values of materialism, profit and loss, consumption, at the expense, so she argues, of 'action'. Modern life represents the triumph of the private over the public, leading to a loss of perspective and understanding, of 'worldliness'. Under certain conditions this can lead to a deepening of feelings of alienation. It can lead to a feeling of what Arendt describes as 'uprootedness' and, worst of all, to a feeling that one is 'superfluous' or unimportant. When these feelings of helplessness and isolation are widespread then 'social atomization' is the result. Such a condition is an enormous danger to the body politic. When people think that their actions have no consequence, no meaning, they become susceptible to the songs of the Sirens telling them that if only they join this movement, believe this ideology, then all their problems will be solved. Of course the simpler or cruder the ideology the more effective this message will be. When people are so distraught by what they see around them, and so alienated by the actions of those charged with ordering social life, then simple messages are more likely to hold sway over the popular imagination. People in these conditions want to be transported from what they see about them. They do not want more of the same; more appeals to calmness, rationality and the process of law. They want action and they want it now. The reason Bolshevism and Nazism were effective is ultimately because they manipulated such feelings in a direct and intelligible fashion. It is because, as Arendt puts it, the 'elements of experience' on which they were built were 'politically more important than those of other ideologies'.[9] They are both radical ideologies; they both see a break with the present as the only solution to the ills of society. In the context of deep social alienation they were thus able to capture the imagination of enough people to make their respective movements viable. Ordinary political discourse had broken down in Germany and Russia and hence room was opened up for the full expression of the implicitly totalitarian character that, as Arendt makes clear, lurks within all ideologies.

In the conditions of a functioning body politic and an informed and actively political public those who seek to advance a particular ideological cause have to temper their message to gain the support of the sceptical, the luke-warm, the uncommitted. This leads to a more plural, more open style of politics in which ideologies compete against one another to attract support. Particularly in democracies, clearly defined rules evolve which curb the more authoritarian traits of political parties, making them more accountable to their members and to the public more generally. Furthermore, because of the difficulty of organising parties on conspiratorial lines ideologies are themselves subject to debate and criticism. Their worst or least realistic aspects can thus be rejected or modified to suit the nature of the circumstances. In other words, under democratic conditions ideologies are prevented from becoming totalitarian because they are constantly subject to examination and criticism. However, in conditions in which the body politic has broken down and where the population has become atomised parties develop along quite different lines. Instead of participating in open and plural debate, they become closed and conspiratorial. Instead of being accountable to their members, they become authoritarian and dominated by an ever-diminishing number of fanatics. Instead of recognising limits to their behaviour they look for every opportunity to challenge and oppose the rule of law. In such conditions what is merely latent in the nature of ideologies is allowed to express itself fully. What this means in practice is, firstly, that a clear leader emerges to take control of the entire organisation and to guide it in its attempts not merely to assume power, but to fulfil the historical destiny outlined in the ideology. Arendt is clear that it does not matter who this leader is, only that there be a leader who can act as the focal point for the movement. It is a mistake to think that only the naturally charismatic, the naturally gifted or talented can become leader. In fact, as she points out, looking at the examples of Hitler and Stalin, virtually the opposite is the case. People do not trust the flamboyant and the gifted, so such a figure will find it difficult to fare well in the internal struggles that are such a feature of totalitarian movements. We only have to compare the careers of Stalin and Trotsky, Arendt argues, to see what an advantage it is for a leadership candidate at least to appear quite ordinary. The leader is, nevertheless, crucially important, because without the leader the movement will lack direction and focus. Ideologies are like religions; to determine what it is permitted to believe, what actions are illegitimate and legitimate, there must be one source of authority, one figure who can rise above disputes and give authoritative verdicts. Furthermore, since ideologies claim scientific insight into the nature of history, since they claim to reveal truth, to have more than one leader would be like having more than one oracle at Delphi. Reflecting their status as seers within the movement, both Hitler and Stalin were thus effectively beyond challenge once they had established their authority. For the movement to rid itself of its leader would be to rid itself of its guiding light. Such movements largely exist because people have expressed their faith in the leader's power to discern the forces shaping history. The notion, therefore, that the leader should be accountable to the membership, or should even listen to what they have to say, is one that rails against the logic informing the development of the movement. The leader is the key to its success; it is the leader who possesses special powers, and thus it is to the leader, not the movement or party organisation, that the members and supporters owe their allegiance.

Reflecting the special role accorded the leader, the structure of these movements deviates strongly from the pattern of other political groups and organisations, particularly those found within democratic states. Discussion is held to a minimum, and is confined to practical matters to do with tactics and organisation. Party meetings are purely celebratory occasions and are normally in the form of rallies, parades, and so forth giving the leader the chance to appear before his adoring followers. Organisationally, movements resemble, as Arendt in her highly original formulation puts it, an 'onion', with the leader 'in a kind of empty space' in the middle of the entire operation. All the important questions facing the movement are resolved by him and thus he is the axis around which it revolves. The next 'layer' is formed by the leader's most trusted lieutenants, the heads of the most important party organisations, and those entrusted with the security of the leader and his entourage. Subsequent layers are formed by those with slightly less responsibility, slightly less prestige, and so on, right the way to the outermost layer which is composed of the newest, least encumbered members and sympathisers. What this onion structure reflects, in Arendt's view, is the varying degree of fanaticism within the movement. The leader is of course the most convinced of his own powers and of the truth of the ideology, and he forms the heart of the whole structure. The next layer is, on the one hand, buoyed by the fanaticism of the leader, but, on the other, given a greater sense of perspective by contact with those closer to normality in the next layer out. As Arendt remarks, the unique structure of the movement helps it to become 'shockproof' against the intrusion of the outside world. As she notes:

All the extraordinarily manifold parts of the movement: the front
organizations, the various professional societies, the party membership, the party bureaucracy, the elite formation and police groups, are
related in such a way that each forms the façade in one direction and
the center in the other, that is plays the role of normal outside world
for one layer and the role of radical extremism for the other.[10]

The movement must come to terms with reality, it must finance itself,
attract members, and so on; but those upon whom this task of
negotiating with the real world fall are generally those furthest away
from the core of the movement. The fictitious world generated by the
ideology is thereby preserved along with the fanaticism and energy
needed to secure and maintain power.

What contributes to the novelty of totalitarian movements is that
on assuming power their essential characteristics remain unchanged
although they have taken over the offices of the state. In other forms
of dictatorship the assumption of power by a given group or clique
normally results in its members taking over the functions of the state.
Loyal followers are rewarded by being given the most prestigious
posts and offices within the state's hierarchy. Despite the change in
personnel, the character of the state does not usually change
significantly. There are still distinct ministries or offices with particular tasks to achieve and a particular manner of achieving them.
There are still laws, rules and regulations governing the manner in
which officials act. What changes is that the power of the state is used
to serve the interests of a new elite. This elite thus uses the state for its
own benefit. It does not normally seek to reshape the state for some
entirely different purpose.

Under a totalitarian regime, on the other hand, the entire state
apparatus is made subordinate to the movement, eventually
becoming a part of it. The reason for this difference is that
totalitarian movements regard the capture of the state as a means
rather than as an end in itself. Possession of an ideology is not the
same as a set of goals. Totalitarian movements do not set out simply
to complete a given programme, but to keep everything 'in motion'.
The ideology is at odds with the real world and thus reality has to be
prevented from destroying it. Only by maintaining momentum can
the movement preserve reality from impinging upon and eventually
destroying the fictitious world that it has created to mirror the logical
structure of the ideology. In this sense, the very idea of the state is
entirely anathema to the movement. A state represents solidity and

permanence; it embodies laws and rules that in the Weberian ideal
are supposed to possess validity independent of the particular values
or beliefs of those who rule. It is a neutral entity, playing the role of
umpire in the conflicts and antagonisms that beset daily life. For
totalitarian movements there is, however, no neutrality, no independence; there is only history and the onward march of the 'idea'. As
Arendt remarks:

> The seizure of power through the means of violence is never an end in
> itself but only the means to an end, and the seizure of power in any
> given country is only a welcome transitory stage but never the end of
> the movement. The practical goal of the movement is to organise as
> many people as possible within its framework and to set and keep
> them in motion; a political goal that would constitute the end of the
> movement simply does not exist.[11]

Accordingly, what characterises totalitarian regimes is the complete
breakdown of institutional autonomy. Instead of the clear
delineation of offices and departments, we see the creation of a
multitude of overlapping fiefdoms and petty empires. Instead of
particular tasks being allocated to particular officials we see various
officials being allocated to the same task. Thus although both the
Nazis and the Bolsheviks presented themselves as the very acme of
organisational efficiency, the only principle in operation in either of
these regimes was that of the *Führerprinzip*. In these regimes the
offices of the state are completely subordinate to the word of the
leader. The leader is the only fixed and enduring element of the
system. Everything else is in motion, in flux, and therefore beset by
instability and uncertainty. It is the leader who decides everything:
which institutions are to do which tasks, which officials are to be
given which responsibilities, and which resources are to be supplied
to which projects. Only the leader can decide these things because
only the leader knows how the system works and how its various
parts are related to each other. Of course, this in turn strengthens the
position of the leader within the movement's hierarchy. Everyone
has to pay obeisance to the leader because there is no other means of
getting the power needed to carry out the tasks that have been
allocated to them.

Reflecting on the novel manner in which the movement transforms
itself into regime, Arendt believes commentators are mistaken if they
think that totalitarian systems are in some sense authoritarian. An

authoritarian regime is one in which there are rules and laws that are in principle knowable and which circumscribe the powers of the rulers. Authoritarian regimes are in this sense like every type of political system, stable, hierarchical, governed by laws and conventions. The main difference between them and authoritarian regimes is that the size of the elite ruling the country is smaller. Thus, even the worst tyrannies are, she thinks, better than totalitarian systems. It is still possible in an authoritarian system for people to be aware of the laws and thus to be aware of what sort of behaviour is expected of them. At least here, as Arendt puts it, people are able to know why they have been arrested. This is never the case in totalitarian systems. Here, since the regime aims at nothing less than 'total domination', ordinary notions of guilt and innocence are irrelevant. Everyone is in a sense 'guilty' because everyone's existence as a distinct autonomous entity represents a risk to the regime. In these regimes there are no fixed or permanent rules, because that would suggest that there is a source of authority existing independently from the leader's will.

The other difficulty she finds with contemporary accounts of totalitarian regimes is the notion that such regimes are 'monolithic', i.e. that power is exercised in a vertical direction moving from the leader to the led. In her view, the opposite is the case.[12] The main characteristic of these systems is their relative lack of structure, their 'shapelessness' as she puts it. To describe a system as monolithic is to imply that relations of power are fixed and known, set in concrete as it were. It suggests that such relations are unchanging, static, and that over any given period of time little change takes place to them. However, Arendt argues that in totalitarian regimes the opposite is the case. The reality, she thinks, is that everything is in motion. Nothing is certain in totalitarian regimes, except the certainty that the ideology is correct. However, since the content of the ideology constantly changes according to the needs of the leader, it is impossible to know on a daily basis what constitutes the truth. Thus the great difficulty for the citizens of such systems is that the regime is not interested in eliciting mere obedience. They are not even interested in the more ambitious task of creating a core of convinced followers: people who are persuaded of the legitimacy and veracity of the ideology. Totalitarian rulers realise that the only means of safeguarding their fictitious world and hence their power is to destroy the capacity to think and hence the capacity to tell the difference between reality and falsity. Totalitarian rulers understand

that the existence of individuals represents the possibility that the]
ideology will be understood for what it is, a farrago of lies. They
understand that each new individual is born with the capacity to
think and hence with the capacity to reflect on his or her own
condition and the nature of the world. As Arendt comments:

> The category of the suspect thus embraces under totalitarian condi-
> tions the total population; every thought that deviates from the
> officially prescribed and permanently changing line is already suspect,
> no matter in which field of human activity it occurs. Simply because of
> their capacity to think, human beings are suspects by definition, and
> this suspicion cannot be diverted by exemplary behaviour, for the
> human capacity to think is also a capacity to change one's mind.[13]

It therefore follows that if the delicate web of mendacity spun by the
regime to justify its power is to be maintained, human nature will
itself have to be changed. There is no room in these regimes for
thinking, reasoning or reflecting individuals. People must thus be
terrorised to the point where they are incapable of thought.

It is this desire not merely to control individuals but to construct a
new type of subject that Arendt believes forms the logic behind the
setting up of concentration camps. It would be wrong, she thinks, to
regard these novel institutions simply as contemporary equivalents
of the dungeon. Although they also provide a means of punishing
enemies and other undesirables, their real purpose is as 'laboratories'
in which the regime can experiment to find new ways of creating its
model citizen. 'If we take totalitarian aspirations seriously', she
argues,

> and refuse to be misled by the common-sense assertion that they are
> utopian and unrealizable, it develops that the society of the dying
> established in the camps is the only form of society in which it is
> possible to dominate man entirely. Those who aspire to total domi-
> nation must liquidate all spontaneity, such as the mere existence of
> individuality will always engender, and track it down in its most
> private forms, regardless of how unpolitical and harmless these may
> seem. Pavlov's dog, the human specimen reduced to the most
> elementary reactions, the bundles of reactions that behave in exactly
> the same way, is the model 'citizen' of the totalitarian state; and such a
> citizen can be produced only imperfectly outside of the camps.[14]

Within the camps individuals can be isolated from the world. They
can be detached from the familiar and the known, and be subjected

to treatment that anywhere else would be regarded even by those carrying it out as unimaginable. Only here therefore can 'total terror' be achieved, because it is only here that the regime can confront individuals with the prospect of their own death for every moment of every day. Outside the camps domination is far more difficult to achieve. Terror can never be total because there are always times and places when individuals can be alone with their thoughts. Yet, try as it might to make the whole of society one great concentration camp, the regime is doomed to fall short of that ideal and hence to fall short of its goal of total domination. Populations are after all finite. Not everyone can be placed in camps and subjected to the extremes of terror only possible within them because the regime would soon run out of people to run the country, fight its wars, and so on. To turn the whole of society into a giant camp would thus very quickly lead to the disintegration of the regime.

Nevertheless, despite the impossibility of making the concentration camp the model for all social relationships, the presence within the system of such institutions enables a greater depth of subjugation to be achieved. Where there are death camps there is terror, and where there is terror there is social control. It is this fostering of pervasive terror throughout the population that is the most tangible benefit of the camp system. Terror, Arendt explains, destroys the 'space' between men. It imposes an 'iron band' around individuals preventing them from acting independently of each other. People are thus not merely denied access to the public realm in these systems: they are encased in an all-embracing 'loneliness' that deprives them of any meaningful social life. People who suspect all those around them, who are terrified of the environment in which they live, are those who live completely at the mercy of the regime. They depend on the regime for their idea or sense of the world because they cannot communicate their own experiences to others lest they are thought of as enemies. As a result, 'man loses trust in himself as the partner of his thoughts and that elementary confidence in the world which is necessary to make experience at all. Self and world, capacity for thought and experience are lost at the same time'.[15]

The product of totalitarian domination is not, as others argue, the convinced follower of a distinct ideological creed. Since conviction is itself a sign of the capacity to make judgements and hence a sign of the subject's independence of mind, this is a quality that totalitarian regimes must destroy if they are to succeed. People living within totalitarian states are not therefore simply manipulated or persuaded to think and behave in certain ways. Their autonomy is so under-mined that they become in effect part of a herd of utterly uprooted and superfluous creatures 'for whom the distinction between fact and fiction (i.e. the reality of experience) and true and false (i.e. the standards of thought) no longer exist'. The real novelty of totalitarian regimes is thus that they are able to dispense altogether with coercion as that word is ordinarily understood. Because terror is total, because it permeates the life of every person within the system, it becomes natural. When terror is total people lose their capacity to reflect upon their condition. They lose the sense that they are being forced or manipulated to think or behave in certain ways. Thus in fully developed totalitarian systems it is true to say that autonomy has effectively disappeared. Here, people are so terrorised, so coerced all that remains is one 'highly deficient sub-jectivity'. So successful are totalitarian techniques in undermining the ability of individuals to distinguish themselves from the herd created by mass society that it is quite possible to regard the popu-lations of these systems as 'one man'.

*

As should now be clear, for Arendt the key to understanding the nature of totalitarian systems is ideology. However, she is not talking about any specific ideology being totalitarian. She is not agreeing with Hayek that it is socialist ideology that is to blame for totalitarianism. She does not agree either with Popper's view that we should blame 'historicist' ideologies calling for 'utopian social engi-neering'. The problem is ideology *per se*. The reason for Arendt's mistrust of all forms of ideological belief is that she believes ideologies contain the seeds of tyranny. An ideology is no mere statement of preference about what form of society is best or most in keeping with the needs of the individual. It contains an entire account of our origins, development and future. It is, so those possessing ideologies claim, scientifically rigorous. Nothing is left to interpretation or refutation. Because they are logical, systematic systems of belief, possession of an ideology represents the abdication of responsibility for one's own thoughts and ideas. It represents the surrender of autonomy and self-consciousness to a closed, logically flawless system of thought. However, as she makes clear, ideologies are constantly forced into confrontation with the world because reality is far more complicated than ideologies suggest. Individuals are unpredictable creatures; they act spontaneously, making knowledge about the future course of society impossible in principle as well as in practice. The only way, therefore, to protect the ideology from refutation and collapse is to control every person, for only when everyone is under control and their actions co-ordinated with each other can the ideology be maintained. Only through total domination, in other words, can the ideology's fictitious world be prevented from imploding. It is this desire or, rather, need to control and master every element of the outside world that is unique to totalitarianism. It is this feature that gives these systems their unrelenting, 'total' air. An ideology drives a movement to seek total control of everything and everyone yet because it is impossible to achieve such a goal the regime is forced in effect to resort to terror to keep people from reflecting on their predicament. Motion, flux and uncertainty is thus the essence of totalitarian forms of rule.

The real strength of Arendt's account of totalitarianism lies most obviously with its descriptive vigour. Arendt wants not merely to tell us what a totalitarian system is, what its constituent parts are, and so forth. She wants to describe what it is like to live in such a system. She wants us to know what it means to be subject to such a form of rule. She wants us, in short, to understand the essence of totalitarianism, not merely its morphology. It is this effort to bring to life the historical experience of totalitarianism that is the most remarkable aspect of *Origins*, and which gives it much of its value.

The other apparent source of strength is that, unlike Hayek for example, Arendt's account of totalitarianism refuses to engage with the vexing question of whether certain ends could be said to be more totalitarian than others. She does not, that is, want to tell us that it is bad, irrational or despotic ideologies that lead to totalitarian regimes. As she appears to realise, the problem with such accounts of totalitarian ideologies is that they have to show how apparently different sets of beliefs, for example Nazism and communism, are essentially the same with respect to ends and goals. This is not easy, as Hayek's less than successful attempt to do just that shows. Arendt's account, on the other hand, escapes such questions altogether. She focuses on the *form* of ideological belief, attributing to all ideologies the capacity to inspire totalitarian movements and parties. As with contemporary critics of 'totalising discourse' such as Jean-François Lyotard, her argument is not with particular ideologies, but with the whole way of thinking implied in ideological systems. She therefore has no problems with the question of ends and goals since it would appear to follow from what she says about ideologies that, for example, liberalism and conservatism are just as potentially totalitarian as Nazism and Bolshevism. That the totalitarian regimes of the twentieth century were erected by Bolsheviks and Nazis is thus a quirk of history. It is not implied in the content of the ideologies, their aims and goals, themselves. As she puts it,

> all ideologies contain totalitarian elements, but these are fully developed only by totalitarian movements, and this creates the deceptive impression that only racism and communism are totalitarian in character. The truth is, rather, that the real nature of all ideologies was revealed only in the role that the ideology plays in the apparatus of totalitarian domination.[16]

Unlike Hayek's theory of totalitarianism, which relies for its cogency on convincing us that the Nazis and the communists wanted to construct the same sort of society (i.e. one in which scarcity would be overcome through central planning), Arendt's theory stands or falls largely on her account of the actual nature of ideologies. To assess the validity of her account of totalitarianism we therefore need to ask, is she right about the character of ideology? Are all ideologies potentially totalitarian? Does the possession of an ideology imply the desire for total domination and the eradication of the human subject? The answer to these questions will reveal how useful Arendt's account of totalitarianism is.

Arendt certainly seems to be justified in regarding ideologies with some suspicion. Her description of ideologies as essentialist systems of thought in which certain aspects of human existence are elevated into the determinant of all others certainly has a degree of plausibility. It is true that it is not only Marxists and Nazis who possess all-encompassing social theories purporting to explain the nature of the historical process. Even conservatives, for example, have a particular view of human nature and a particular view about how societies develop, how problems arise within them and so on. In this sense, they do have a way of ordering the world, of making sense of particular actions and events. We could even say that they possessed a systematic *Weltanschauung*, one enabling them to make sense of the events they see around them. Arendt therefore appears to be right on this matter at least. Ideologies do not have to be radical or extreme to be all-embracing. Adam Smith's system is after all just as 'total' as Karl Marx's.

It is also possible, as Arendt argues, that possession of an ideology might make people intolerant of other beliefs or ideologies. They may, in other words, become so convinced that their particular ideology gives the most accurate explanation for why things are as they are that they become quite unwilling to listen to the views of anyone else. There certainly seems to be a case for saying that once people believe they have an explanation for human behaviour, social development, and so on it is quite likely that they will become intolerant of those who disagree. Even liberals, after all, can become so convinced of the rationality of their belief in the benefits of tolerance and the 'open society' that they will refuse to countenance the views of those who disagree. The phenomenon of McCarthyism in the United States is surely proof enough of that.

Arendt thus appears to be on the right lines: possession of an ideology can lead to an attitude of intolerance. An ideology can induce a feeling of infallibility on behalf of those who believe it to be true, and hence lead to the attitude that the opinions and values of others are not worth hearing. If we accept that the institutionalised acceptance of intolerance is a hallmark of totalitarianism, then it seems logical to make the connection between ideology and tyranny. However, Arendt wants to say more than that; much more. She wants to say that possession of an ideology necessarily entails the desire totally to dominate everything and everyone. Possessing an ideology does not, in her view, merely entail being intolerant of others. It entails wanting to destroy the subjectivity of each one of us. It demands that we submit to the view of the world propagated by the ideology and thus that we relinquish our capacity for thought and action. It is not intolerance that leads to the Gulag and the concentration camp, but the desire for infallibility and absolute certainty.

For Arendt an ideology engenders the desire to dominate because the view of the world contained within it is constantly at odds with reality, with the world 'out there'. To protect the ideology from refutation by the real world those who follow the ideology have to ensure that those who do not are unable to see the ideology for what it really is, i.e. a deeply restricted view of history. An ideology can only survive, Arendt seems to be saying, if those who might other-wise be able to judge its merits are effectively dispossessed of their capacity to do so. Since such an end can only be achieved by terrorising people, it follows that a regime in which the elite is intent on enforcing ideological conformity amongst the populace will necessarily be totalitarian.

Arendt is certainly on to something when it comes to ideology. Many people who adhere to one regard the presuppositions of that ideology as being based on fact. A liberal such as Hayek would, for example, argue that it is a fact that self-interest forms the primary basis of human behaviour. He would say that much of the way we live our lives is shaped by self-interest and hence that any attempt to create institutions and structures based on social justice or ideas of collective responsibility are doomed to failure. He would say therefore that it is a fact that capitalism is a better, more rational form of society than a society based on central planning. A Nazi, on the other hand, would say that it is a fact that the Aryan race is superior to all other races, and hence that it is a fact that other races and creeds should be made subordinate to the needs of the Aryans. A Marxist would regard it as a fact that wage labour is exploitative and that it leads to the alienation of the individual, and he or she would argue that it is a fact that wage labour has to be abolished to construct a just society. People who possess ideologies have a system for looking at the world; they have a set of assumptions and expectations that form an internally coherent, yet entirely self-referential whole. The danger, as Arendt sees it, is that such systems betray the essentially contingent character of human life. They assume that everyone behaves in essentially the same way, that they have the same needs and the same expectations, the same 'nature'. They assume in short that *what* we are is more important than *who* we are. In this sense, ideologies of all hues, left and right, radical and conservative, suffocate the possibilities open to the individual.

What Arendt has put her finger on is the rather deceptive nature of ideologies. She sees that they have in common a claim to have understood certain fundamental characteristics of human existence and hence the ability to prescribe the best or most just form of society for us. She sees that the alleged facts about human nature, social development and so on are not really facts but generalisations. She sees therefore that although ideologies claim universality and truth they are really rooted in preference and prejudice. People who say that we are all self-interested are not *actually* describing a quality possessed by all individuals. They are really recommending or prescribing that we be self-interested so that the system they regard as rational and just, capitalism, will be regarded by everyone else in the same light. All this is clear. What is not clear is why Arendt nevertheless thinks that to sustain their belief in a given ideology some people are compelled to seek mastery over others.

The mistake she seems to have made is in thinking that to expose the mythical character of the presuppositions underpinning an ideology is tantamount to refuting it. She thinks, to go back to our example, that if it were possible to locate a person who is not self-interested, who acts through completely unselfish motives all the time, then Hayek's thesis would be rebutted. To preserve his position, his 'fictitious world' as it were, Hayek would, she supposes, have to terrorise us. He would have to undermine our capacity for thought and action to prevent us from convincing others that he was wrong. For only through domination, she insists, is it possible to preserve the myths or metaphysical assumptions upon which the credibility of the ideology rests. The question is, why should this be the case at all?

What she seems unwilling to acknowledge is that it is precisely because ideologies are more mythical than scientific that they are so durable and so apparently immune to refutation. Whilst facts can usually be disproved by weight of evidence, it is immensely difficult to disprove the metaphysical assumptions and generalisations that underpin ideologies. Someone, for example, who is convinced that people are primarily motivated by self-interest is rarely going to give up that view because it is possible to give examples of people who seem to be motivated by altruistic motives. He or she can always reply that they are freaks, or, more sneakily, that their altruism is itself the product of self-interest. In other words, if he or she really believes that people are essentially self-interested a way will always be found of accounting for examples that appear to contradict that belief. The Nazi who believes that the Aryans are superior to other races is probably not going to change those views because he or she knows individual Jews who happen to be brilliant, attractive or creative. It is not the particular example that he or she is interested in, but the general characteristics of races. Neither should we expect the Marxist to abandon the belief in the fundamental importance of class characteristics when he or she is shown examples of philanthropic capitalists or contented workers. As before, such examples can always be written off as exceptions that prove the rule.

Contrary to what Arendt is saying, ideologies do not put forward hypotheses or propositions which it is possible to falsify. In this sense they are very different from scientific propositions, which, if we follow Popper, are defined as being falsifiable or capable of refutation. Indeed we might say that this is precisely what distinguishes ideological statements from scientific ones. Ideologies put forward what essentially amount to value judgements, judgements of taste or preference. They are thus primarily prescriptive, having in view the justification of a desired state of affairs. An ideology cannot therefore be proved right or wrong; it can only be more or less convincing, more or less appealing. If, for example, it seems to me that people are not primarily motivated by self-interest, then I will hardly want to concur with Hayek that the most just state of affairs is one in which people are left to fend for themselves in a market order. I will want to argue that society should be based on social justice, that it should reflect people's concern to provide for others within the community, or some other such formulation precisely because in my view people are not primarily self-interested; we care about other people and we want the state to be the vehicle of caring.

Given that what defines ideologies is the moral or prescriptive character of the propositions that compose them, it is difficult to see why Arendt is so insistent that the possession of an ideology is tantamount to a declaration of war on the human race. If, as seems clear, an ideology is not falsifiable then it surely follows that whilst events in the real world can make an ideology more or less attractive, more or less convincing, they can never actually disprove it. We can see this clearly with Marxist ideology. Marxists of course pride themselves on the fact that their doctrine is scientifically rigorous. Indeed, part of the reason Marxists claim that their version of socialism is superior to other 'utopian' varieties is that they are able to comprehend the process of historical development. Yet the key prediction Marx made, i.e. that capitalism would inevitably collapse due to the very nature of the system, has not so far been realised. There have of course been periodic crises and depressions, but so far nothing more. Now, whilst there are many who have taken this as a sign of the lack of credibility of Marxism, there are many others who seem prepared to carry on believing it. Perhaps they hope that Marx will eventually be proved right. Perhaps they regard the 'scientific' aspect of Marx's work as of secondary importance when compared with his vision of a communist society. That his prediction has not been realised has not, therefore, fatally undermined the attractiveness of the doctrine. It has certainly made it less credible to many who might otherwise have been attracted to it; but it has not 'disproved' it in the manner Arendt apparently believes it would. If, furthermore, it cannot be disproved or falsified, then it follows that Arendt is mistaken in thinking that Marxists or followers of any other ideology are forced to dominate others to sustain the 'fictitious world' of their ideology. It is perfectly possible, in other words, for Marxists to tolerate the existence of others who do not agree with them. They might hold such non-believers in contempt, charging them with suffering from 'false consciousness'; but there is no necessity for them to attempt to dominate them or destroy their subjectivities in defence of their ideas. Of course there are many Marxists who dogmatically refuse to engage in meaningful debate and discussion about their ideas, but there are many others as well who want to refine and develop their thinking by engaging with others, particularly other socialists.

What this discussion shows is that Arendt's novel attempt to find the roots of totalitarianism in the form of ideological thought is less than entirely convincing. The fact is that ideologies do not carry within them the seeds of despotism as she suggests. She is certainly right in arguing that ideologies are not what they may well claim to be, i.e. rigorous 'total explanations' of the historical process. However, she is surely wrong in thinking that what they do offer is some form of testable, and hence falsifiable, empirical account of the world. They are, as I have argued, essentially collections of assumptions, prejudices, preferences, values; that is what makes them ideologies. The notion that the possession of an ideology forces individuals into a hostile posture against the world and mankind is therefore a dubious one to say the least. It is just not convincing to say of people that because they are Marxists, conservatives, or whatever, that they have to seek the total domination of humanity. 'Totalising discourse' can be corrosive of debate and discussion. There is nothing like being confronted by a hatchet-faced hard-liner of whatever ideological hue to inject a sense of futility into proceedings. However, to suggest that lurking within that person lies a proto-Hitler or Stalin is to stretch a valid point beyond acceptable limits. It certainly seems to be true that to start from a position of absolute certainty when discussing the nature of the individual or society is a sign of the weakness rather than the strength of an argument; but it is a long way from this observation to the idea that people with firm ideas about such matters are dictators-in-waiting. The conclusion we have to come to is that if it is possible to discern the origins of totalitarianism in ideologies it must be in ideologies whose aims and goals would somehow make necessary the domination of those subject to them. As we have seen, the way in which ideas are presented is not necessarily a guide to telling whether they contain the seeds of tyranny. We have to look at the content of the ideas, at what sort of society these ideas prescribe. We have to see whether those ideas are injurious to liberty. Although Hayek's assumption that socialist ideas are to blame for the evolution of both Stalin's and Hitler's regimes looks suspect, his assertion that what we need to look at is the content of ideologies, not the manner in which they are presented, looks more convincing than Arendt's argument that we need to look at the form of ideological discourse. This is a conclusion that, as we shall see, most other theorists of totalitarianism tend to agree with, and hence one to which we shall be returning.

Although Arendt is under a misconception about the nature of ideologies, about what it means to possess an ideology, this is not to say that her account of the actual character of totalitarian systems is necessarily flawed. What it means, I think, is that there is a significant weakness in her account of why totalitarian systems *became* totalitarian in the first place. There remains much of value, however, in what Arendt says about the nature of totalitarian rule. In particular, her argument that a key feature of totalitarian rule is the attempt to construct a hermetically sealed 'fictitious world' remains compelling, even if her explanation for why they attempt to construct such an entity does not. There is no doubt that one of the more significant similarities between the regimes of Hitler and Stalin was the attempt to manipulate information to create the desired impression of omnipotence and infallibility. A characteristic of both regimes was after all the control of the media, the censorship of cultural products leading to a policy of fostering 'positive' images of the regime, and the cracking-down on the dissemination of any material that might contradict that put out by the state. There is no doubt, in other words, that both dictators wanted to control the sources of information upon which the experiences and opinions of their subjects was formed. As they well understood, if you can control what people know about the world then the ability to influence their beliefs and behaviour will be enhanced. In this sense they did attempt to construct 'fictitious worlds'. They did attempt to cocoon their subjects in a web of manufactured images and lies to control them more easily. All of this is not only perfectly true, but crucially important, as Arendt argues, to understanding the nature of these regimes. It is, as she points out, precisely this gap between reality, the people's lived experience, and the regime's account of reality that caused the uncertainty, scepticism and sense of dislocation prevalent within the populations of these regimes. It is this gap that helps sustain the sense of flux and uncertainty she so graphically describes. Yet the notion that all of this was caused by the clash between the version of reality contained within the ideology and reality itself is one that, as I have shown, is deeply problematical. The question remains, however, if it is not the ideology that lies behind the desire to create fictitious or mendacious worlds, what is it?

Surely Orwell is right on this point. In *Nineteen Eighty-Four*, a graphic exploration of the dynamics of power within a totalitarian system, we see Big Brother's regime attempt to construct precisely the manufactured reality Arendt describes in *Origins*. There is total control of the media; every 'fact' is subject to constant review by the party; lies and propaganda surround the entire population for every moment of the day. Yet, in Orwell's account it is not any need to defend an ideology that lies behind the systematic manipulation of information at the Ministry of Truth. Indeed, the character of the governing ideology (always assuming there is one) is comparatively irrelevant for understanding the actions of the regime. The only important consideration, as Orwell makes clear, is power, absolute power, power as an end in itself. The Inner Party understands that knowledge is power. They realise that through controlling all sources of information they will guarantee infallibility for themselves because control of the facts gives control over the means of verifying whether any given event took place, whether a person existed, and so on. Furthermore they know that infallibility makes them immune to challenge. How can a person challenge someone who is always 'right'? In other words, the reason for constructing a fictitious world is to safeguard the power of the Party and to ensure that opposition is made effectively impossible. What Orwell understands is that the construction of a fictitious world is seen by the regime as a means for securing power. It is not an option that has somehow been forced upon them, but rather a method or technique that they have at their disposal to control the population. The problem with Arendt's analysis is that it gives no room to the possibility, articulated by Orwell, that the regime *chooses* to exploit the means at its disposal. For her, the regime is itself just as much a victim as the population at large. They are, she thinks, victims of the fact that the ideology cannot control or contain reality and thus has to be propped up by terror to prevent people from seeing the true nature of the world. This is a significant weakness in her argument. To suggest that Hitler and Stalin's manipulation of the media, their control over the dissemination of information, and so on, was in some sense forced upon them by the nature of their own ideologies is a very curious position to hold. It is almost to excuse the cynical Machiavellianism that is otherwise acknowledged as being such a central characteristic of each man's rule. Are we really sure we want to argue that totalitarian dictators are *forced* to manipulate the media, that they have no other choice but to do so? Do we not really want to say that they *want* to manipulate the media so as more easily to control people? Arendt's formulation appears, in other words, to get this important issue back to front.

The insistence on ideology as the primary shaper of the character of totalitarian regimes also has a corrosive effect on Arendt's otherwise compelling account of their structure. As we have seen, Arendt's view challenges the idea of totalitarianism as simply an updated version of an ancient political form, the dictatorship. She points to the lack of authority in the system, the breakdown of the conventional pyramid structure of command in favour of a more fluid arrangement, and, most influentially, she points to the extreme state of flux and uncertainty within the system. In other words, she has produced a convincing argument demonstrating that these systems are the opposite of what many commentators claim them to be, that is, monolithic and authoritarian. Unlike many other theorists of totalitarianism, she also attempts to account for the genocidal tendencies of Nazi and communist regimes by reference to the logic of the system, rather than seeing them as mere by-products incidental to its essential functioning. Yet what we are being asked to believe is that the way in which the structure of power evolved within these regimes was determined by the need to protect the ideology from the cold light of reality. Hitler's and Stalin's actual intentions are irrelevant as far as Arendt is concerned. That such confusion, flux and uncertainty perfectly suited their need to make themselves impregnable to challenge within their own regimes appears to be incidental. Once again the actual, real intentions of particular historical actors are put aside to accommodate the sweeping tide of historical and political necessity.

Perhaps the weakest part of Arendt's account of totalitarian regimes is, however, her characterisation of the relationship between regime and society. In her view an important distinguishing feature of totalitarian systems is the fact that the regime is able to exercise total power over the entire population. The great novelty of totalitarian systems is in this respect that the division between regime and population has been completely broken down. In a situation where 'total terror' is the norm, people are unable to distinguish their own will from the will of the regime. They have lost the capacity to control their own thoughts and ideas and hence have lost the capacity to distinguish themselves from the atomised 'crowd' manufactured by the regime. A crucial assumption of Arendt's account is thus that politics has been extinguished. Since people are unable to think for themselves, the notion that 'the people' might have a life, will or interest separate from that of the regime is misguided. The population is itself swept along by the whirling movement and so cannot have an existence independent of it. Totalitarianism really does mean *total* power, *total* control. It is the final realisation of a system in which *all* disharmony and antagonisms have been overcome. In these systems, therefore, unity really is achieved, but through terror, not consent.

Such an account of the relationship between rulers and ruled in totalitarian systems is deeply troublesome. To begin with, it is clear that people living within Nazi Germany and the Soviet Union under Stalin were not uniformly dominated in the manner Arendt describes. They were not, that is, incapable of acting or thinking for themselves. As, for example, research into the *alltagesgeschichte* of Nazi Germany shows, there was a vast spectrum of responses to Hitler's regime ranging from the outright hostility of many religious dissidents, socialists, members of youth cults, and so forth, to the fanatical support of Nazi Party members, fellow-travellers and racists.[17] As is clear from the copious intelligence reports compiled by the Gestapo itself, at no point did the Nazis enjoy total power over the population, or anything like it. On the contrary, although the Nazis enjoyed a great deal of support, they were constantly aware of and alarmed about the possibility of the emergence of dissidence and opposition. Yet what is also evident is that the Nazis enjoyed actual popular support for much of the time from much of the population. To put this support down to the efforts of the Party to indoctrinate the population is to ignore the fact that at least some of this support was built up when the Nazis were in opposition and thus without the means of imposing their views without reply. It also ignores the fact that the Nazis did actually possess a concrete programme of proposals designed to improve the lot of certain designated groups and classes. They did seek popularity and, moreover, they did it in much the same manner as political parties in modern liberal-democracies, i.e. by promising an increased standard of living, jobs, better services, and so on. Just as in other political systems, notice therefore had to be taken of the reaction of ordinary people to the policies being pursued, hopes, fears and expectations had to be met or answered, strategically important groups appeased or conciliated. In other words, although both Hitler and Stalin attempted to foster an image of unanimity and harmony, the reality was quite different. Lurking beneath the surface was all the petty squabbling, rivalry, clashes of interest and favour begging familiar in every other form of political system. In other words, at no point was politics abolished or transcended. It was at best concealed or temporarily hidden.[18]

Many of the most interesting questions about the nature of the relationship between rulers and ruled in these systems are never asked by Arendt. She has chosen in effect to believe the boasts of the dictators regarding their ability to control the populations, and to dismiss the notion that any independently minded person or any non-regulated group could have survived under them. In doing so her account of totalitarianism floats away from historical reality and towards dystopian fantasy. What she ends up describing is not Germany under Hitler or the Soviet Union under Stalin. In fact she is not describing any system that even might exist in the future. What she is describing is a form of society that could only exist in our worst nightmares, a negative ideal. It is clear that what she has done is to base her account of totalitarianism on the experience of those who, like herself, were exposed to the hell on earth that was the concentration camp. Whilst the camps and equally the Gulags are indicative of the type of savagery such regimes are capable of inflicting on their populations, it would surely be wrong to extrapolate the nature of totalitarian society from the nature of the camps. Yet this appears to be exactly what Arendt has done.

Both the strength and the weakness of Arendt as a theorist of totalitarianism derive from her awareness of the extraordinary nature of the regimes she describes. On the one hand, it is a great strength of Arendt's account that she never loses sight of the uniquely grotesque nature of what Hitler and Stalin did. Totalitarianism without the concentration camp, the torture, horror and humiliation was for her a contradiction in terms. She had little time for those who wanted to weaken the identification of totalitarianism with Hitler and Stalin. Although the term was quickly adopted by the Cold Warriors as a means of berating virtually any system that deviated from the liberal-democratic ideal, she herself remained adamant that its use should be restricted to genocidal, terroristic regimes of the sort she described. She was, for example, adamant that the Soviet Union ceased to be totalitarian after the death of Stalin when a more settled oligarchic pattern of dictatorship was established. On the other hand, the fact that she wanted explicitly to equate totalitarianism with the actual attainment of total power and total domination means that the term effectively becomes an ideal-type or dystopia that systems can only approximate, never realise. Not even Hitler or Stalin were actually able to attain the degree of power described by Arendt. As many have forcefully argued, both of them in fact fell well short of that model.

Arendt's study must be regarded as compelling and highly original despite her account of totalitarianism, not because of it. Broadly considered as a contribution to political thought *Origins* is undeniably brilliant. The sheer scope of the work, the way in which it pans over the ideas, assumptions and arguments of an entire culture, is quite startling. So too is the attempt to render totalitarianism a lived experience for the reader. Here, it has to be remembered, is a person who was herself touched by the cold hand of a barbaric regime, and it shows. There is nothing flippant about the book; there is no attempt at points scoring for the Free World or for any other cause save that of truthful inquiry. It is a work of enormous integrity and passion, and for these reasons alone deserves respect. However, considered as an analysis of totalitarianism, its origins and subsequent development, its utility is rather more limited. As I have already argued, there are useful insights into the character of totalitarian regimes. Her description of the 'shapelessness' and lack of authority certainly represents a challenge to one of the prevalent images of such regimes as 'monolithic' or static. Her insistence that the character of totalitarian regimes is shaped by the character of totalitarian movements, and that the movement, not the state, remains the true source of power is also illuminating. Yet the conclusion we have to come to is that although much of her description of totalitarian systems is compelling and original, her explanation for why such systems arise and develop is flawed. Of course she is right in stressing the centrality of ideology in totalitarian systems; but she is surely mistaken to argue that it is the ideology that shapes the manner in which the system develops. As one commentator remarks, if ideologies really were as dangerous as Arendt suggests we would need an explanation for why there remain systems in the world that are *not* totalitarian.[19]

Notes

1 Hannah Arendt, *The Origins of Totalitarianism* (London 1986), pp. xxiv.

2 See, for example, Agnes Heller's essay 'An Imaginary Preface to the 1984 Edition of Hannah Arendt's The Origins of Totalitarianism', in *Western Left, Eastern Left. Totalitarianism, Freedom and Democracy*, edited by Ferenc Fehér and Agnes Heller (Cambridge, 1987).

3 *Origins*, p. 469.

4 *Ibid.*, pp. 457–8.

5 The concept of 'natality' is a motif of Arendt's political philosophy. For a full explanation of its meaning and significance see her work *The Human Condition* (London, 1958).

6 *Origins*, p. 458.

7 *Ibid.*, p. 392.

8 On the nature of mass society and a prescription for the revival of a more authentic way of life see *The Human Condition* especially the chapter on 'action'.

9 *Origins*, p. 470.

10 Hannah Arendt, *Between Past and Future* (Harmondsworth, 1977), p. 99.

11 *Origins*, p. 326.

12 As she notes in the preface to Part Three of *Origins*: 'We always suspected, but now we know that the regime was never "monolithic" but "consciously constructed around overlapping, duplicating, and parallel functions", and that this grotesquely amorphous structure was kept together in the same Führer principle – the so-called "personality cult" – we find in Nazi Germany', p. xxxii.

13 *Origins*, p. 430.
14 *Ibid.*, pp. 455–6.
15 *Ibid,*, p. 477. On the destruction of meaning and understanding in the totalitarian world see also Arendt's articles 'Understanding and Politics', *Partisan Review*, 20 (1953) and 'Totalitarian Imperialism: Reflections on the Hungarian Revolution', *Journal of Politics*, 20 (1958).
16 *Ibid.*, p. 470.
17 There is now a copious literature on the variety of responses of ordinary people to the Nazis. Readers will find reference to some of the most important work on the subject in the bibliography.
18 For a particularly scathing examination of Arendt's account of Nazi Germany see in particular Pierre Ayçoberry, *The Nazi Question. An Essay on the Interpretations of National Socialism (1922–1975)* (London, 1981). So divorced from reality is Arendt's analysis that he concludes that *Origins* is 'a shocking, even scandalous book', p. 132. More sympathetic accounts of Arendt's analysis can be found in Stephen J. Whitfield, *Into the Dark: Hannah Arendt and Totalitarianism* (Philadelphia, 1980) and in Noel K. O'Sullivan, 'Politics, Totalitarianism and Freedom. The Political Thought of Hannah Arendt', *Political Studies*, 21 (1973).
19 See the comments of Robert Burrowes in his article 'The Revised Standard Edition', *World Politics*, 21, no. 2 (January 1969).

3

Carl J. Friedrich and Zbigniew Brzezinski
Totalitarian Dictatorship and Autocracy

If Arendt's analysis of totalitarianism is regarded as the 'classic' work in the field, then Carl J. Friedrich and Zbigniew Brzezinski's *Totalitarian Dictatorship and Autocracy* (first published in 1956) must be regarded as the 'standard' work. As we argued in the last chapter, the enduring appeal of *Origins* lies essentially in the scope of the inquiry, and the sheer dexterity with which Arendt attempts to manage it. More than any other work on totalitarianism, it comes closest to conveying the madness and irrationality of the regimes of Hitler and Stalin. Yet brilliant though this account may be, considered as an account of a totalitarian political system it has serious flaws. The idea, for example, that the logic of totalitarian domination is contained in the very nature of ideological belief looks persuasive until this form is looked at more closely. Furthermore, much recent research on the regimes Arendt describes has also cast doubt on her view that one of the hallmarks of totalitarian rule is the ability of the regime totally to control the population. Even if such a feat is possible in theory, it was certainly never achieved by either Hitler or Stalin. Arendt's account thus suffers as a result of her exaggerated perception of the amount of power able to be exercised by totalitarian regimes. What she ends up arguing is, in effect, that totalitarian rule is synonymous with the attainment of total power. For reasons already expressed such a view does not provide a promising basis for providing us with a workable definition of totalitarianism.

Friedrich and Brzezinski had a quite different goal from that of Arendt and, indeed, Hayek. They wanted above all to develop a neutral, value-free understanding of totalitarianism that could be used for the purposes of comparative analysis. They recognised that there was a significant danger that the concept would simply be hijacked by those with a vested interest in using it as a weapon in the propaganda battle being waged between East and West. They could see that the term had a strong association in people's minds with Nazi Germany, and hence that calling a regime totalitarian was akin to comparing it with Hitler's dictatorship. However, they believed that there was strong reason for keeping the term and developing it for comparative use. Modernity had, they argued, greatly improved the potential for social control and hence for the establishment of more refined forms of tyranny. There were vastly increased opportunities for propaganda and for communicating with the now literate and politicised masses. There were many new methods of surveillance and indoctrination available that increased the potential for controlling not merely the actions, but also the values, beliefs and thoughts of those subject to rule. In short, there had been a qualitative leap forward in the capacity to tyrannise, and this had to be recognised by political scientists.

It was this desire to put the study of totalitarian systems on a more empirical footing that led Friedrich and Brzezinski to construct what became the standard reference point for virtually all subsequent discussion on the nature of totalitarianism, namely the 'syndrome of interrelated traits and characteristics'. They attempted to provide a check-list of essential characteristics belonging to totalitarian systems. By doing so, they hoped to make use of the concept of totalitarianism more acceptable and more objective. In this sense they were moving in the opposite direction to Arendt. As we have seen, she was determined to convey the idea that totalitarianism was an event, a happening, a once and for all phenomenon. For her, therefore, the word 'totalitarianism' was inevitably bound up with the horror of the Gulag and the concentration camp, and with the desperate uncertainty of life in a context of mutual hostility and suspicion. Friedrich and Brzezinski's model signalled, on the other hand, a dramatic shift in the meaning and significance of the term. Like Arendt they were certain that the regimes of Hitler and Stalin were totalitarian, but they were equally adamant that there were a number of other regimes such as communist China, and Mussolini's Italy that possessed totalitarian characteristics as well. Moreover, they thought that far from being an extraordinary aberration of the past, a moment of madness as it were, totalitarianism represented the present and the future. We could not rule out, in other words, the possibility of a growth in the number of totalitarian regimes, or indeed a further refinement in the manner in which such regimes were able to control those subject to their rule. As the longevity of various communist regimes made clear, totalitarianism was here to stay and the sooner it was understood exactly what a totalitarian system was the better.

Friedrich and Brzezinski's model thus marks a considerable departure from earlier attempts to define the concept of totalitarianism. From being a term almost exclusively used to describe the systems constructed by Hitler and Stalin, emphasis was now placed on developing the concept for use in comparative political analysis. The question that remains is to what extent Friedrich and Brzezinski's much copied and commented upon model is successful in achieving this ambitious task.

*

As has just been mentioned Friedrich and Brzezinski were not interested (as Arendt was) in explaining the origins of totalitarianism. In fact they regarded the task of constructing 'genetic theories of totalitarian evolution' purporting to provide an all-embracing explanation of totalitarianism in terms of its philosophical, intellectual and cultural antecedents as inevitably ideological. It seemed to them obvious that to impute a similarity of 'purposes' and 'intentions' to movements as diverse as those of the Nazis and the communists was to misunderstand the nature of their respective ideologies. Such movements did not share the same vision of how society should look; they did not share the same values and beliefs; nor was their rise caused by the same historical factors. To argue that totalitarian movements and regimes are characterised by a shared attachment to a particular ideology is mistaken. Such an argument could only undermine the utility of the term and discredit its use by political scientists. They aimed, therefore, to avoid such holistic explanations. They wanted to produce a model that would demonstrate the similarity of 'the structures, institutions, and processes of rule' of the regimes in question. In this way they hoped and anticipated that they would rescue the concept from the ideological uses to which it was otherwise prone to be put.

In Friedrich and Brzezinski's view there is no one feature or characteristic that distinguishes a totalitarian system from any other. Unlike Hayek and Arendt, that is, they do not believe that totalitarianism has an 'essence' or that it is possible to isolate certain core beliefs forming a totalitarian ideology. In their view what makes one regime like another is a similarity in the 'structures and processes' of rule, and in the 'morphology' of the system. In other words, what they are looking for is a certain 'family resemblance' between regimes that in other respects might be regarded as quite different from each other. What the aims or goals of the rulers might be is comparatively irrelevant. What is important is how the regime appears to the interested observer.

The conclusion they came to is that the presence of six particular features is enough to warrant describing a given system or regime as totalitarian. As they put it in their celebrated formulation:

> The 'syndrome', or pattern of interrelated traits, of the totalitarian dictatorship consists of an ideology, a single party typically led by one man, a terroristic police, a communications monopoly, a weapons monopoly, and a centrally directed economy.[1]

The point to stress immediately is that Friedrich and Brzezinski are not claiming that each factor is itself totalitarian. The fact that all states claim a monopoly over the use of force is not to say that all states are in some sense totalitarian, or, indeed, that they are on the road to becoming totalitarian. It is not the factors themselves that are totalitarian, but their combination together. Totalitarianism, they argue, is the sum of the parts, not the parts themselves. Thus, as they point out, a system such as 'socialist Britain' (i.e. Britain during and after the Second World War) could possess three of the factors, namely monopolies on communications, weapons and the economy, without necessarily being considered totalitarian. That Britain, a liberal-democracy, could possess at least half the traits shared by totalitarian systems does not show that Britain is half-totalitarian. What it shows is that there is a notable proximity between totalitarian systems and other types of modern rule. Totalitarianism, they think, is really the 'logical exaggeration' of certain tendencies inherent in modernity. Totalitarianism is a product of mass society, and it should not be surprising that totalitarian systems share characteristics with other mass political systems because in their view there is a comparatively narrow spectrum of possible political systems within modern settings. Whilst totalitarianism and democracy are at opposite ends of the spectrum, they are still in important senses members of the same family.[2]

What becomes immediately clear, however, is that certain traits are more significant than others. Possessing a monopoly on the use of force is an example of a trait that is relatively insignificant in shaping the character of rule. All states claim a monopoly on the use of violence, but not all states are the same; far from it. Similarly there are many regimes that have been led by one man. Tyranny, i.e. in Aristotle's terms 'imperfect' rule by one man, is one of the oldest forms of political association. Other systems such as police states have also employed terroristic police services, and others have been based on the rule of a 'party' or clique whose claim to rule rests on their allegedly superior wisdom or knowledge. What really distinguishes totalitarian states from all other systems is the possession by the elite of an ideology, that is, a vision or blueprint of a future society that it seeks to realise. Moreover, it is the ideological character of these systems that helps to make sense of all the other characteristics possessed by totalitarian systems. It helps to explain why these systems are monopolistic, why they employ a 'terroristic' police force, and why totalitarian parties survive after the seizure of power. Coming to terms with the nature of totalitarian ideologies is thus the key to understanding the nature of totalitarian systems themselves.

For Friedrich and Brzezinski ideologies are very simply 'action-related "systems" of ideas' whose purpose is 'to unite (integrate) organisations that are built around them'.[3] Ideologies are systems of belief. They typically involve criticism of the existing state of affairs, and some idea about what sort of society would best fit the needs of mankind. Thus all ideologies are inherently political; they concern the institutions and structures governing the life of the community, the values and norms by which we should live and an idea of what the 'best' or most harmonious form of society would be like. However, there is nothing inherently suspicious about ideologies; neither is there anything about the form of ideological belief that is necessarily totalitarian. They therefore disagree with Arendt's assertion that the rise of ideologies is due to the general rootlessness and alienation of modern man. Ideologies are not symptomatic of the decay in our ability to perceive reality; they are simply collections of beliefs, values and aspirations. To argue that a given ideology leads to totalitarianism therefore requires us to examine what the particular ideology contains, and what it proposes.

What distinguishes totalitarian from non-totalitarian ideologies is, in their view, quite simple. Normally ideologies are based on the beliefs of a given section of the population. They are the concrete expression of a particular frame of mind or temperament. Conservative parties reflect the views of those who are cautious about change. Such parties therefore seek to preserve traditional ways of organising social, political and economic life. They see institutions as evolving gradually, over time, as circumstances require. Conservatives are therefore critical of those who seek somehow to test an institution's rationality or fitness. Other parties, on the other hand, are organised to promote different ideals and a different way of organising the affairs of the community. Yet the important link between parties in a democratic state is that they are all inspired by already existing beliefs and sentiments. They do not confront society with novel or alien beliefs, but, rather, reflect the needs and hopes of people within society. Totalitarian parties and movements are, however, quite different. As Friedrich and Brzezinski remark: 'In place of more or less sane platforms of regular political parties critical of the existing state of affairs in a limited way, totalitarian ideologies are perversions of programs. They substitute faith for reason, magic exhortation for knowledge and criticism.'[4]

Unlike ideologies found in democratic states, totalitarian ideologies do not arise out of the sympathies of ordinary people. They are not in this sense a reflection of how people feel and think about themselves and their society. They are not organic, that is, they do not develop gradually over time to reflect the changing perceptions of the population. Totalitarian ideologies are doctrinal. They are typically the product of one man's efforts to explain the world and provide a blueprint for human happiness. Communism, for example, is not the product of the interplay of ideas and beliefs in society. It is a doctrine created and built upon by Marx, Engels and those who claim to be able to interpret correctly the meaning of their texts. Indeed, far from being inspired by the beliefs of ordinary people Marx regarded such beliefs as manifestations of 'false consciousness', and thus as an obstacle to social progress. Although less identified with one man, both Nazism and Italian fascism at least had an ideological figurehead claiming to be the inspiration for the success of the respective movements. Hitler was not of course a particularly original thinker, but his *Mein Kampf* did at least possess many of the properties of a holy text, being comprehensive in outlook and obscure in content. Mussolini was even less original than

Hitler. However, he made up for his own lack of ideas by employing a competent court philosopher, Giovanni Gentile, to do much of the work for him. What this concern with ideas and ideology shows according to Friedrich and Brzezinski is, again, totalitarianism's modernity. Hitherto regimes that claimed legitimacy on the basis of the infallibility of the ideas they propounded were all religious. Most people could not read, thus the appeal to certain texts or ideas had limited value. However, the increase in reading ability meant that for the first time people could be mobilised behind 'literate ideas'. Moreover the fact that these ideas claim universality and everlasting value means that those who produce them come to be regarded by those believing in them as prophets, seers and demi-gods.

The most significant attribute of totalitarian ideologies is not so much their doctrinal quality, but the fact that they are 'totalistic'. Although, as Friedrich and Brzezinski make clear, there is little similarity between the actual ideas being espoused by various totalitarian movements, they remain closely tied in form. The essential point is that all such ideologies are radical, uncompromising and intolerant. Thus, though ideologies such as communism and Nazism may call for completely different forms of society to be constructed, they share certain very distinct characteristics. As Friedrich and Brzezinski explain, what characterises a totalistic ideology is that

> it is concerned with total destruction and total reconstruction, involving typically an ideological acceptance of violence as the only practicable means for such total destruction. It (i.e. the ideology) might accordingly be described as 'a reasonably coherent body of ideas concerning practical means of how totally to change and reconstruct society by force or violence, based upon an all-inclusive or total criticism of what is wrong with the existing or antecedent society'.[5]

Totalistic ideologies are not merely artificial or alien collections of ideas, they are also revolutionary; they call for the complete dismemberment of society and its reconstruction along some new, ostensibly more rational lines. Marxism, for example, regards all hitherto existing societies as exploitative and degrading. Marxists therefore demand the destruction of the entire fabric of society, its institutions, structures, traditions and practices to promote equality. Only through a complete rejection of the past, they argue, can a new society be built in which people are allowed to develop their full talents and capacities. Nazis and fascists are similarly antagonistic towards the existing state of affairs. They see contemporary society as weak, decadent, corrupt and divided. They therefore call for the 'sweeping away' of the *ancien régime* to promote social harmony. Thus although the particular visions of the ideal society put forward by totalitarian movements may differ, the demands are the same: society is to be totally destroyed and reconstructed according to the blueprint of a new Messiah. Yet, as Friedrich and Brzezinski argue: 'It is precisely this attempt to impose on society a rationally, or rather pseudo-rationally, conceived pattern of distinctly novel forms of social organisation that leads to totalitarian oppression. Since, furthermore, this oppression is justified in terms of the ideology, the ideology is totalitarian.'[6]

The reason totalistic ideologies are despotic is, in their view, quite clear. Ideologies like Nazism and communism are radical and revolutionary, and they regard everything that already exists as in some sense a barrier to the realisation of a better form of society. The problem as Friedrich and Brzezinski see it is that what already exists has been created and sustained by the people themselves. When someone says everything must be changed, he or she is talking about changing not merely the formal institutions and structures governing the conduct of individuals, businesses, and so on, but about the entire way of life of a given population. It is not enough therefore merely to change the way in which social life is organised; social life must itself be changed to conform with the dictates of the ideology.

In Friedrich and Brzezinski's view the assault on the pre-existing form of social life is necessarily tantamount to a declaration of war on the people. Societies are after all shaped by those who live in them. Furthermore, the way people live is not normally the product of force. Neither on the whole are the institutions by which social life is regulated. To take an example, the institution of the university has developed over centuries. No one designed the university or forced its acceptance upon an unwilling population. It developed in response to the need for a place where knowledge could be pursued for its own sake. However, totalitarian movements regard such institutions as an obstacle to the creation of an entirely new life. The ideal of the university as an independent institution in which received truths can be examined, scrutinised and if necessary rejected is part of an anachronistic social order that has failed the people. In their desire to sweep away such institutions totalitarian movements represent not merely the novel, but the artificial and the alien. What they are in effect promoting is a form of life created not by society, but essentially by one man. What they are seeking to destroy is a plurality of ways of living developed over centuries. Totalitarians cannot tolerate the tried and the tested, the familiar and respected. They must seek, therefore, to impose, to coerce and to dominate. As Friedrich and Brzezinski explain, the elite

> by their almost complete rejection of the status quo, are inclined to attempt to force history to fit their conception of it. And when such a conception involves a far-reaching idea of the desirable, that is, historically inevitable scheme of social organization, the efforts to mold society to fit it, and the consequent measures to break down the resistance to it, call for such a massive deployment of organised force that the result is totalitarianism.[7]

It is this confrontation between what is and what must be that makes necessary the use of terror in totalitarian systems. For Friedrich and Brzezinski it is obvious that where a movement seeks so completely to change the pattern of life resistance and opposition will necessarily arise. Whilst certain sections of the population may be swayed by the promise of utopia, many others will feel intimidated and threatened. And indeed they are threatened, for totalitarian movements cannot allow people their private space in which to live. They cannot allow people to live according to a different moral code. These movements seek total power; they seek to change everything and everyone. A person whose behaviour, opinions, beliefs or values challenge the orthodoxy must therefore be forced to relinquish them. The existence of people who do not wholeheartedly support the movement remains evidence of its lack of power and is a threat to the project they are trying to complete.

There are different degrees of terror in totalitarian systems, and different ways in which terror is organised and controlled. Terror is greatest, Friedrich and Brzezinski believe, immediately after the seizure of power when large numbers of the population will still be thinking and behaving in conformity with old values and norms. It is at this point that resistance is likely to be greatest. People find the totalitarian regime strange and unfamiliar, its new ideas about life alien and intimidating. Of course there are those for whom the movement represents a new beginning, a fresh start. These supporters are the bedrock of the system and without them the regime

will quickly founder. However, for the others life becomes a series of
confrontations as the state seeks to accumulate the power needed to
pursue utopia. Because the state possesses a monopoly on the dissemination of ideas and of public communication, because it controls the educational apparatus, because it is able to regulate the
interaction of all individuals whether at work or in the home, this
confrontation is an uneven struggle. Many of those who initially
opposed the regime, or who might have been expected to oppose the
regime, are simply swamped by a welter of disinformation and
propaganda. It is this capacity to monopolise the public realm that is
part of the great novelty of totalitarian regimes. So complete is their
hold on society that even those who are not sympathetic to the
regime's ideology end up acquiescing. Yet, as Friedrich and
Brzezinski hopefully point out, 'while it might be the intent of the
totalitarians to achieve total control, it is certainly doomed to dis-
appointment; no such control is actually achieved, even within the
ranks of their party membership or cadres, let alone over the population at large'.[8] What gives the regime its terroristic quality is thus
the fact that it faces a constant struggle to achieve the abolition of
spontaneity and individuality at the heart of its 'passion for unanimity'. It is a terror born of the regime's hostility towards certain
enduring human institutions: the family, the church, the university,
and towards all manifestations of independence. 'It can be said',
Friedrich and Brzezinski assert,

> that even within the grip of the total demand for identification with a
> totalitarian regime, some persons and even groups of persons manage
> to maintain themselves aloof, to live in accordance with their personal
> convictions, and perhaps to organize some minor opposition to the
> regime. They are often inspired by hopes that the regime might be
> forcibly overthrown, farfetched as such hopes have proved in the past.
> Yet such islands of separateness are not only eloquent testimonials to
> the strength of human character, and to the unquenchable thirst for
> freedom; they are also helpful in preserving some human beings for a
> better day.[9]

Despite the heroic attempts by some isolated individuals to remain
aloof from the crowd, it is evident that the longer totalitarian regimes
maintain themselves in power the more difficult it becomes for
ordinary citizens to keep a hold on their own subjectivity. To begin
with, enjoying a monopoly over the means of public communication,

the regime is able simply to bombard the entire population with its propaganda. Totalitarian regimes have at their disposal a vastly increased capacity to manipulate and deceive. It is thus inevitably the case that the sheer weight of this propaganda, the constancy with which it is repeated, undermines the individual's capacity to resist. Here, as Friedrich and Brzezinski point out, 'even the more or less determined enemies of the regime fall prey to its insistent clamor, to the endless repetition of the same phrases and the same allegations. A general pattern of thought, almost a style of thinking, proves increasingly irresistible as the regime continues in power'.[10] Referring to the tests carried out by American political scientists such as Alex Inkeles and Raymond Bauer, Friedrich and Brzezinski note that: 'It has been the frequent experience of interviewers of former Soviet citizens to find that even those who profess the most violent hostility to the Soviet system tend to think in patterns instilled into them by that regime'.[11] In contrast to Arendt's evocation of a Bosch-like form of existence in which the shadow of the concentration camp looms over the entire population, the accent in Friedrich and Brzezinski's work, particularly in the second edition of *Totalitarian Dictatorship and Autocracy*, is on the gradual transformation in the style of thinking of the population. According to them what the regime is effectively ensuring in the control and regulation of public communication is the prevention of the development of genuine forms of subjectivity. In these systems the regime is virtually able to define the meaning of words, and is therefore able to control the thoughts of the population. If the regime can control the language then it can control the manner in which people think. As Friedrich and Brzezinski make clear, 'words laden with propaganda-derived value-judgements are used as part of their daily vocabulary. They (i.e. the people) thus serve unconsciously as unwitting propagandists for the regime they abhor'.[12] The key to the longevity of totalitarian systems is thus their ability to disguise the fact that people are being forced to adopt a form of behaviour effectively serving to perpetuate and legitimate the system. Although the method of rule in totalitarian systems can still be described as terroristic, the 'war' between system and subject is fought to the point where 'often the victims of such terror are quite unaware of their own psychic states'.[13] As totalitarian rule continues, therefore, the fact that people are forced to behave and think in the way they do becomes progressively less obvious to the people themselves.

Beyond the terrorisation of those people who were brought up before the totalitarian regime came to power, there remains the task of 'socialising' those born under the regime into the ways of thinking and behaving expected of them. Since it is those individuals born under the regime that are to be indoctrinated, it is the schools and colleges that provide the means of securing compliance and control. As Friedrich and Brzezinski explain: 'The entire educational process is utilized for the propaganda efforts of the regime and is part of this process in ever larger measure as the totalitarian nature of the dictatorship unfolds. As such, it is the mainstay of the process of consensus formation, as in turn the growing consensus obscures the propagandistic nature of the instruction'.[14] In other words, 'education, like ideology, becomes an instrument in the hands of the regime that takes upon itself the definition of the truth'. As they see it, although even in a democracy education necessarily involves an element of what Aristotle terms *paideia*, or education in civic responsibility, in a totalitarian dictatorship what might otherwise appear to be a similar process is really 'a technique for "making" fascists and communists'.[15]

The end product of the 'indoctrination' and 'brainwashing' of the 'defenceless citizen' is thus the creation of an ideologically manipulated 'consensus' effectively concealing the reality of the 'psychic fluidum' in which the subjects of totalitarian systems find themselves. Whilst the construction of an elaborate façade of democratic and popular legitimacy may appear to presage the passing of totalitarian dictatorship, the truth is quite different. With the intensification of the propaganda barrage people are simply no longer able to understand the nature of their own predicament. Whilst they may feel free, whilst they may, for example, willingly participate in the myriad procedures of mass legitimation, they are simply being manipulated in more efficient ways; the rationalisation of forms of coercion coinciding in effect with the elite's attainment of an absolute grip on the people. The result is, they believe, an 'internalized totalitarianism' in which repression is 'self-inflicted'. Yet, as they remark: 'Since the controls remain all-permeating and the dictator continues to have the last word, it remains a system of total power, even though the techniques are changed'.[16]

The point Friedrich and Brzezinski are therefore keen to stress is that the overt use of terror to elicit compliance is a sign of the *immaturity* of a totalitarian system. This represents a notable shift from Arendt's position, which is that it is the open use of genocide that ensures compliance. Sheer, naked aggression in her view is the mark of the authentic totalitarian regime. Friedrich and Brzezinski's view, however, is that the longer the totalitarian regime manages to survive the more likely it is to be able to create mass legitimation. Thus, whilst the Nazis had very limited opportunities for creating a basis of genuine mass support and hence had to rely heavily on the use of force to elicit compliance, communist regimes in, for example, the Soviet Union and China have both been successful in indoctrinating their respective populations with the dominant ideology. As a consequence, both have been able to exercise power without the need for the overt use of coercion.

In recognition of the marked change in the dynamics of legitimation in totalitarian systems by the second edition of *Totalitarian Dictatorship and Autocracy* published in 1964, Friedrich and Brzezinski talked about the development of 'popular totalitarianism', that is a totalitarianism backed by a 'substantial consensus'.[17] What they seemed to be saying was, in effect, that the totalitarians had won, that they had established what the world knew to be autocratic dictatorships, but which the people living within them believed to be the acme of rationality and justice. In short, these regimes appeared to have solved the problem that had plagued every previous tyrant or despot. They had elicited mass legitimation from their subjects, whilst at the same time maintaining total power over the decision-making apparatus. Reflecting this shift in the fundamental character of totalitarian systems, the conclusion Friedrich had reached by the end of the 1960s was that the connection between terror and totalitarianism was not as solid as both he and Brzezinski had earlier thought. It was evident that these systems were maintained by, as Barrington Moore puts it, 'a diffuse system of oppression'; but it was also evident that this oppression was 'more or less willingly accepted by the mass of the population'.[18] Thus in one of his last major articles on totalitarianism Friedrich was now prepared to broaden considerably his original definition of the concept. 'Totalitarian dictatorship', he wrote,

> is a system of autocratic rule for realizing totalist intentions under modern technical and political conditions. Since modern political conditions signify a general acceptance of democracy, a totalitarian dictatorship can also be described as a 'perfect democracy' in the sense that the people, represented by the party, which in turn is represented

by its leaders, exercise total and unrestrained power.[19]

From being a concept redolent in people's minds of a system in which the people are held in sway by the most brutal and overt forms of domination, totalitarianism had, particularly in Friedrich's later work, come to mean something markedly different. The accent was now on the proximity of totalitarian to other modern types of rule. In Friedrich's view, the key to understanding modern political systems is the importance placed on legitimacy and consent. The difference, ultimately, between democracy and totalitarianism was now regarded as the manner in which that legitimacy is established. Whereas the legitimacy of the totalitarian regime is the product of deception, propaganda and lies, democratic legitimacy is the product of a genuine trust in the institutions, laws and practices of the polity. Whereas in a democracy people exercise choice on the basis of what they themselves feel they need or want, in a totalitarian dictatorship the 'will' of the people has become inseparable from the will of the regime. Totalitarianism is thus not so much different from democracy, as its mirror image. Totalitarian dictatorships had come to possess all the surface characteristics of democracy but without its substance, essence or authenticity.

*

Although Friedrich and Brzezinski stress the importance of regarding totalitarianism as a syndrome of interrelated traits and characteristics, it should by now be clear that in their view what really distinguishes totalitarian dictatorships from other forms of autocracy is the stress on the achievement of ideologically formulated goals. Many of the traits that they include within the syndrome are found within other systems. Only the 'totalist ideology' seems to be missing from other systems that might be regarded as near relatives of totalitarian states. The most important characteristic of totalitarian regimes is that they are uncompromisingly radical. For the totalitarian elite the ideology is not just a mere device to secure compliance or to cement together the members of the ruling class. The ideology forms the very *raison d'être* of the system. It explains why these people are in power and what they are in power to achieve. It explains why there are concentration camps, Gulags and executions, why the regime wants a monopoly over every aspect of social, political and economic life, and why it seeks to expand indefinitely. It is therefore the totalist ideology that is the key feature of totalitarian systems. Without it such states would be difficult to distinguish from many of the other forms of autocracy that have sprung up in the twentieth century and which support themselves with the use of modern technology.

It should be clear that part of the sub-text of Friedrich and Brzezinski's analysis is an attack on revolutionary ideology. In their view there is a chasm between the sort of ideologies normally found in democratic states and revolutionary, radical ideologies. The former are rational and 'open' in that they reflect the antipathies and sympathies of ordinary people, the 'common man' as Friedrich puts it. Although these ideologies may be critical of some aspects of contemporary life, they never go so far as to suggest that 'the system' should be demolished. They want piecemeal incremental changes to promote a more just, more prosperous, more contented form of life. By contrast, totalitarian ideologies do not reflect the existing hopes and aspirations of the population, but are based on the doctrinal teachings of a small number of men, if not of one man. They are not inspired by, nor accountable to, the views of ordinary people, holding such views to be a part of the problem, not part of the solution. The ideas of the totalitarian movement thus challenge and confront the accepted norms and values of society for the sake of advancing some entirely novel idea about what must be. Because these ideologies are 'totalist', because they demand destruction followed by total reconstruction, it follows, Friedrich and Brzezinski argue, that totalitarian regimes must seek and achieve total power if they are to realise their vision. They seek to build a new society and to do that they must change the habits of thought and behaviour, the norms and values of those who remain. However, such a radical goal can only be achieved if every person is dominated in every aspect of his or her life. Totalising ideologies are therefore the source of totalitarian practices. That, briefly, is Friedrich and Brzezinski's account of the novelty of totalitarian systems. The question is, is this an adequate account? Does it give us the necessary means for distinguishing between totalitarian systems and other forms of autocracy?

As has already been argued, the fundamental assumption underlying Friedrich and Brzezinski's account is that it is possible to isolate a certain category of ideologies as being totalitarian or, rather, 'totalist'. Rather cleverly, they have avoided the sort of difficulties that arise in attempting to argue that, for example, Nazism and communism are really the same ideology dressed up in different clothes. As they see it, such an argument is wrong on historical grounds, and serves to distract from the important point, which is that the Nazis and communists both built similar types of rule albeit to realise quite different ends. They have also avoided Arendt's argument, i.e. that all ideologies are essentially totalitarian, but that some are more totalitarian than others. In their view, ideologies do not have a similar form; they do not all breed intolerance (as the history of democratic politics shows); and they do not all require the world to be conquered to remain credible in the eyes of their followers. Instead, following Popper, they argue that the really important consideration is whether the ideology calls for far-reaching, radical change to the nature of society. As they see it, most people are not radicals; they live perfectly happily within the established framework, and thus do not crave a fundamental revision to the pattern of life. Since in their view society is itself the product of the regular, habitual interaction of individuals, it rails against common sense to expect people to want to tear up the fabric of the life they lead for the sake of some abstract, untried vision of another society. 'Totalist' ideologies are therefore totalitarian because, they call for changes that the vast majority of people do not or, rather, would not want.[20] The only way they can be put into practice is thus by coercing people into accepting them. Ultimately it is this gap between what people want and what the totalitarians want that gives the lie to the idea that consensus can ever be real in totalitarian societies. People do not want what the totalitarians have to offer, therefore where there is consent to the ideology that must indicate that the consensus is the product of brainwashing and indoctrination.

There certainly appears to be some justification for the point Friedrich and Brzezinski are making. Most people are not revolutionaries; they do not regard the wholesale destruction of the political, social and economic system in which they live as an immediate priority. Nor are most people normally attracted to the ideas of self-styled prophets or saviours who claim to be able to solve all the problems facing humanity. Most people, in other words, do not have the energy or will to overturn the *status quo*. However, they are surely overstating the case if they are arguing, as they seem to be, that in every political system there is always consensus about the norms and values under which people should and do live. The truth is surely rather different. Every political system has its moments of crisis, and many have suffered and continue to suffer partial or complete breakdown. Political systems are not permanent, unchanging entities, and a system that cannot adapt and change will likely be replaced by one that can. One of the effects as well as one of the causes of crisis is political ideas; ideas about how the system should be run, who should do the ruling, what principles will be followed and so forth. At moments of crisis to suggest that what is required is the sweeping away of the old order and the creation of a new one might be less likely to be regarded as threatening or irrational than at times when there is apparent consensus about how the system should be governed. Indeed, as has often been the case, such ideas might prove to be one of the factors that cause the old system finally to crumble. We can in this regard point to such ostensibly 'popular revolutions' as those that occurred in America to rid the New World of the British, the 'Velvet Revolutions' of Eastern Europe, and the multitude of other revolutions that have swept away colonial or imperial rule around the world to the general satisfaction of the subject peoples involved. It is no escape to claim that in all of these examples the revolutions were in effect 'restorative', that is, merely returning the nation to the state it was in before it had been conquered, overrun, or annexed. In many cases, for example in the United States, the revolutionaries were not merely inspired by thoughts of restoring rights and liberties that they mistakenly thought they had enjoyed, but of inventing new practices, new institutions, new ways of living, even a new nation. In other words, the process of the formation of the new state was in many senses a genuinely revolutionary moment. It was a moment of experimentation, of novelty and of iconoclasm. The American revolutionaries were quite self-conscious in their desire to sweep away what they regarded as the old and the moribund and to institute entirely new practices for what they considered to be a New Age. It is not too difficult surely to argue, in the terms offered by Friedrich and Brzezinski, that this new ideology was 'totalising'; but do we want to say that because it was totalising it was at the same time totalitarian? Were these the first tentative steps on the road to the Gulag?

It is hard to believe that Friedrich and Brzezinski want to claim this at all, and yet it is equally difficult to escape the conclusion that their logic would lead them along this path. Their view of change, political action and ideology appears so thoroughly imbued with a Burkean-inspired mistrust of reason, argument and the power of words that it is unimaginable how they could be reconciled to the concept of the 'just revolution'. It is possible to imagine them sympathising with those who sought to overthrow the tyrannical Jacobites in the name of the 'rights of Englishmen', because the whole issue was framed in terms of restoring something that was in danger of being lost. We can wonder, however, what their reaction would be to those who in 1989 and 1990 called for the 'total destruction' of communist power in Eastern Europe and the 'total reconstruction' of civilised norms of political conduct.

The notion that revolutionary ideologies contain the seeds of totalitarianism within them is a plausible one when applied to settled democratic states, or other well-established, consensual political systems. However, not all political systems are democratic and settled in this way and, as the discussion above indicates, where we move further away from this pattern such a notion becomes progressively less convincing. This creates considerable difficulty within the context of this discussion because of course the systems thought by Friedrich and Brzezinski to be totalitarian have not in general been created in a settled and harmonious context. On the contrary, if the history of totalitarian movements tells us anything it is that they arise at times of the most profound political crisis, not during times of peace. The popularity of the Nazis, for example, rested to a certain extent on their promise to dismantle the unloved Weimar system, which had been in crisis practically since the day it was constructed. It was a system regarded as having been foisted on the Germans after defeat in the First World War, and was associated with the profound economic and social crisis of the 1920s and early 1930s. Many Germans therefore regarded the Nazi promise to construct a New Order based on traditional values as a relief from the uncertainty and apparent anarchy of Weimar Germany. The Bolsheviks, on the other hand, took over a political system that was not merely in crisis, but which had practically ceased to exist. Tsarism had disappeared some months before, forced out by a people fed up with fighting on an empty stomach. Its replacement, the Provisional Government, was a self-appointed committee of well-meaning, but ineffectual men whose hold on power was at all times tenuous. The Bolsheviks thus hardly needed to 'destroy' the old order to begin the march to socialism. As Lenin himself remarked, the Bolsheviks did not take power, they 'found it on the streets'. The promise totally to construct a new social and political order was not in this sense revolutionary, but a question of necessity given that the old order lay about in ruins. Indeed in many senses the problems the Bolsheviks faced in the early months of rule were due to the almost complete absence of a state system to take over. They therefore had to improvise institutions in a the most difficult of contexts. Of course it would be perfectly legitimate to argue, as many have done, that the sort of 'reconstruction' the Bolsheviks had in mind was one likely to lead to the misery and unhappiness of a majority of the people; but this is not the point Friedrich and Brzezinski are making. What they are saying is that it is the *desire* to reconstruct society from scratch that contains the seeds of tyranny. Yet so far it is not clear why this should be the case.

What Friedrich and Brzezinski seem unwilling to countenance is the possibility that people might not like the society they live in. They think that the beliefs, values, norms, and attitudes of people are essentially static and hence that a people's vision of the natural order of things remains unchanging. They do not, in other words, believe it significant that people have the facility to change their minds. Thus in their view an ideology that challenges or undermines the received truths of a given society must be suspicious. If people's minds never change, then an ideology that called for the casting off of old, anachronistic ideas would be regarded by people as a threat. A revolutionary regime wanting to create an official ideology would have to change people's minds for them; it would have to confront old beliefs, old values to make society work at all. However, people can change their minds, and, moreover, they do. They can lose faith in the institutions and structures of social life under which they have lived with apparent equanimity for many generations. We might note that societies that have staved off fundamental change for over a century are comparatively rare. Revolution and change are, if anything, the norm not the exception. Moreover, they are often signs of a people sloughing off the sort of 'consensus' that holds that only kings and priests possess the necessary judgement to rule.

Friedrich and Brzezinski have, however, a further argument to show how revolutionary, totalising ideologies engender totalitarian forms of rule. In their view the call for the total destruction and reconstruction of society makes necessary the establishment by the new regime of total power. Totalitarian ideologies are inherently utopian; they call for a 'heaven on earth', a paradise in which antagonism, conflict and scarcity are but a distant memory. This

88 *Making sense of tyranny*

sounds fine on paper, but as they (among a multitude of others) are keen to point out, blueprints for the construction of utopia can never, by definition, be realised in practice. Where a regime attempts to put such a programme into action the result will necessarily be failure. Antagonism, conflict, and scarcity are it seems always to be with us, and thus the attempt to get rid of them is akin to a person banging his head against a brick wall. Of course for a regime to admit failure would be to expose the emperor as having no clothes. What such regimes are inevitably forced to do therefore is to seek greater amounts of power. Power allows the regime to control people, and if the regime can control every person absolutely then it can convince them that its attempt to produce utopia has been entirely successful. In Friedrich and Brzezinski's view the pursuit of a utopian programme requires seeking total power; for only with the attainment of total power will the carping voices of dissent be silenced and the illusion of unanimity for which all such regimes have a 'passion' be secure.

One difficulty with this account of how totalitarianism comes about is the assumption that the desire to construct utopia necessarily leads to total domination. Why does the fact that a given movement wants to construct some particular vision of the good life determine the actual manner in which that vision will be pursued? The answer implicit in Friedrich and Brzezinski's view is that a movement seeking to construct a utopia will not want to wait for the right conditions to develop before proclaiming success. Totalitarians, in their view, crave utopia the moment they seize power. Totalitarians, they are saying, are impatient people; they cannot wait for developments to make the move to utopia easier, but have to pursue their goal here and now. Of course given the revolutionary nature of their demands, given that what they are seeking is the total reconstruction of the fabric of society, they are doomed to frustration. The result must inevitably be terror.

Plausible as this account may seem, the evidence is hardly conclusive. Bolshevik ideology certainly resembled in many respects the 'totalising' ideology that Friedrich and Brzezinski believe to be at the heart of the totalitarian project. The Bolsheviks believed that existing society had to be radically changed or transformed to bring about a more just state of affairs. They also believed that it was not merely the people who ruled that were the problem, but the institutions, practices and values of 'bourgeois society'. It would seem to follow that they did desire wholesale change or, as Friedrich and Brzezinski put it, the 'total reconstruction' of society. Moreover, although the Bolsheviks claimed to possess a 'scientific' as opposed to a 'utopian' doctrine, if there is a vision of society that is utopian it is Marx's. Attractive though it may well be, a society in which each person is by dint of the alleviation of scarcity free to be a hunter in the morning, a fisherman in the afternoon, and an artist and critic in the evening can without difficulty be called utopian. What is not clear, however, is whether any Bolshevik believed the creation of this society to be anything other than a long and arduous process, particularly given the conditions prevailing in Russia when they came to power. To begin with, it is a cardinal tenet of Marxism that progress to socialism and thence to communism can only happen with the complete development of the means of production. Indeed, in the *Critique of the Gotha Programme* Marx stresses that communism is incompatible with want. Communism, he believed, was a society in which goods would be distributed according to 'need'. It follows that communism could never be established before the capacity to meet all needs was met. The Bolsheviks give every indication of having been aware of what Marx meant by a communist society: they knew that 'utopia' was not at hand at all, and hence that a period of transition would have to be undergone before they could proclaim the achievement of the socialist phase, let alone the communist phase of development. There were important differences between the Bolsheviks as to exactly how long this transition was going to take. Some, like Bukharin, argued that it would take decades, if not generations, to develop the productive base to the sufficient point. They therefore argued that the best policy would be to allow the market to develop over time thereby encouraging industrial growth at relatively little cost to the state. It was this argument that found practical fruition in the New Economic Policy which was established in the Soviet Union between 1921 and 1928. Others, however, argued that socialism had to be introduced immediately to serve as a model to the 'toiling masses' of the world, and to preserve the Revolution. It was this argument that crystallised into Stalin's programme of 'Socialism in One Country' and which found fruition in the introduction of the Five Year Plans, heavy industrialisation and the collectivisation of the peasantry. There was little talk of how long it would be before communism would be reached, all sides appreciating the problems that lay ahead in even staying afloat. It is difficult, therefore, to see how Friedrich and Brzezinski's comments could have any relevance here. No Bolshevik expected utopia to break out overnight, and indeed most of them realised with grim realism how hard it would be to construct any sort of durable socialist society in the Soviet Union, particularly after the expected European and world revolution failed to materialise. It was precisely this apparent lack of idealist fervour that lay behind the implementation of the deeply pragmatic NEP programme. The notion that the Bolsheviks wanted to achieve total power over the population because of their failure to achieve the construction of utopia is one that appears difficult to show. It may well be true that the Bolsheviks wanted total power and wanted completely to dominate all those unfortunate enough to be subject to their rule. It is certainly arguable that Stalin in particular wanted 'total power', and that his policies were designed specifically to achieve that end. Yet it would not be true for the reasons given by Friedrich and Brzezinski. The Bolsheviks knew perfectly well that utopia could not be built overnight. They knew that global revolution would have to have taken place before a move to communist forms of organisation could even be contemplated. Why then would they seek total power to give the appearance of having constructed a perfect society?

What this discussion shows is that it is more difficult than is often argued to show that there is a causal link between utopian ideology and practices of despotism. The fact that a movement or political party wants us all to live in a harmonious or perfect society in which *inter alia* there is no illness, want or unhappiness tells us very little about the way in which that project is to be pursued. It is perfectly consistent with the possession of a highly idealistic policy of this sort to say that a great passage of time will have to be undergone before the vision becomes a possibility. It is perfectly possible to say that people's attitudes, values and behaviour will have to have changed before the New World can be created. In other words, a person can be a utopian without being a revolutionary. He or she may argue that his or her form of society is only possible after the human race has evolved a little further in its habits and characteristics. William Morris, for example, was undoubtedly a utopian in the sense of being interested in the creation of a 'perfect society' of the sort outlined in his dreamy *News from Nowhere*. However, not even the most determined enemy of the eco-anarchy propounded by Morris could have accused this mild-mannered humanist and artist of harbouring totalitarian desires to control all those around him. Thus there is nothing inherently violent about utopian ideologies. That violence often accompanies the birth of a new society is undeniable; but the idea that the violence of a revolution is caused by or inherent in the ideology underpinning the actions of those involved in it is more questionable. As often as not, violence is the product of the confrontation between social forces competing for power after a revolution has taken place.

Another difficulty with Friedrich and Brzezinski's account of totalitarian ideology is one of applicability. They are sure that if any regimes are to be called totalitarian then it is those of Hitler and Stalin. The problem is that one can see how communism conforms to their idea of a totalising ideology. Most Bolsheviks called for the total destruction of the old order and the total reconstruction of the new. Most of them also regarded violence as a necessary means for getting rid of the former, and that violence would probably be needed during the transition period to safeguard the gains of the revolution. However, it is more difficult to say the same of the Nazis and fascists. It is true, as we have already noted, that the Nazis espoused ideas that could arguably be said to be revolutionary, i.e. desirous of a fundamental change in the structure of society. Hitler's *Mein Kampf* does after all contain the outlines of manifesto that could be regarded as in essence revolutionary. It called for the abolition of the Weimar system; for the destruction of the 'Jew-dominated capitalist system'; and the creation of a *Volksgemeinschaft* that would meet the needs of ordinary German people for food, housing and security. It was outwardly revolutionary as well, regarding the destruction of the international order and the capture of *Lebensraum* for the German people as immediate priorities. Yet, despite the apparently far-reaching ambitions of the Nazis, once in power many of these ambitions appeared to have been progressively watered down. Hitler was quite prepared to deal with existing elites and to safeguard the interests of many of the most powerful groups in German society. In contrast to the Bolsheviks, Hitler allowed the ownership of land, capital and the means of production to remain in private hands. He allowed the military to remain dominated by the staunchly conservative Prussian Junkers. He allowed many of the officers of the judiciary, many academics, state officials, and so on to remain in post so long as they joined the Party. It is true that the Nazis relentlessly enforced a policy of

Gleichschaltung or co-ordination ensuring that every institution and structure of civil society was effectively enveloped by the tentacles of the movement. However, what is not clear is that this process can be regarded as tantamount to a revolutionary transformation of the system. Certainly it does not seem to have been so regarded by many of the more radical elements in the Nazi Party who called for nothing more than the implementation of the programme Hitler had earlier outlined. Indeed, so aware was Hitler of the threat posed by the disgruntled 'socialist' wing of the Party that he felt compelled to arrest and even assassinate its principal members on the Night of the Long Knives. What this points towards is that some time before or immediately after the Nazi seizure of power Hitler relinquished the more overtly revolutionary elements of his own ideology. It remains true, on the other hand, that at no point did he relinquish the search for ever greater amounts of power. At all times and for all purposes Hitler strove for mastery of the system and for a position of absolute supremacy. In this sense, it could, as Friedrich and Brzezinski argue, reasonably be said that Hitler strove after 'total power'. What is not clear, however, is that this striving was caused by, or was the product of, the attempt totally to reconstruct society. This is because it is not clear that Hitler had any fundamental desire to reconstruct society by the time he came to power and was in a position at least to attempt to do so. He certainly wanted to redraw the map of Europe and to extend German control over much of the land to the east. However, accumulating land for a given people is not the same as reconstructing the framework of social, political and economic relationships. He certainly wanted to make Germany a more orderly as well as a more racially pure nation. Yet neither of these goals apparently involved the 'total reconstruction' of society. It is far from clear, in other words, that it was Hitler's frustrated attempts to realise a utopian, totalist ideology that is to blame for his seeking total power and extending a reign of terror across society. Surely it makes more sense to regard his quest for total power as being fuelled by the age-old concern of tyrants to secure for themselves a position of omnipotence.

It is not just their account of the link between ideology and power that is problematical in Friedrich and Brzezinski's account of totalitarian systems. What is in many senses more worrying is their preparedness to argue, particularly in the second edition of *Totalitarian Dictatorship and Autocracy*, that the novelty of totalitarian dictatorship rests on the ability of the regime to secure by coercive means legitimacy and the consent of the masses. Reading the account of totalitarianism given by Arendt we are immediately struck by the connection between totalitarianism and terror. What she describes is not so much 'psychic' or 'mental' terror, not terror that is somehow hidden away, but terror that is palpable and overt. Totalitarian regimes cannot in her view be fitted into the normal spectrum of autocratic systems precisely because they are so extreme in their use of force. The quantitative leap forward which such regimes make in terms of the depth of subjugation represents, she argues, a qualitative leap towards a new type of system. They are so extreme, so barbaric that a new word is needed to describe them. It is this necessary connection between terror and totalitarianism that is part of the reason she regards totalitarianism as a historical moment rather than a mode of practice institutionalised within an established political system. A political system implies a certain permanency or durability of institutional arrangements. Yet, given the self-destructive character of totalitarian regimes permanency and durability are never achieved. The moment a totalitarian regime stabilises it ceases in her view to be totalitarian. Friedrich and Brzezinski's account is, on the other hand, quite different, as indeed is their perception of what totalitarianism represents. The extreme brutality that Arendt thought to be the essence of totalitarianism is a mark, as they see it, of a system's immaturity. There is, they believe, a necessary connection between terror and totalitarianism, but the nature of the terror changes as the system becomes established. Whereas in the early phases of rule terror is as Arendt describes (i.e. openly exercised against large parts of the population), as the regime's attempts to brainwash the population bear fruit so the nature of terror itself changes. Terror moves to the background becoming part of everyday life. Whilst in developed or 'mature' totalitarian systems such as China or the Soviet Union the naked and open use of force diminishes as the regime remains in power, coercion and force remain as constant as ever, they are just not noticeable to the unpractised eye, or indeed to the population itself. It is as if the regime had implanted a commissar in the mind of each individual ensuring that 'anti-social' or negative thoughts are held in check. Whatever needs, thoughts or desires were not found acceptable the commissar would not allow to pass. In such fashion the true self is regulated and controlled, but without the subject being aware that this was going on. Thus, as Friedrich and Brzezinski argue, although it is true to say that terror has disappeared from view in such systems, it is still present in the form of a coercive power acting upon the subject. The difference is that terror is now covert instead of overt. Terror is now insidious and internal, and acts upon people by promoting feelings of guilt. If they do not vote in the single-party elections, or turn up to the victory parade, and if they do not wave a red flag on May Day they will feel guilty and inadequate. However, these feelings are not the product of their own consciousness, their own desires or needs. They have been implanted in people, and are the product of the 'psychic fluidum' in which they find themselves. Friedrich and Brzezinski are not then disagreeing with Arendt's identification of totalitarianism with terror. What they are saying is that terror takes a number of different forms, and that in the really 'successful' totalitarian systems it takes a form so subtle as to be barely discernible either to those subject to it or to many of those studying the society in question.

The difficulty with this account of totalitarianism becomes immediately apparent once one starts to reflect upon what is really being said. When we talk about people 'living in terror' or being 'terrorised' we surely mean that they are fully aware of the fact that they are being terrorised. We are talking about people who feel that their lives and the lives of others are under threat. We are talking about people who are palpably afraid. People who are terrorised surely understand very well that they have to behave in a certain way because if they do not they know they will suffer some tangible punishment or sanction. People who are terrorised do not therefore think in ways engendered by the regime, nor do they hold the beliefs, norms and values encouraged by it. It is precisely because they do not that they feel threatened and fearful. If people are so completely convinced of the legitimacy and wisdom of the regime and its ideology that they willingly obey its command why, therefore, should those people be regarded as being 'terrorised'? Far from being in terror surely they would feel quite satisfied. After all, their own views are mirrored in those of the regime and its policies. Of course it is perfectly legitimate to argue that people believe in what they do because they have in some sense been indoctrinated or brainwashed, and hence that given other circumstances they might have developed different beliefs. What appears mistaken is to argue that individuals possessing such beliefs can be said still to be suffering from coercion as they hold those views. It is reasonable to argue that a person's conversion, say, to the faith of the Moonies was the product of coercion or 'brainwashing', but it makes little sense to regard his or her continuing to hold the faith as evidence of the fact that the coercion is being continued.

The problem with Friedrich and Brzezinski's analysis of the connection between terror and 'mature totalitarianism' is thus that they stretch the meaning of 'terror' so far that it loses touch with the experience and feelings it was intended to convey. They may be right that the apparent consensus and legitimacy found in particular in the long-established communist regimes is initially the product of coercion and indoctrination. Nevertheless, as Arendt realised, once it is argued that legitimacy and consent have developed then we are talking about the development of a different sort of political system. In other words, either totalitarianism and terror are inextricably linked, in which case the development of legitimacy and consent harbour the end of the totalitarian phase of a system's development; or, totalitarianism is defined without reference to terror at all but by reference to certain other qualities, traits or characteristics. To have it both ways, as Friedrich and Brzezinski appear to want, is surely to widen the meaning of the term to the point where it not only possesses little utility, but it becomes a hindrance to understanding.

*

Friedrich and Brzezinski's account of totalitarianism appeared to represent a new departure in the study of the subject in that what was being sought was the definition of a concept rather than an explanation for a seemingly unique historical phenomenon. However, despite their apparently 'value-free' stance it is quite evident that far from remedying the difficulties of earlier studies of totalitarianism Friedrich and Brzezinski's 'syndrome' reproduces them albeit in new and interesting ways. To begin with, their attempt to escape an essentialist definition of totalitarianism by talking about a number of 'interrelated traits' shared by totalitarian regimes is at best partially successful. It is immediately obvious that one of their traits, namely the possession by the regime of an ostensibly 'totalist' ideology is considerably more important than any other. Although literally every state possesses at least one of the 'traits' (i.e. a monopoly on the use of armed force) and many others such as 'socialist Britain' possess considerably more, only totalitarian regimes possess totalist ideologies. Thus, far from escaping the concern with ideology and hence with the relative assessment of values and beliefs which Friedrich and Brzezinski believed to be at the source of the difficulty with previous attempts to define totalitarianism, they are themselves stuck with showing how admittedly disparate movements and regimes come to construct similar forms of rule. However, as with the attempts of Hayek and Arendt, Friedrich and Brzezinski's distilling of a core totalitarian ideology is not entirely convincing. Their assertion that totalitarianism is the product of the attempt to put into practice revolutionary ideologies is too widely drawn. It ignores the fact that there are many differences between revolutionary ideologies, and that some would seem to pose a much greater threat to liberty than others. What they end up arguing is that since any call for the radical transformation of social institutions and structures is 'totalist', it must at the same time be totalitarian. What they appear to forget (or ignore) is that without the actions of people regarded at the time as revolutionary there would not be any democratic assemblies, constitutions, elections or guaranteed human rights.

On a different note, it is difficult to see how the policies of those regimes regarded by Friedrich and Brzezinski as typically totalitarian were caused by totalist ideologies. It is arguable that Hitler at some point possessed a revolutionary or 'totalist' ideology. The programme outlined in *Mein Kampf* and by other Nazis such as Gregor Strasser and Ernst Röhm certainly called for radical change. However, it is not clear that the actual policies of Hitler and the Nazis were really 'totalist' in the manner Friedrich and Brzezinski use the term. Whilst the Nazis had of course a dramatic impact on German society, the actual framework of social relations remained largely unchanged, particularly compared with what occurred in the Soviet Union. Indeed, what changes there were largely mirrored those taking place in other advanced industrial countries such as Britain, France and the United States. On the other hand, it is difficult to see why such an apparently totalising ideology as Marxism should necessarily be regarded as totalitarian. Of course Stalin justified everything he did by reference to Marx's writings; but it was the arguments of Marxists that also justified the policies of the NEP period, destalinisation, and so on. It is therefore what people do with utopian, totalising ideologies, how they interpret and put them into practice, that is important. It is not the content of the ideology that determines the actions, but rather the actions that determine the content of the ideology.

Finally, although Friedrich and Brzezinski appear justified in asserting that there is a necessary connection between terror and totalitarianism, their insistence on stretching the meaning of terror beyond the point where it can make any sense stretches the meaning of totalitarianism in a similar way. What this stance suggests is that they are unable to contemplate the existence of a 'totalistic' system that was not at the same time totalitarian. What this means is that they are unable to distinguish between phases in the development of communist systems. In their view all communist systems are totalitarian because they all profess adherence to an ideology that is radical and revolutionary. Yet no matter what one's view of communism and communist systems might be it seems undeniable that there are great differences both between individual regimes and between 'immature' and 'mature' systems. Not to recognise this critics argue points to the rather indiscriminate nature of the way Friedrich and Brzezinski formulated their concept. It also leaves their account very much open to the charge of ideological bias. As I have attempted to show, the sub-text of *Totalitarian Dictatorship and Autocracy* is that all ideologies calling for radical change to the institutions and structures of society are totalitarian, and that all ideologies that defend or justify existing procedures are rational and good. This hardly seems an adequate starting-point for the development of a neutral, value-free or indeed useful model of totalitarianism.

Notes

1 Carl J. Friedrich and Zbigniew K. Brzezinski, *Totalitarian Dictatorship and Autocracy* (London, 1956), p. 9. A second edition of the work revised and updated by Friedrich appeared in 1965. Unless otherwise stated all further references to this work will be to the second edition.

2 The syndrome, it can be noted, has long provided a focus for debates about the nature of totalitarianism with critics and sympathisers revising and re-revising the basic formula laid down by Friedrich and Brzezinski. Some interesting discussions about the utility of the syndrome can be found in: Hugh Seton-Watson, 'On Totalitarianism', *Government and Opposition*, 2 (1966–67), pp. 154–7; Frederic Fleron, 'Soviet Area Studies and the Social Sciences: Some Methodological Problems in Communist Studies', *Soviet Studies*, 1, (1968), pp. 329–35; Sigmund Krancberg, '1984 – The Totalitarian Model Revisited', *Studies in Soviet*

Thought, 29 (1985), pp. 71–8; William Welch, 'Totalitarianism: The Standard Critique Revisited', *Rocky Mountain Social Science Journal*, 10, no. 2 (April 1973), pp. 60–2, and Henry Reichmann, 'Reconsidering "Stalinism"', *Theory and Society*, 17 (1988), pp. 60–4.

3 *Totalitarian Dictatorship and Autocracy*, p. 88.
4 *Ibid.*, p. 26.
5 *Ibid.*, pp. 88–9. Further discussion of the difference between the types of ideology found in totalitarian and non-totalitarian systems of rule can be found in Friedrich's *Man and his Government*, pp. 89–91, and in his article 'Political Philosophy and the Science of Politics', in *Approaches to the Study of Politics*, edited by R. A. Young (London, 1958), pp. 185–7.
6 *Totalitarian Dictatorship and Autocracy*, p. 105.
7 *Ibid.*, pp. 102–3.
8 *Ibid.*, p. 16.
9 *Ibid.*, pp. 288–9. 'All these groupings', Friedrich remarks elsewhere, 'find it necessary for purposes of survival to resist the total claim of the totalitarian rule which seeks to reduce the persons subject to its rule to isolated "atoms" – the "mass-man" of modern industrialist society – or to keep men in this state whenever they have already reached it', *Man and his Government*, p. 640.
10 *Totalitarian Dictatorship and Autocracy*, p. 143.
11 *Ibid.*
12 *Ibid.*
13 *Ibid.*, p. 129.
14 *Ibid.*, p. 148.
15 *Ibid.*, pp. 148, 149. In a footnote on p. 405 Friedrich goes on to criticise the comparative studies of education in the Soviet Union and the United States undertaken by Charles Merriam. These studies, Friedrich asserts, 'are all built upon the assumption underlying Merriam's entire enterprise, that the "making of fascists" and the "making of citizens" is essentially the same kind of undertaking. Actually the difference is as great as that between liberating and enslaving a man'.
16 *Totalitarian Dictatorship and Autocracy*, p. 43.
17 Although the revised edition of the work appeared under both their names it should be noted that these revisions were made by Friedrich alone, Brzezinski having evidently decided that most communist systems could no longer be regarded as totalitarian precisely because they had overcome the need to terrorise their populations.
18 *Totalitarian Dictatorship and Autocracy*, p. 43. Friedrich and Brzezinski are here quoting from Barrington Moore Jr, *Political Power and Social Theory: Six Studies* (Cambridge, Mass., 1958), p. 80.
19 Carl J. Friedrich, 'The Evolving Theory and Practice of Totalitarianism', in *Totalitarianism in Perspective: Three Views*, edited by Carl J. Friedrich (London, 1969), p. 136.

20 This view of the individual as essentially a respecter of pre-existing authority and tradition comes through very strongly in other works by Friedrich such as *Man and his Government, Tradition and Authority, Constitutional Government and Democracy,* and *The New Image of the Common Man.*

4

Herbert Marcuse
One Dimensional Man

The suspicion that the concept of totalitarianism was formulated specifically to tar the image of communist systems with the brush of Nazism is, as the preceding chapters indicate, one that appears more than amply justified. All the theorists hitherto considered have started with the premise that communism and Nazism are two sides of the same coin, and this assumption strongly colours the manner in which they have used the concept. The criticism of those who say that the concept of totalitarianism must be rejected because it is possible to show that there are fundamental differences between communist systems and the Third Reich seems, therefore, to be based on sound reasoning. However, the problem with this line of argument is that it assumes that the concept is only ever applied to these regimes or to regimes strongly resembling them. Yet, whilst it is certainly true that this has very largely been the case, it is not exclusively so. As we shall see in this chapter the concept has also been used to describe industrialised systems more generally. In this chapter we will be looking at the theorist best known for this much broader application of the term, namely Herbert Marcuse. Examining his idea of what totalitarianism is should therefore give us a fuller picture of how the concept has been used and what continuities and similarities there are, if any, between those employing the term for comparative analysis.

The fact that the concept of totalitarianism has been used to equate Nazi and communist rule means that socialists and those of the Left have tended to shy away from employing the term. As we have seen, it is a commonplace assumption of many who use the concept that totalitarianism is what occurs when people armed with radical policies and visions of a better life are allowed to take power.

It should hardly be surprising, therefore, to find that theorists sympathetic to radical or collectivist solutions to humanity's ills should feel lukewarm about the concept. However, there have been exceptions, particularly among those disappointed by the course of events in the Soviet Union. Two early examples of socialists using the term in this manner are Trotsky in the *Revolution Betrayed* and Victor Serge, the anarchist-Bolshevik, in his *Memoirs of a Revolutionary*. Both men made the same basic point, though from slightly different political positions. They both believed that Stalin's rule represented a 'betrayal' of the Russian Revolution and the socialist legacy of Marx and Lenin. Both used the term more for political effect than for serious purposes of comparison with Hitler's Germany. Nevertheless, the point was made. With the consolidation of a bloc of communist regimes continuing to betray the revolution after the Second World War so other 'libertarian' socialists continued the line of attack. To those such as Claude Lefort, Cornelius Castoriadis, and members of the Budapest School such as Agnes Heller and Ferenc Fehér, there was indeed very little difference between 'actually existing socialism' and the practices of the Nazis. They therefore felt quite comfortable about calling the former totalitarian. Contrary, then, to what many critics of the term appear to believe, it would be quite wrong to regard the concept of totalitarianism as simply 'right wing' or as expressive of conservative or liberal sentiments. Many on the Left critical of the way in which socialism had been hijacked to legitimate the rule of communist apparatchiks freely employed the term to give vent to their understandable belief that socialism is incompatible with the Gulag.

Whilst entirely sympathetic with this view, 'the Frankfurt School' of Marxist theorists, whose most prominent members were Theodor Adorno, Max Horkheimer and Herbert Marcuse, had a much more radical and far-reaching suggestion.[1] For them the emergence of regimes in which genocide and terror are the norm is symptomatic of a more general alienation pervading modern life. In this sense Auschwitz and the Gulag were not aberrations or mistakes in the otherwise unsullied march of 'progress'. They were not extraordinary in the sense of being unforeseeable or irrational. They were a manifestation of a deep-rooted sense of dislocation and anomie. Echoing themes found in the work of Weber and Lukacs, they believed the problem to lie in the actual nature of modernity.[2] For them, modernity represents a hostility to life and to spontaneity. It is a world in which control, co-ordination and calculation are held up as ends in themselves. It is thus a world in which the sensual, the aesthetic and the playful are sacrificed in the name of 'civilisation'. Instead of promising liberation and emancipation, the advance of 'instrumental reason', of science and technology, implies, rather, an increased capacity for domination and subjugation. Implicit in the School's outlook was thus the idea that the more apparently 'advanced' the society the worse off people are within it. Domination, they reasoned, is most effective when people do not realise they are being dominated, when they cannot see the strings controlling their every move. What the School claimed was that the most virulent and penetrating forms of domination were therefore to be found in those systems where the appearance of freedom and rationality are greatest (i.e. Western liberal-democracies). It is precisely here, they believed, that totalitarianism was most deeply embedded, for by being presented as systems based on popular sovereignty and the rule of the 'demos' they perpetuate an illusion of harmony and reconciliation that fails to cohere with reality. Domination is worst where people believe themselves to be best off, where liberties and freedoms are greatest, and where the living standard is the highest. It is here that control is most effective because it is here where people comply with and consent to their own powerlessness.

This idiosyncratic not to say provocative thesis found its ultimate expression in Marcuse's *One Dimensional Man*. Whilst the theme of the growing 'rationalisation' of society had been a constant refrain of the School since the 1930s, it was only in this work, published in 1964, that the argument found a wider audience. Indeed, such was the impression made by the book that it became essential reading for every would-be radical or student leader. Emerging as it did at the start of a period of profound disillusionment among young people in the West, Marcuse struck an immediate and powerful chord, particularly in the United States where he lived and worked as an academic philosopher. As an early edition of the book proudly boasts, *One Dimensional Man* was to sell 'more copies than Mao's *Little Red Book*'. Yet it would be wrong to think that the only significance of Marcuse's work is as a guide to the character of New Left activism and student protest in the 1960s (although it is also important for assessing those movements as well). The argument presented within it raises important methodological and substantive issues about power relations in modern states, about the character of ideology and about the nature of domination. All of these issues are, as we have seen, crucial to the question of what differentiates totalitarian rule from other forms of dictatorship. As we shall see, although *One Dimensional Man* represents a radical departure from earlier theories of totalitarianism in that it seeks to apply the concept to Western liberal-democracies, there are also powerful lines of continuity between his work and the work of theorists with whom in most other respects he appears to have little in common.

*

The starting-point for Marcuse's inquiry is the failure of capitalism to develop in conformity with Marx's account of it.[3] Marx of course held that capitalism was inevitably doomed. The logic that impels the development of capitalism is one that cannot be sustained and thus capitalism will either give way to higher forms of society or stagnate and perish. As Marx puts it, the choice facing humanity is either 'socialism or barbarism'. In his view there is an internal contradiction in the logic of capitalist production. Those who own the means of production are forced to sell an ever greater quantity of goods to compete. To make sure that their goods are cheaper than their rivals and thus that they are able to prosper in the market-place they have to drive down the basic costs of production of which the most basic component is the cost of wages. However, because every capitalist has to seek cuts in the price of labour the net result is the impoverishment of the working class and the overproduction of goods. In other words, although it is in the interest of all capitalists to pay their workers less, by doing so they ensure that the workers are unable to buy the goods offered by other capitalists. A vicious circle thus inevitably develops, fuelled by the desire of factory and land owners to make a profit and raise their own standard of living. If, Marx reasons, it is inevitable that workers will be paid less and less for their labour, it is also inevitable that there will come a point when they can take no more. There will come a point when they are so impoverished that the only way they can ensure their survival and the survival of their families is to take to the streets and revolt. Thus although it is by no means certain that socialism let alone communism will eventually be built, revolution certainly is inevitable. Once the masses feel their stomachs tighten nothing will stop them erecting barricades. Or so Marx thought.

Despite the seemingly cast-iron logic informing this account of the development of capitalism, global revolution did not occur, and, furthermore, has rarely looked like occurring. The Russian Revolution was of course regarded as a harbinger of the collapse of capitalism, but to the surprise and annoyance of many Marxists failed to be so. There were numerous crises in Europe after the First World War; various 'red' republics, movements, and parties came and went, but all to little avail. Capitalism not merely survived, but carried on much as before, minor and not so minor crises and depressions being followed by periods of sustained growth and consolidation. However, what was just as worrying from the Marxist point of view was not merely the continued survival of capitalism but the, if anything, growing legitimacy that capitalist systems seemed to enjoy. Such systems appeared able not merely to stave off crisis and revolution on a daily basis, but to convince those whose position in society should have made them support radical change that the *status quo* was worth preserving. In other words, capitalism was winning the battle for the 'hearts and minds' of the population against those who advocated building a society more in keeping with humanity's needs. Moreover in Marcuse's view the longer capitalism survived the better able it was to negate those forces and feelings that otherwise represented a threat to it. The cause of crisis in industrial society seemed not merely to have been staved off, but eradicated. The 'crisis of overproduction' had been negated by the evolution of a consumer culture in which consumption was regarded as an end in itself. The divide between the working class and the bourgeoisie which Marx believed to be the fundamental constituent of social relations in capitalist society had given way to an atomised mass of shoppers who craved nothing more than the latest gadget. In short 'negativity', the feeling people have when they are alienated from their surroundings, their work and their fellow individuals, appeared to have evaporated only to be replaced by a dissolute yet all-pervading 'happiness'. In short, society had somehow come to feel at ease with itself. Either, therefore, Marx was entirely wrong about modernity or something quite unforeseen had occurred to knock history off the tracks leading to socialism.

Observing the manner in which advanced industrial societies were evolving, many theorists concluded that Marx was indeed wrong. The 1950s and 1960s were years during which the 'end of ideology' was proclaimed and it was declared that we had 'never had it so good'; and, indeed, the 'contradictions' of capitalism did seem to have been overcome.[4] Since capitalism seemed capable of delivering economic growth for the years ahead, there was no reason to be 'radical', or to call for fundamental social change. Most people's standard of living was increasing, and they could afford many of the new products that were being laid in front of them. Marx's belief that there was a limit to economic growth and hence that overproduction and immiseration were necessary aspects of the capitalist process appeared not merely pessimistic but utterly flawed. If growth was sustainable, then everyone could have a stake in society. They could all be consumers as well as producers, and thus could all reap the benefits of a system designed to 'pile it high and sell it cheap'. In other words, whatever feelings of envy and resentment working-class people had could be channelled into more positive feelings by allowing them the means to participate and direct the process themselves. A new world had been born in which the old social divisions between the 'haves' and 'have nots' were rapidly disappearing. Moreover it was now evident that the difference between types of industrial society was one of form not one of substance. Although communist regimes proclaimed their adherence to norms and values different to those adhered to in the West, in reality the goals set by communist leaders were quite similar. They wanted economic growth, increased productivity and a higher standard of living for their workers as well. Khrushchev's boasts were after all about beating the United States, about overtaking the West, about producing more goods at a better rate than anything hitherto achieved. The communists were not talking about a radically different set of goals; they were talking about different means to achieving the same goal, i.e. material bounty.[5]

Amidst the cheers of triumphant self-congratulation of those who argued that fundamental antagonism had been banished from contemporary society was raised the discordant voice of Marcuse (among others). For him the claim that social conflict was at an end was merely the latest attempt by the bourgeoisie to present its hegemony as the incarnation of rationality. In his view Marx was not fundamentally wrong; the problem was that his analysis of the development of modernity needed substantial revision. Marx's view that alienation and exploitation are what characterise capitalist production is basically correct. The fundamental nature of capitalist production remains unaltered. The vast majority still work for others, though who those others are is increasingly difficult to see given that everyone appears to be engaged in the same sort of activity. However, work still involves the act of expropriation: the worker makes something and the bourgeois sells that product for more, pocketing the surplus value, the profit, for whatever purposes he or she has in mind. Moreover, although capitalist society projects an image of unity and harmony the reality is quite different. Strife and antagonism are still produced by capitalist production. The difference is that instead of radically affecting all areas of social life conflict and antagonism are transferred to areas that do not affect the functioning of the system. That class conflict is now most keenly felt at the international level between the industrial and the developing nations means that the individual now no longer experiences conflict on a daily basis. The nature of employment is such that most people who have a job are engaged in performing similar tasks to most others. There are differences in status between employees; but what they do, the nature of their job, does not differ nearly so much as, say, the employer and the employee of a nineteenth-century mine, factory or farm. Everyone is rewarded according to similar criteria of performance; they wear similar clothes, aspire to own similar products, and so on. Moreover, the cult of teamwork and collective endeavour that characterises most industrial enterprises encourages the individual to suppress any feelings of unhappiness or discontent for the sake of the collective. The point is that individuals are not expected to reflect on the condition of their existence or to wonder at the nature of what they are doing. What is important is simply that they work, eat, sleep, play, get up the next morning and start the process again. As Marcuse reasons, if this is not the sign of a deeply alienated form of existence, then what is?

However, the important point from the standpoint of thinking about the potential for revolution is that the principal source of conflict within industrial society is not between employers and employees, but between those who have a job and those who do not. It is between those who enjoy the fruits of the relentless industrial growth that Marcuse thinks characterises such systems, and those who do not.[6] The great difficulty from the point of view of the latter is that they are invisible to society. Modern consciousness is deeply influenced by the media, but the media has little interest in the margins of society. Those who have nothing to spend are not of interest to advertisers, and what is not of interest to advertisers is not of interest to the media. The margin remains hidden, sealed off from the concerns of the public and thus the concern of politicians and policy-makers. Marcuse's conclusion therefore differs significantly from those who proclaimed the 'end of ideology'. The latter argued that industrial society had effectively overcome the problem of alienation by giving everyone a stake in society. If everyone could see that their happiness was bound up with the continuing existence of the system then they would be unlikely to rebel. Marcuse, on the other hand, argues that whilst alienation is still a very real aspect of daily existence, the difference between life in early industrial society and in more advanced societies is that the system has now found ways of containing alienation, of preventing it from bursting out and provoking rebellion. The question Marcuse asks in *One Dimensional Man* is: how does industrial society manage to contain what should be uncontainable? How, in other words, do you convince people in a state of existential alienation that their best interests lie in continuing to support the *status quo*?

As with Marx Marcuse believes that to answer such questions it is necessary to look at the process that legitimates the governing ideas of the system. In other words, we have to look at the manner in which an ideology perpetuating relations of domination is seen as valid not merely by the dominators but also by the dominated. In his view the origins of the ideology legitimating contemporary society are to be found in the Enlightenment. The starting point of much Enlightenment thought is the idea of progress. More specifically, it is the idea of progress through the exercise of reason and the conquest of nature. Progress was regarded by Enlightenment thinkers in very instrumental terms; it represented the increasing ability of humanity to understand the world, to order it, and use it to increase human happiness. Thus what characterises Enlightenment thought is the belief that there is a direct correlation between the ability to master nature and self-fulfilment. Marx, who on this view fully embraced many Enlightenment assumptions about progress, believed that freedom was only possible once necessity had been overcome. To increase freedom he thought it was imperative to develop the forces of production. The more developed the machinery of production becomes, the more goods it will be able to produce, and the freer we will be. In a society in which most of the work is done by machines people will have more time to develop their own talents and capacities. In this sense the conquest of alienation is intimately bound up with the development of science and technology, for only with the greatest possible exploitation of the knowledge and materials available to humanity will we be able to conquer need. Such a view is not the exclusive province of Marxists, but is the basis of much post-Enlightenment thought. The difference between Marxism and other ideologies is essentially to do with how the pursuit of progress is organised and how the knowledge available to us is fully exploited. Marxists and other socialists believe that the free market is an obstacle to the rational utilisation of social knowledge. They believe that knowledge ought to be used for the benefit of all and hence controlled by society as a whole. On the other hand, liberals like J. S. Mill and Hayek believe that only by allowing individuals the freedom to use knowledge for commercial gain will progress continue. The point, however, is that they all agree that progress is measured in material terms, because only with economic growth and the exploitation of the resources available to us will the potential for liberty increase. There is then a basic similarity here: if freedom means the ability of people to do what they want then the obstacles preventing them from doing what they want to do must be removed for them to be really free. The chief obstacle to freedom is necessity, the constant call of physical need. In Marcuse's view the dominant modern ideology is not therefore liberal-capitalism, nationalism or socialism, but what he terms 'Logos', the will-to-knowledge. It is the belief that our freedom is won from nature, from the struggle to transform the raw materials nature provides us with into products of value. Though Marx and Mill may disagree on the means to achieving human happiness, they are both essentially agreed on what the nature of that happiness is: the alleviation of necessity through the harnessing of the potential contained within nature.

Plausible as such an account of the relationship between reason and freedom might once have been, in Marcuse's view, and in the view of other members of the Frankfurt School such as Horkheimer and Adorno, it is now obvious that the form of reason so beloved of the Enlightenment is the handmaiden of domination not liberation. According to Marcuse what Marx and other Enlightenment thinkers failed to understand is that the end of Logos is not as they argue neutral; it is not simply a means for the pursuit of ends that we choose to set ourselves. The desire to compute, calculate, and order goes hand in hand with the desire to limit, control, and ultimately to dominate. The end of science is to understand and quantify. It is to construct a complete view of the universe and everything within it including ourselves. There is no room, therefore, for the unpredictable, for the spontaneous or uncontrollable. To admit the possibility that there may be events or actions that cannot be foreseen is to give up the goal of ordering reality and thereby to recognise limits to what can be known. Science as understood by Enlightenment thinkers and as practised in the modern world is thus far from being the necessarily useful activity that earlier thinkers supposed. Implicit in the goal of science is the domination of Man, for only when our autonomy and independence have been snuffed out and we have become conforming automatons can we be said to be a fit object for quantification and utilisation. As Marcuse argues:

> Science, by virtue of its own method and concepts has projected and promoted a universe in which the domination of nature has remained linked to the domination of man – a link which tends to be fatal to this universe as a whole. Nature, scientifically comprehended and mastered reappears in the technical apparatus of production and destruction which sustains and improves the life of the individuals while subordinating them to the masters of the apparatus.[7]

Science is thus in a sense an ideological Trojan horse. As it ordinarily appears to us science is nothing but a series of techniques for comprehending the world. What the aim or *telos* of scientific knowledge might be is entirely dependent on the uses to which it is put. Thus knowledge of the atom has been used to construct weapons capable of mass destruction. However, it has also been used for positive purposes, i.e. to provide domestic and industrial power. In other words, we appear to be able to put science to whatever service we want to put it. Science is not normally credited with containing a hidden agenda or hidden ends quite separate from the ones we devise for it. Yet as Marcuse insists:

> Formalization and functionalization are, prior to all application, the 'pure form' of a concrete societal practice. While science freed nature from inherent ends and stripped matter of all but quantifiable qualities, society freed men from the 'natural' hierarchy of personal dependence and related them to each other in accordance with quantifiable qualities – namely, as units of abstract labour power, calculable in units of time.[8]

The point Marcuse is making is that science is not merely an activity whose results we can choose to ignore or employ, it also fosters a distinct world view. Science, he argues, has become the ideal against which to measure the rationality of the organisation of social life as a whole. Thus, to take the example of the economy, one of the great innovations in the productive process in the twentieth century has been the introduction of Taylorism. Taylor is noted for recommending the replacement of the rather haphazard practices of the craftsman with the streamlined efficiency of the production line. Instead of having an individual working slowly and carefully on constructing a particular product, he argued that it would be much more efficient to break down the process of production into small, easily learned tasks. Workers could be trained to perform one task and to repeat it to a rhythm set by the management. What this represented was of course the introduction of scientific principles into the workplace. It was the attempt to rid production of all those irrational extraneous considerations such as the degree of satisfaction involved in the work, the happiness of the worker, and so on for the sake of increasing output and maximising profit.

In Marcuse's view the rationalisation of daily life by the application of scientific methods shows clearly how, far from being neutral, the logic of 'instrumental reason' contains a clear blueprint or 'project' for the reconstruction of social life. There is a form of society already implied in instrumental reason, and it is one in which everyone has his or her set place, in which what people do is wholly determined by 'objective' criteria of efficiency, and in which individual thought and action is replaced by the machine process. A 'scientific' society is one in which, therefore, individuals suffer the deepest possible alienation. The dilemma confronting those critical of the existing state of affairs is that this project seems capable of sweeping away the possibility for the emergence of alternative visions of how society might be ordered. 'As the project unfolds', Marcuse explains,

> it shapes the entire universe of discourse and action, intellectual and material culture. In the medium of technology, culture, politics, and the economy merge into an omnipresent system which swallows up or repulses all alternatives. The productivity and growth potential of the system stabilize the society and contain technical progress within the framework of domination. Technological rationality has become political rationality.[9]

In this new social formation in which stability is maintained by subordinating everything to the needs of technological rationality and productive efficiency, the whole notion of political mastery, of domination exercised by one group or class of people over another becomes completely irrelevant. Here, instead of the productive apparatus being controlled by, and in the interests of, the ruling class, it is the logic of the productive process that determines the development and character of social life. This is because, he argues, 'the technical apparatus of production and distribution (with an increasing sector of automation) functions, not as the sum-total of mere instruments which can be isolated from their social and political effects, but rather as a system which determines a priori the product of the apparatus as well as the operations of servicing and extending it.'[10]

According to Marcuse people are now prevented from acting, from taking control of their lives. Instead of society reflecting the desires and wishes of a given group acting in the name of their own readily identifiable interests, society is shaped by the imperatives of a rationality whose logic is the expansion of technological, and hence productive capacities. Once established, as in the advanced economies, as the only legitimate or justifiable principle upon which social life can be ordered, this technological logic (which can be summed up in the phrase 'the means justifies the end') simply moulds reality to conform with its idea of what must be. Anything that does not meet the required standards of efficiency and productivity is simply crushed by the weight of scientific and technological necessity. In this way, Marcuse argues,

> the productive apparatus tends to become totalitarian to the extent to which it determines not only socially needed occupations, skills and attitudes, but also individual needs and aspirations. It thus obliterates the opposition between the private and public existence, between individual and social needs. Technology serves to initiate new, more effective, and more pleasant forms of social control and social cohesion.[11]

In Marcuse's view an important shift has taken place in the nature of the relationship between ideology and existence. In earlier forms of industrial society there was always a gap between the promises of the rulers and the lived reality of the subject population. The explicit claim of bourgeois rule was always to promote 'equality', 'social justice' and 'liberty'. Yet these ideals were betrayed by the actual condition in which people lived and inequalities were fully apparent for people to see. Whilst the bourgeois class enjoyed the fruits of industrial expansion, building palatial mansions, riding around in luxurious carriages and eating in expensive restaurants, the workers endured a life of drudgery and servitude. It was thus only too obvious that the bourgeois vision of the good life was merely a means of controlling society. However, in contemporary society this is no longer the case. Here what we see is 'the absorption of ideology into reality'. People are no longer fooled into believing that society is rational, because it only makes sense to talk about fooling people where those people have in theory the capacity to distinguish between lies and reality. People can therefore no longer be said to be the victims of a process of deception that could in theory be shrugged off in the truth-revealing process of revolutionary struggle. Where the organisation and character of all social practices is wholly determined and directly controlled by the imperatives of technological rationality the individual is in a very real sense produced by his or her society. As Marcuse explains:

> The productive apparatus and the goods and services which it produces 'sell' or impose the social system as a whole. . . . The products indoctrinate and manipulate; they promote a false consciousness which is immune against its falsehood. . . . Thus emerges a pattern of one-dimensional thought and behaviour in which ideas, aspirations and objectives that, by their content, transcend the established universe of discourse and action are either repelled or reduced to terms of this universe. They are redefined by the rationality of the given system and of its quantitative extension. [12]

Just as the control and coercion of individuals is maintained by determining the choices that are available to them, so the social and political institutions of society are shaped to extend the mirage of freedom and autonomy perpetuated by the operation of the 'free market'. In contrast to those anachronistic and inefficient systems of domination that rely on force to retain authority, a 'rational' totalitarian system is one that is best able to nourish the illusion of its 'openness' and 'responsiveness' to the wishes of its citizens. Of course, in no sense do these systems provide the opportunity for the deliberation and execution of meaningful choices, of choices, that is, between competing systems or ways of living. The choices presented here are between parties that essentially agree on all the important questions. A person chooses between competing management teams, not competing ideas of the good life. Thus, as Marcuse notes, the 'free election of masters does not abolish the masters or the slaves'.[13] On the contrary, the stability of these systems depends entirely on their ability to seal off the possibility for the formulation of real alternatives before the need for them even occurs to the population. In its most developed form, as in the 'plural' system of the United States, stability is maintained because the system is able to manipulate the needs of the population in such a way that whatever choices they make politically will coincide with whatever is in the interests of 'the apparatus'. By monopolising all sources of information and all forms of cultural dissemination, the system is able to present 'choices' to the people that appear to cater for all possible needs and positions. In actuality these choices are manipulated to maintain the logic of that never-ending technological and productive expansion upon which the apparatus depends for its power. By exercising what Marcuse terms a 'repressive tolerance' over the population the mirage of political debate can be sustained without bringing into question the principles upon which the system is based. Television programmes 'examine' political questions, newspapers are free to criticise government, people are free to demonstrate, but only as long as no really fundamental questions are asked about the nature of the system itself. A person can criticise the masters, but he or she cannot suggest that the system of masters and slaves be abolished. As a result, Marcuse observes, under the conditions of a rising standard of living, 'non-conformity with the system itself appears to be socially useless, and the more so when it entails tangible economic and political disadvantages and threatens the smooth functioning of the whole'.[14] 'As long as this constellation prevails', he argues,

> it reduces the use-value of freedom; there is no reason to insist on self-determination if the administered life is the comfortable and even the 'good' life. This is the rational and material ground for the unification of opposites, for one-dimensional political behaviour. On this ground the transcending forces within society are arrested, and qualitative change appears possible only as a change from without.[15]

Part of what makes this form of totalitarianism so successful is that in these systems 'opposition' is an integral part of the whole illusion. There is no need for naked shows of force, for the rounding up of dissidents, or the imposition of overt censorship and control on the cultural life of the community. Since for any form of action to be intelligible requires the actor to conform to the expectations of a population whose conception of the world has already been shaped by the standards of the apparatus, protest and 'transcendence' do not present a threat to the dominant forces and hence are no longer 'negative'. They are, rather, 'the ceremonial part of practical behaviourism, its harmless negation' and as such 'are quickly digested by the status quo as part of its healthy diet'.[16] Protest and opposition effectively legitimate the system because to protest is to imply that the system can be changed from within. It implies that the institutions and structures of society are amenable to the wishes of the people and hence that the people control the system.

The vaunted pluralism of contemporary liberal-democracy is thus only a façade hiding the manipulations of those 'vested interests' whose position requires that the underlying justification for the system is left unchallenged. By defining satisfaction, autonomy and desire with 'the vicious circle of consumption' ('the more you have the more you need'), by constantly reiterating the necessity for vigilance against the threatening ideals of outside powers, opposition to the system loses all sense. In these self-contained 'welfare-warfare states' (the description of whose logic uncannily resembles Goldstein's analysis of the totalitarian world system in *Nineteen Eighty-Four*), every conceivable avenue of spontaneity and individuality is first negated, then absorbed and finally eliminated in 'a comfortable, smooth, reasonable, democratic unfreedom'.[17] For the 'citizens' of such states all that is left is thus to lie back and enjoy the fruits of a process whose logic and rationale is immune to challenge.

For Marcuse totalitarianism means the creation of a hermetically sealed world whose development is determined not by the actions of individuals, groups or classes, but by 'technological rationality'. Within this 'whole' the individual is simply another object or role subject to the needs of the system. All thought and behaviour simply reflect the requirements of a face-less, subject-less apparatus whose own actions are determined by the need for increased production and the creation of an ever-growing catalogue of new desires. In Marcuse's view as long as the organisation of individual and social life remains bound by this hidden dynamic society remains one-dimensional, that is, totally administered, completely integrated and, above all, a pleasantly suffocating totality from which its somnambulant citizens can offer no challenge and imagine no escape. The final triumph of 'positivity', of total conformity, is thus the reduction of the human subject to a mechanistic process, a series of 'mimetic' impulses. As the denial and subversion of all spontaneity such a subject is the absolute inversion of 'liberated Reason'. If ideology has really come to an 'end' then it is only because there are so few souls left who are able to reflect on the true nature of their own predicament.

*

Marcuse's account of totalitarianism is, on the face of it, virtually a complete inversion of the accounts already considered. For theorists such as Hayek, Arendt and Friedrich totalitarianism and liberal-democracy occupy opposite ends of the political spectrum. Liberal-democracies embody the rule of law; they enshrine – or at least respect – the right of individuals to free speech, freedom of religious belief, and freedom of movement; and they allow everyone to vote and stand for elections. Totalitarian states are quite the opposite: they deny freedoms and rights, they deny the individual the right to voice his or her opinions, and regard all deviation from an officially prescribed ideology as an act of opposition punishable by imprisonment or worse. Marcuse sees matters quite differently. He argues that far from representing the antithesis of totalitarianism, liberal-democracy is actually the most refined version of it. The difference between, say, a communist system and the United States is not one of substance but one of form. Whereas in the former the inculcation of the dominant ideology is only partially successful, making necessary the use of force against large sections of the population, in the latter this process of indoctrination has been wholly successful. Force is thus rarely required to maintain social order, most of the population being apparently quite happy with their state of servitude. It seems safe to say, therefore, that there is little ground of agreement between Marcuse and other theorists. Indeed, so wide does the gulf appear that it is difficult to understand how they could be using the same language and concepts as each other.

It is entirely true that the way in which Marcuse applies the concept of totalitarianism is thoroughly at odds with the way in which it has been applied by most other theorists, and not only the ones we have been considering. Nevertheless it is evident that there are overlaps and continuities between them. Like Hayek, Arendt and others, Marcuse is convinced of the modernity of totalitarianism. Like them he thinks that one of the distinguishing qualities of such a form of rule is the attempt to impose ideological uniformity on the

subject population. Of course Marcuse disagrees with the others on
what the nature of a totalitarian ideology is. Whereas they are
virtually unanimous in arguing that ideologies calling for radical
change or for the total reconstruction of society are those most likely
to lead to totalitarianism, he thinks totalitarianism is the product of
the demand to keep things as they are. In his view, it is the denial of
the necessity for radical social change that is threatening and
totalitarian, because to maintain the *status quo* is to maintain a
system based on domination and hierarchy, on alienation and
anomie. Although he disagrees with them on the nature of the
ideology to be imposed, he agrees, however, that totalitarianism
would be impossible outside a modern context. Without the
development of mass communications, machine technology,
weapons of manipulation and surveillance, and so on, the control of
thoughts and actions would have been a mere pipe dream. As
Marcuse notes: 'The capabilities (intellectual and material) of
society are immeasurably greater than ever before – which means
that the scope of society's domination over the individual is immeasurably greater than ever before.'[18] If, as seems to be agreed, one of
the hallmarks of totalitarianism is the ability of the system to break
down the barrier between the private realm of life and public
authority, then such a system can only subsist in a modern setting.
Without the establishment of a monopoly over all aspects of individual existence individuals would be able to gain the space and time to
contemplate the nature of their predicament and to mount opposition to the system. If, however, all a person's life is public, open to
scrutiny and review, then conformity is essentially his or her only
realistic option. In Marcuse's view it is this inability to escape the eye
of the system that is destructive of human liberty, all the more so
when this is combined with a demand that the individual not merely
conform to prevailing norms and standards, but celebrate their
rationality and virtue.

   From the point of view of this discussion probably the most
significant feature of his analysis is his insistence on the achievement
of total domination. As we have seen in preceding chapters, most
theorists of totalitarianism are agreed that the aim of totalitarian
movements and parties is to seek the total domination of all those
subject to their rule. It is generally agreed that one of the novelties of
such movements is their desire to achieve complete control of the
subject, and in doing so to break down the barrier between the

individual and the state. Tyrants want people to do what they want them to do. Totalitarians, on the other hand, want not merely obedience, but love. They want people to obey them because they *want* to obey, not because they *have* to. They want, in other words, willing supporters, not grudging servants. What theorists of totalitarianism appear less able to agree on is the extent to which this desire has ever been realised in practice within totalitarian states, or, indeed, whether it is actually possible to achieve at all. Whilst Hayek seems uncertain on the matter, Arendt, for example, thought total domination was only completely achievable within the confines of the concentration camps where individuals are so terrorised they lose sense of themselves. By the time he came to revise *Totalitarian Dictatorship and Autocracy* Carl Friedrich clearly thought a form of total domination was possible, hence his suggestion that with the development of a 'substantial consensus' totalitarian systems could now be regarded as 'popular'. Since by the 1960s and 1970s most people living in the Soviet Union and China had little experience of life under a different set of values they had become totalitarian subjects. The only way of knowing that these systems were totalitarian was through knowledge of how people had in fact been forced to adopt their habits of thought and behaviour, and through seeing how the regimes dealt with those who obstinately refused to succumb to the brainwashing. In other words, only a long-term perspective and careful scrutiny of the activity of dissidents gave the lie to the claim that these regimes had acquired genuine or authentic legitimacy. Marcuse, however, goes one step further. Not only does he suggest that totalitarian societies are capable of acquiring long-term legitimacy and the outward support of many of its citizens, but that the happier and more contented the citizens of such systems appear to be the more totalitarian it is. Thus, to establish which systems are the most totalitarian one has only to look where the people appear to enjoy the greatest liberty, the highest standard of living, the most opportunities for the expression of 'dissent' and 'opposition'. Since domination increases with 'technical progress' it is where people enjoy 'many liberties and comforts' that 'unfreedom' will be greatest.

Although Marcuse's thesis looks radically at odds with those of the other theorists we have been considering, there are, as I have just shown, considerable areas of overlap. The question that remains to be asked is how useful Marcuse's highly controversial thesis is.

Novel it may be, but does it help us to get clear about what totalitarianism is and how it may best be applied?

To begin with, Marcuse's assertion that in advanced industrial systems there exists a consensus about the importance of economic growth, about the nature of progress and technological rationality does not seem entirely without basis. There is now little argument in most political systems about the priority of economic growth, the importance of productivity and competitiveness, and the development of new goods and markets. In a sense, as Marcuse argues, the realm of politics has therefore virtually ceased to be a realm of argument and debate about the nature of the 'good life', about what sort of society we want to live in, or about the ends of human life. Politics is now almost exclusively concerned with the *oikos*, that is with the technical question of how best to ensure continuing economic growth. Of course there is some deliberation about how the fruits of economic success are to be distributed, about what the most just apportionment of resources might be. There remains, in other words, a realm of contestation, for there remains substantial disagreement still about what the best means is for making sure prosperity increases. Nevertheless, it is a realm in which the really fundamental ethical and moral issues facing humanity are never raised. There is no clearer illustration of this stunted political discourse than the contest between the major political parties in most liberal democracies. As every undergraduate textbook on American politics explains, little difference can be discerned between the dominant parties on the basic issue of what the priorities of the United States Government should be. They both campaign to promote growth, wealth and a constant rise in the standard of living. Indeed, to campaign for anything else is, as Marcuse argues, to remove oneself to the outer fringe of American political life. Much the same can be said of the party contest in states such as Britain and Germany. Ideological differences are slowly giving way to differences in emphasis, differences in the manner in which growth should be promoted. In a sense therefore Marcuse is right. There does exist a consensus about how economic, social and political life should be organised that runs deep throughout not merely American society, but that of most other advanced industrial systems. As Francis Fukuyama from a completely opposed intellectual viewpoint has argued, it does seem that the imperatives Marcuse talks about have transcended whatever differences between societies and cultures might once have existed.[19] There does seem to be a universal desire to sacrifice everything in the relentless drive for the creation of newer, better, faster products.

The novelty of Marcuse's argument is not so much in pointing out that the values of the consumer seem to have driven out all others. Many theorists of modernisation like Bell and Fukuyama have said much the same thing. What is different is that Marcuse regards the development of this culture as the product of coercion. Whereas theorists such as Fukuyama see the ultimate triumph of economic liberalism, the market and 'bourgeois' values as in a sense a verification of the Hobbesian view of man as a restless seeker of recognition, 'glory' and power over others, Marcuse sees it as a sign of the success of the process of indoctrination to which everyone is subjected. In his view it is simply nonsense to see the evolution of 'one-dimensional' consensus as the sign of 'the end of ideology'. The Darwinian struggle between ideas has not been won in favour of instrumental reason because people have somehow come naturally to believe in the rationality of the existing state of affairs. It is due to the efforts of those with a vested interest in making sure that their view of the world remains beyond challenge. Marcuse's view is that we have been prevented from questioning the values and ideals of our society by brainwashing and indoctrination. There is, he argues, a concerted effort to undermine people's capacity to decide what type of society they wish to live in. From the earliest age we are bombarded by propaganda designed to convince us how happy we are with the goods and products manufactured by society and hence with the institutions and structures of the system. The entire world of 'discourse' is designed constantly to affirm the rationality of what already exists as a way of short-circuiting the discussion of what might be. Alternative viewpoints are marginalised, ridiculed and dismissed in the media. As a result, a 'repressive tolerance' is sustained which, whilst not actually outlawing opposition or dissent, makes it extremely difficult to raise fundamental questions about the direction in which society is heading. People thus think they are free, and that is the great triumph of modern liberal-democracy. If people think they are free then in a sense the battle of ideas over. All other visions of freedom will seem not merely unattractive, but also threatening, thereby justifying further repressive measures to ensure the safety of the Free World. However, in Marcuse's view the freedom enjoyed by citizens of modern states is strictly illusory. Whilst it may be possible to air views not in conformity with the prevailing consensus the fact that our world view is so thoroughly imbued with the prevailing norms of 'technics' means that they are almost unintelligible to all but those at the fringes of society. Thus it is not through the banning of opinions contrary to the interests of the *status quo* that the latter retains its grip on social consciousness. It is through depriving people of their capacity to judge between competing conceptions of the good life and hence by rendering challenging opinions senseless.

Marcuse has a point: the idea that modern societies can without complication be regarded as 'open' is one that appears at the very least naïve if not wrong. It is surely beyond question that where most of our information about the world comes through the media, money buys influence. With money comes the ability to fund campaigns, buy newspapers, purchase advertising, and so on. Without money it takes a great deal more effort to generate the same impact on public consciousness. In a democratic society a person may be free to oppose prevailing views, but without money may find it difficult to do so. It is also surely a truism that those with a great deal of money tend to share a similar world view. They tend to want to justify a system in which it is possible to become wealthy and to enjoy the luxuries and privileges that go with it. They tend, therefore, to support the values and norms of a system that has after all allowed them to become rich in the first place. In a system in which there is a free market in ideas it is only to be expected that the ideas of the free market will come to predominate.

Marcuse's argument that far from being plural and open, modern society is monopolistic and closed is not entirely unreasonable. It is certainly true that the media is dominated by those with the money to air their views, and that those with money are normally supportive of the existing state of affairs, of big business, of economic growth. There is undeniably a consensus in most advanced industrial systems about the ends of society. Most people want economic growth, they want an increase in their standard of living, and to enjoy the fruits of modernity. At the same time, as Marcuse argues, there are vested interests that seek to promote and reinforce the values that sustain the system. The fact that such forces have direct access to people through advertising, newspapers, and other media gives them influence over the way people think about themselves and their society. However, what still remains to be shown is that there is a direct link between the efforts of the 'hidden persuaders' to make us believe in the system and the consensus giving the system its legitimacy. It is one thing to say that there are groups in society with an active interest in making people think in a particular way, but quite another to argue that the way people think is *determined* by these groups. How, in other words, does Marcuse know that our consent to the system is a product of the efforts of 'vested interests'? What makes him so confident in asserting that the relationship between 'us' and 'them' is one of coercion?

The key to understanding why Marcuse considers force is necessary to make people conform with the values and norms of the system is because these values and norms are at odds with people's 'true needs'. As he sees it, if people had the chance they would never freely choose to live in a society of endless striving and one-upmanship. They would never choose to spend their time shopping and consuming the latest fad or fashion. They would never want to live in a highly competitive society that requires us to trample over each other to get to the 'top'. This is because the form of life prevailing in modern societies does not meet our 'true needs', the needs we feel deep down. What we really need, he argues, is solidarity, reciprocity and community. What we need is to satisfy our most basic instincts, the instincts that cry out for a more aesthetic, erotic, playful form of existence. What we therefore need is a world in which there are no onerous duties to be performed, a world in which necessity, hunger, want, and avarice has been banished. This is the world we really need, and, furthermore, this is the world we could have if only society was organised along different lines. The technical level of production is such that we could create the material bounty Marx promised. We could have a society in which we are freed from want and thus able to pursue a more meaningful form of existence. The conditions to implement such a transition are already in place. 'Civilization', Marcuse idiosyncratically explains,

> produces the means for freeing Nature from its own brutality, its own sufficiency, its own blindness, by virtue of the cognitive and transforming power of Reason. And Reason can fulfil this function only as post-technological rationality, in which technics is itself the instrumentality of pacification, organon of the 'art of life'. The function of Reason then converges with the function of Art.[20]

All that is needed is an effort of will, a casting off of the delusions and lies upon which the legitimacy of the current system depends. What is needed is a change in the way we think about ourselves and the world and a corresponding change in the manner in which social, economic and political institutions are regulated. Everything is in place. All that is required is, as Marcuse puts, 'the Great Refusal', a refusal, that is, to tolerate the current state of affairs coupled with the desire to put humanity on 'a new footing'.[21] So what is it that prevents humanity simply shrugging off the empty, ritualistic craving of our 'false needs' and recognising our 'true' subjectivities? Why can we not find the effort of will to move to the Promised Land of state planned satisfaction? The answer, to Marcuse, is of course painfully apparent. We have been deprived of our capacity to imagine a better form of life.

The difficulty with Marcuse's thesis is knowing what might count as evidence supporting his analysis. Marcuse is insistent that the sort of radical or oppositional activity that we might cite as evidence for the existence of disapproval of the system should not be counted. Thus although we might ordinarily want to say that protest marches or demonstrations are evidence of discontent or disillusionment with certain policies or even with the system as a whole, for Marcuse they are, as we have seen, merely 'the ceremonial part of practical behaviourism', 'its harmless negation', and thus affirmative of the *status quo*. As he explains in *One Dimensional Man*, the real novelty of totalitarian regimes is to make such activity appear to represent a challenge to the system when really it is part of its 'healthy diet'. Protest provides an outlet for what might potentially become negative energies, whilst preserving the illusion of openness and tolerance necessary for the legitimation of the system. The point Marcuse is making is that nowhere do we see the radical activity or even radical thinking that would really serve to undermine the existing state of affairs. No one, in other words, is confronting the entire system of oppression with a blueprint for the form of life he or she thinks we need. What demonstrations there are are usually aimed at producing some piecemeal change in a particular policy or initiative. A demonstration, for example, against the building of a motorway through a particular area is not really 'negative' in the sense of challenging the system. This is because implied in such a campaign is a recognition that the system as a whole has legitimacy. If it did not then the marchers would not be demonstrating on this particular issue, but would be rebelling against the system as such. In other words, such actions are 'affirmative' because they promote the idea that whilst certain policies require review the system itself is perfectly rational. Why would people bother to demonstrate if they did not believe that by doing so their actions will have some tangible effect on the decisions of government? So it is the *absence* of radical demands, the absence of calls for the wholesale demolition of the entire system, that for him is really telling. What it signals is the continuing success of the apparatus in preventing people seeing what their 'true needs' are and acting upon them to bring about a better world. 'Whether or not', Marcuse asserts,

> the possibility of doing or leaving, enjoying or destroying, possessing or rejecting something is seized as a need depends on whether or not it can be seen as desirable and necessary for the prevailing societal institutions and interests. In this sense, human needs are historical needs and, to the extent to which the society demands the repressive development of the individual, his needs themselves and their claim for satisfaction are subject to overriding standards.[22]

However, if the expression of discontent in the form of protests, marches, demonstrations and so on cannot be taken as evidence for the existence of unfulfilled 'true needs' then it is difficult to see what his evidence might be. What is still left to be shown is that we possess 'true needs' opposed to and contradictory with our 'false needs'.

From the discussion above, it seems clear that Marcuse is attempting to draw a clear distinction between 'need' and 'want'. Ordinarily we tend to use the words in an overlapping way in the sense that much of the time what we need is also what we want, and vice versa. When I say 'I need a drink' I am also expressing what I want because I want a drink as well as needing one. Of course the fact that the words often overlap does not mean that they have the same meaning. It is possible for us to want something that we do not need, and to need something that we do not want. For example, I may need to go to the dentist because I have a toothache. However, it would only be human to say that I do not *want* to go to the dentist, particularly if I have painful memories of my previous visits. If I go to the dentist it is not, therefore, because I want to go, but because I have to go, because I need to go. On the other hand, I may want something that I do not need. I may, for example, want a convertible Mercedes roadster, but I certainly do not need one. I have already got a perfectly serviceable car catering for all my 'real' needs.

Marcuse's point is that we *need* the sort of liberated society he discusses, even though at this particular moment we might not *want* it. Ask people in modern societies what they want and the chances are they will say that they want more of the same. They would want their own position to be materially better, they would want more money, more leisure time, a bigger house, a faster car, more holidays, and so on. Ask them if they want a new political system or an entirely new form of life and they would probably say they do not. Most people are reasonably content with the *status quo*, particularly if they can see some benefit to themselves in maintaining the existing state of affairs. That of course is the problem. To Marcuse, asking ordinary people such a question is like asking happy slaves if they would like to have their own freedom. One or two slaves might say they would; but most would say they would not. The point is that slaves have been trained to lack adventure, they have been educated to be thankful for whatever they receive. Most of us are, it seems, happier to remain as we are than to risk all for the great unknown. We are the happy slaves, unwilling to shrug off our alienated condition for the promise of a better world. We do not want the better world, therefore, but we certainly need it; or so it seems.

The question of whether Marcuse is right, i.e. that we need a society in which all our 'true needs' are taken care of, can be put aside for the moment. What it is important to consider are the implications of what Marcuse is saying, for if his analysis is correct then obviously more thought will have to be given to the nature of domination.

Normally we use words such as domination, coercion and force to describe a situation in which someone is being made to do something that they do not want to do. Someone is being forced to do x when they do not want to do x. Someone is being coerced when, instead of being able to do y, they are made to do z. Someone is suffering domination when they are unable to do c because someone else insists that they do d and is in a position to make sure that they do d and not c. In other words, when we use such words we are talking about situations in which people are not able to do what they want to do because another person or group is forcing them to do something else. The novelty of Marcuse's analysis of domination is that he is talking about a form of domination which is exercised not against the will, not against what a person wants to do, but against ostensibly objective needs that all of us are alleged to have in common. In his view we have to get away from the idea that people are coerced when they are forced to do something they do not want to do and adopt an entirely different way of looking at the issue. What we should ask is, what do people really need? If those needs are not fulfilled then we must regard those people who remain, so to speak, objectively unsatisfied as subject to domination. Thus, in Marcuse's view, it is perfectly consistent to talk about people being dominated or being forced to do something despite the fact that people themselves deny that they are being coerced. If it is decided that, for example, we need access to painting lessons to enjoy a happy and fulfilled existence, then according to the logic of Marcuse's argument my not having access to painting lessons can be taken as evidence of the fact that I am being dominated or coerced by another person or group. The fact that at this moment I do not want painting lessons is entirely irrelevant on this logic, because it is not what people want or do not want that we should be worried about, but about what people 'need'.

A moment's reflection on what is being said here reveals how problematical such an argument is. To go back an earlier example, if I have a toothache we can say that I need to go to the dentist. However, the fact that I need to go to the dentist does not necessarily mean that I want to go to the dentist. So clearly it is possible, as Marcuse infers, to separate what a person wants from what they need. What is less clear is how a person who needs something but does not want it can be coerced by being prevented from having it. If I want to go to the dentist but am prevented from doing so by someone's actions, then we could say that I am subject to coercion. I want to do something I have the ability and the right to do, but I am prevented from doing it by someone else's actions. Here there is a clear exercise of force to prevent me doing what I want to do and thus I can with some legitimacy claim to be coerced. If, on the other hand, I do not want to go to the dentist, if I declare myself wholly against even the idea of having my teeth seen to, how is it possible to say that I am being coerced by not going to? No force has been exercised against me, no one has imposed their will upon me, or made me obey their command. I have simply decided to ignore the signals from my own body telling me to do something. The fact that my need remains unsatisfied cannot therefore be taken as *prima facie* evidence that force has been used to prevent a particular need from being satisfied.

The conclusion I think we have to come to is that it is meaningless to regard the existence of unsatisfied needs as evidence for the exercise of domination. The existence of unsatisfied needs may well be evidence for the existence of injustice or inequality in a society, that is beyond dispute. However, use of terms such as domination, coercion, and force only makes sense in a context when those needs are linked to the desire for their satisfaction. If I need something and also want it and am prevented from having it then it is possible to begin talking about domination. Where, however, it is alleged that unsatisfied needs exist but yet there is no demand for their satisfaction then it seems unwarranted to regard those possessing these needs as subject to domination. We can simply ask the question, if the needs are so pressing why do those who have them not make manifest their desire to have them fulfilled?[23]

It can now be seen that with Marcuse's *One Dimensional Man* the connection between the concept of totalitarianism and domination – as that word is ordinarily used – is finally severed. In Marcuse's analysis totalitarianism is no longer employed as a term describing the palpable domination of one group over another. In his 'totalitarian' systems the people who are allegedly the victims of this process of subjugation themselves deny that the system is oppressive at all. Space is given for people to speak their minds, to form political parties, to set up newspapers, even to demonstrate against the system itself. All adults have the right to vote, individual rights are protected by the courts of law if not enshrined in constitutions, people may travel unimpeded, and so forth. Yet to Marcuse all of this is a red herring; it is a lie concealing relations of subordination and coercion. The more open and free a system appears to be to the naked eye the more oppressive are the conditions within it. With Marcuse the concept of totalitarianism therefore comes full circle. Instead of being used to describe systems in which domination is apparently at its worst, it describes systems where liberty is apparently most fully developed. Instead of referring to a society in which people suffer the worst excesses of terror and privation of freedom, it now refers to one in which they enjoy the highest standard of living, the most 'liberties and comforts' and the greatest amount of space in which to develop their talents and capacities. Domination in Marcuse's totalitarian systems is thus transparent. It is something intangible, unfelt, and invisible to all those said to be affected by it, except of course to Marcuse and his followers.

Given that there is little or no empirical evidence which Marcuse can call upon to show that the citizens of advanced industrial societies are dominated or coerced in the manner in which he feels we are, it follows that his account of totalitarianism will only be convincing to those who share his presuppositions concerning the nature of the human condition. If we believe, as he does, that individuals are all endowed with a set of 'vital needs' that require satisfaction in order for us to be fully liberated then of course his argument may well seem highly plausible. If I 'know' that every individual requires an aesthetic, playful, erotic form of existence in which to be fully satisfied then it will seem obvious that a system in which these 'needs' are denied satisfaction is one that has to be founded on force in order to keep it in being. Freud thought along much the same lines, although he believed that we were ultimately better off living in a repressed society since that made 'civilisation' and social order possible, and in his view we cannot be against civilisation. In other words, although he saw that force was needed to prevent the seams holding society together falling apart, he thought there were greater advantages in living within society than the alternative which was living a Hobbesian existence within the 'primal horde'. However, showing that these fundamental needs really exist and hence that force at the instinctual level really is required to keep us from rebelling is difficult indeed. What sort of evidence might we regard as acceptable as showing us that such needs exist and are a primary factor in determining our innermost feelings? What are our innermost feelings, if not those we actually feel and are able to give account of? Why should we suppose that there is only one set of 'vital needs'? Why could not different people possess different vital needs? And so on. In short, what is the nature of the evidence being used to show the existence of relations of domination? Moreover, there are strong ethical and moral reasons why we should balk at the suggestion that it is possible to speak of the existence of 'vital needs' at all. One of the basic presuppositions informing the development of liberal societies has been the belief in the right of individuals to define their own needs and to pursue their satisfaction in the best way they see fit. The notion that there exist vital needs that all of us share by virtue of our membership of the species is corrosive of such a belief and hence corrosive of the practice of toleration that has emerged from it. Although he styles himself a 'libertarian', there is a more than a hint of Platonic hubris about Marcuse's approach, and if Popper *et al.* are to be believed it is precisely such hubris that is itself the root cause of authoritarianism. In this sense, as Richard

Bernstein comments, it is impossible to find in Marcuse's work

> the resources to make the subtle and crucial discriminations between
> individual and public, communal freedom and happiness – the types
> of freedom and happiness that only come into existence and can be
> sustained through the sharing and interactions of individuals in their
> plurality. What always seems to be missing in Marcuse is not 'Man' of
> 'human potentialities', but men – or better, human beings in their
> plurality who only achieve their humanity in and through each
> other.[24]

In other words, the difficulty with Marcuse's account of domination is a reflection of difficulties with his account of the human
subject. The reality is Marcuse is operating with a one-dimensional
account of what it means to be an individual. The object of his notion
of emancipation is not us as we exist now. Rather it is, in his chilling
phrase, the 'new historical subject' endowed with a collective structure of needs and a collective sense of what is required for happiness
and self-fulfilment. In formulating his project in this way he not only
abandons the notion that political struggle should proceed from a
sense of what is morally required for the creation of a free society,
but the notion of freedom as the promotion of individuality, of
difference. As Morton Schoolman remarks: 'The anthropological
conception determines the subject and the subject's mode of being in
advance and in a manner precluding the issues and problems with
which a free subject would contend'.[25] When Marcuse talks about
'true needs' he is not therefore talking about *our* true needs, but the
true needs of some model individual he has invented. It is this model
individual that is the subject of domination in his totalitarian states,
not us.

The conclusion we have to come to is that Marcuse's analysis of
domination lacks credibility when considered as a contribution to
the debate on the causes and nature of totalitarianism. As we have
seen Marcuse's account shares certain characteristics of, as it were,
mainstream totalitarian studies. There is a strong emphasis on the
modernity of totalitarianism, on the ideological character of the
form of rule, and on the achievement of 'total domination'. The great
difficulty with Marcuse's account is, however, the lack of a dominating agent. In all the theories we have so far considered the
assumption is clearly that totalitarianism is the intended end-
product of a given movement or party. The latter begin with a vision

of a society which they want to realise in practice. They take control of the state and attempt to implement that vision in practice. In order to realise the vision radical change is needed in the way people think and behave. This creates conflict between state and society and the state is required to use force in order to pursue its goal. That, in a nutshell, is the argument of theorists like Popper, Hayek, and Friedrich and Brzezinski (Arendt's account of agency is not quite so clear cut). Whether, ultimately, we agree with their accounts of totalitarianism we can at least see the agents or forces alleged to be doing the dominating. The question we are left with in these accounts is whether the theorist has read the relationship between rulers and ruled correctly, whether they have imputed the correct intentions to the regime, and so on. Marcuse, on the other hand, insists that totalitarianism is the product, not of a clearly specified group with an interest in changing society, but of a conception of society contained within the modern *Geist*. Although, as he puts it, there are certain 'vested interests' within modern society with a stake in maintaining the hegemony of 'instrumental reason', these interests do not control the system or shape its development. Everyone in this sense is a victim of the system. The apparent distinction between rulers and ruled is just that, merely apparent. The reality is that our role in society is already determined by the system itself and by the imperatives that underpin it. It is thus not merely a face-less, subject-less form of domination, but also a regime-less one as well. The difficulty with this explanation should be readily apparent. In order to describe a relationship of domination we need to be able to locate a dominator and those who are said to be dominated. We need to be able to say that agent x is using power to make agent y do (or not do) z. If that relationship cannot be found, if, for example, y does z because he himself wants to, then it simply does not make sense to talk about domination at all. Marcuse's account of totalitarianism does not give us a realistic analysis of domination. It gives us an account of a way of life, and the ideas, beliefs and values that characterise it. Ideas may give reasons for dominating others; but ideas themselves do not dominate. Marcuse seems unable and unwilling to see that.

Given the lack of a coherent account of domination in *One Dimensional Man* what emerges is that Marcuse's theory of totalitarianism is really a form of cultural criticism. The not-so-hidden sub-text is that Marcuse does not like modern life in general, and the United States in particular. He does not like the culture of consumerism; the celebration of wealth and plenty in the midst of profound destitution and anomie. He does not like the ritualistic character of liberal-democratic politics, its rhetoric of popular sovereignty amidst the reality of crass manipulation and deception. He does not like the lack of authenticity and sensitivity of the modern citizen, finding our taste for the new, the brash, and the momentary as the pursuit of a singularly hollow form of contentment. For Marcuse there is a world of difference between these values and the values of an emancipated society of free individuals, and many – though not apparently enough – would no doubt agree. Much of what Marcuse says contains a grain of wisdom; but it is the wisdom of the Holy Fool. There are few people, after all, who would be willing to swap a life in a modern liberal-democracy, with all its imperfections, for a life in Stalin's Russia, Hitler's Germany or Pol Pot's Cambodia. An account of totalitarianism that might possibly be interpreted as saying that people are somehow worse off in the former than they were in the latter surely misses the point.

Notes

1 The clearest exposition of Adorno and Horkheimer's view of totalitarianism is contained in their *Dialectic of Enlightenment*, translated by John Cumming (London, 1986).
2 For an excellent analysis of the relationship between the School's criticisms of instrumental reason and Weber's theory of rationalisation see Albrecht Wellmer's article 'Reason, Utopia and the *Dialectic of Enlightenment*', in *Habermas and Modernity*, edited by R. J. Bernstein (Cambridge, 1985), pp. 35–66.
3 There is a vast literature on the subject of Marcuse's relationship both to the rest of the Frankfurt School and to other varieties of Marxist discourse. Some of the most useful accounts of this complex interrelationship are: Martin Jay, *The Dialectical Imagination* (London, 1973); Douglas Kellner, *Herbert Marcuse and the Crisis of Marxism* (London, 1984); and David Held, *Introduction to Critical Theory* (London, 1980), especially chapters 3, 4, 5 and 8.
4 Perhaps the classic statement of this position is in Daniel Bell's *The Coming of Post-Industrial Society* (New York, 1973).
5 By 1958 Marcuse, we can note, had begun to regard all industrial societies as variants of the same system. Capitalism and communism, he argues, 'show the common features of late industrial civilization – centralization and regimentation supersede individual enterprise and

autonomy; competition is organized and "rationalized"; there is joint
rule of economic and political bureaucracies; the people are coordinated
through the mass media of communication, entertainment industry,
education. If these devices prove to be effective, democratic rights and
institutions might be granted by the constitution and maintained without danger of their abuse in opposition to the system'. *Soviet Marxism. A
Critical Analysis* (London, 1958), p. 81. See also *One Dimensional Man*,
pp. 12–13.

6 For a critique of the economic assumptions underlying Marcuse's thesis,
in particular that capitalism has staved off the structural contradictions
present in the capitalist mode of production, see: John Fry, *Marcuse.
Dilemma and Liberation, A Critical Analysis* (Stockholm, 1974); Paul
Mattick, *Critique of Marcuse – One Dimensional Man in Class Society*
(London, 1972); and Göran Therborn, 'The Frankfurt School', *New
Left Review*, no. 63, (Sept.–Oct. 1970).

7 *One Dimensional Man*, p. 135.

8 *Ibid.*, p. 129.

9 *Ibid.*, p. 14.

10 *Ibid.*, p. 13.

11 *Ibid.*

12 *Ibid.*, pp. 26–7. As Adorno and Horkheimer note in similar vein: 'The
effrontery of the rhetorical question, "What do people want?" lies in the
fact that it is addressed – as if to reflective individuals – to those very
people who are deliberately to be deprived of their individuality', *Dialectic of Enlightenment*, pp. 144–5.

13 *One Dimensional Man*, pp. 26–7.

14 *Ibid.*, p. 19.

15 *Ibid.*, p. 53.

16 *Ibid.*, p. 28.

17 *Ibid.*, p. 19.

18 *Ibid.*, p. 9.

19 Francis Fukuyama, *The End of History and the Last Man* (London,
1992).

20 *One Dimensional Man*, p. 187.

21 The idea of the Great Refusal became the most important motif in
Marcuse's later works such as *An Essay on Liberation,
Counterrevolution and Revolt* and *Five Lectures*. As many have noted,
this search for the key to unlocking the rebellious core that he thinks
lurks beneath the surface of the modern individual is really at the heart of
Marcuse's entire theoretical project. On this point see Richard J.
Bernstein's article 'Negativity: Theme and Variations' in Marcuse,
Critical Theory and the Promise of Utopia, edited by R. Pippen, A.
Feenberg and C. P. Webel (London, 1988).

22 *One Dimensional Man*, p. 21.

23 For a further discussion of the the difficulty involved in Marcuse's separation of true and false needs see Alkis Kontos, 'Through a Glass Darkly, Ontology and False Needs', *The Canadian Journal of Political and Social Theory*, 3, no. 1 (Winter 1979).

24 Bernstein, 'Negativity', pp. 24–5.

25 Morton Schoolman, *The Imaginary Witness. The Critical Theory of Herbert Marcuse* (New York, 1980), p. 285.

5

Václav Havel
'The Power of the Powerless'

As should by now be apparent, the heyday of totalitarianism studies was undoubtedly the period from the early 1950s to the early 1970s. We might say that in terms of publications it is a period that stretches from the appearance of Hannah Arendt's *The Origins of Totalitarianism* to Leonard Schapiro's work *Totalitarianism* published in 1972. For a number of reasons use of the concept after this point diminished to the stage where many questioned its continuing relevance for describing contemporary forms of dictatorship. Why?

One of the most important factors in the decline of the concept for describing communist systems is the change in the relationship between the superpowers during the period of *détente*. The West's desire to promote a less hostile stance towards the communist bloc certainly diffused tensions between the two at the diplomatic level. It also led to, or at least coincided with, a toning down of the language used by commentators and analysts to describe communist systems. Just as it seemed inappropriate for politicians to adopt an aggressive stance towards their communist equivalents, so it seemed inapt for academics to continue using language that appeared redolent of Cold War animosity to describe the communist system itself. Symbolic of this 'new deal' for communism was the renaming of Merle Fainsod's *How Russia is Ruled* with the title *How the Soviet Union is Governed* after it had been updated by Jerry Hough. For Hough, as for a growing number of commentators, the Soviet Union had now in a sense grown up. It was quite wrong in his view to continue regarding the Soviet Union as a revamped version of Tsarist autocracy. The Soviet regime no longer relied on the fear of the Gulag to inspire the obedience of the people. Instead, with the promotion of

social programmes in housing, education and welfare a form of
'social contract', albeit a tacit one, had emerged justifying the belief
that the Soviet regime had gained legitimacy in the eyes of the
population. It followed that a concept in which the centrality of
terror in eliciting social control is stressed was now no longer relevant for describing the situation as it pertained in the Soviet Union.

The moderate tone of a new generation of commentators on
communist affairs was, furthermore, backed up by the 'findings' of
modernisation theorists. Inspired in particular by the work of Max
Weber, many social theorists and sociologists had begun to argue
from the early 1960s onwards that the similarities between communist and capitalist systems were greater than their differences. Far
from representing opposite poles of the political spectrum, these two
systems were in fact 'converging' on the same pole. As these theorists
argued, both systems are modern, industrialised and urban. They
both therefore have to contend with similar sorts of problems and
issues, such as how best to provide essential services, how to sustain
growth and unemployment, how to cope with deprivation, crime
and alienation. In sociological, economic, and to a certain extent
political terms capitalist and communist societies share a great deal.
The real opposite or 'other' of this global equation was the Third
World: the developing, the non-developed, and the never-to-
develop. Given that many of these theorists wanted to stress the
similarities rather than the differences between communist and other
modern systems it should hardly be surprising that many of them felt
uncomfortable about using the concept of totalitarianism to describe
the former. It was all too redolent for them of the Manichean
thinking they were trying to get away from.[1]

Quite apart from the sheer unfashionableness of the totalitarian
model as a means of describing the nature of existing communist
systems, use of the concept declined as blows were delivered by
historians to the stock of assumptions upon which the credibility of
the model depended. In particular the image of the totalitarian
system as a monolithic entity in which politics was reduced to the
whim of one man came under severe attack. As historians of the
relevant regimes set out to show, neither Hitler nor Stalin ever
enjoyed the degree of power over their systems that totalitarian
theorists apparently believed. To take the example of Nazi Germany,
the studies of the *alltagesgeschichte* or everyday life of the Germans
revealed that the image of unity and togetherness that the Nazis liked

to project of their New Order was largely fictitious. As the regime's own records show, the Nazis were themselves only too aware of the existence of disagreement, dissent and outright opposition that existed within society, and hence of the care with which their own project had to be pursued. This contrasts strongly with the account of relations between rulers and ruled given, as we have seen, by theorists of totalitarianism. The more we found out about the nature of such regimes the less appropriate the totalitarian appeared. Here, therefore, was a concept lacking a reality to describe. If after all Nazi Germany could not be considered totalitarian then what regimes could?

By the middle to late 1970s, therefore, the credibility and hence the utility of the term appeared to be on the wane. Only those with an interest in stoking the flames of old Cold War animosities seemed still to believe that it could be fruitfully deployed for describing existing communist systems. Herbert Spiro's prediction that the concept would eventually prove to be redundant once its ideological foundations were laid bare was, it appeared, about to be proved correct.[2] Although use of the concept began to diminish in the West, interest was revived by the input of theorists from a highly pertinent source, namely Eastern Europe. Intellectuals from this part of the world had of course long been critical of 'actually existing socialism' and the work of theorists like Milovan Djilas was familiar to those with an interest in communist systems. Yet it was not until the 1970s that the work of other East Europeans such as Leszek Kolakowski, Agnes Heller, Ferenc Fehér, Rudolf Bahro, Jacek Kuron, Karol Modzelewski and Václav Havel began to come to the attention of people in the West. Like earlier East European writers they were all deeply critical of communism and many of them unhesitatingly referred to these systems as 'totalitarian'. This of course should hardly be surprising. Many of them had suffered and continued to suffer at the hands of communist rulers. Some were expelled or ordered out, some were imprisoned and others were simply denied the right to speak or write in public. It is thus no coincidence that their writings were often denied an audience in the West. From the point of view of this discussion what is interesting about the work of these thinkers is that although they employ the term totalitarianism to describe communist systems their intellectual orientation is quite different from the 'totalitarian school' of theorists in Europe and the United States. Whereas, as we have seen, most of those who

employed the term here would regard themselves as being inspired
by liberal or conservative ideas about freedom and the role of the
state, many East European thinkers who subsequently went on to
write about totalitarianism regarded themselves as being if not
Marxists then certainly socialists or, more loosely, of the Left. For
example, the members of the Budapest School which included
Heller, her husband Ferenc Fehér and Georgy Markus, were all at
one time followers of Georg Lukacs, one of the most important
Marxist thinkers of the twentieth century and a hard-line adherent to
the Party line to boot. Leszek Kolakowski was a member of the
Communist Party in Poland until being expelled for his reformist
tendencies in 1966. Jacek Kuron and Karol Modzelewski were also
Party members in Poland, until expelled despite their continuing
adherence to socialist principles. Václav Havel was a member of the
Czechoslovak group Charter 77, a group that criticised the practices
of the communist regime from a position inspired by 'socialist
humanist' principles. Although a number of these thinkers would no
longer regard themselves as being socialists if only because the word
socialism has become for them so polluted, they are far from conforming to the stereotype of the 'militant liberal' either. These are
people who in a sense were driven to their hostility to the systems
they lived in by what they regard as a betrayal of the principles and
values underlying the socialist project. They have arrived at their
analysis of communism not because they were necessarily hostile to
socialism, but because of the actual practice of communist regimes.
What is also noticeably different about the accounts of communism
given by these theorists is that they concentrate on describing the
inside of the system rather than, as with say Friedrich, the outside or
morphology of the system. These thinkers are much less concerned
about mapping the external features of a regime and more interested
in the human dimension, about what it is like to live in these systems.
To put it in more formal terms, their inquiries focus on the fate of
civil society rather than on the form of the state. The fact that all
these theorists lived at one time or another in the society about which
they are writing gives their work an added urgency and immediacy
that other studies of totalitarianism might lack.

   In this chapter we will examine the work of one of the best-known
writers from Eastern or, rather, Central Europe, Václav Havel. As
before our aim will be to present his ideas about the nature of
totalitarian and what he terms post-totalitarian systems. We will

then move on to consider the utility of this analysis for understanding the nature of communist systems, and of totalitarian systems more generally.

*

Václav Havel might at first seem an unlikely subject for a study of theorists of totalitarianism. Unlike the other thinkers we have been considering as well as many of the dissident figures just mentioned, Havel has never been a professional academic or commentator on political affairs. He is best known, rather, as a playwright, as a member of the dissident group Charter 77, and latterly as the president of what until recently was Czechoslovakia. He was born in Prague in 1936 and after completing his schooling and military service worked in various capacities at the Theatre of the Balustrade in Prague. During this period he began to write plays the best known of which are *The Garden Party* and *The Memorandum*. Both were performed all over the world and earned the author a degree of celebrity. These works were followed by a number of others including two short autobiographical plays, *Audience* and *Private View* which were first broadcast on television in 1978. From 1968 onwards Havel's plays were prohibited from being published or performed, the authorities regarding Havel's satirical and subversive brand of black comedy as potentially disruptive. In 1977 Havel was arrested for his political activities and from that point until the fall of the communist regime was either in jail or under police surveillance. During this period Havel did, however, manage to continue writing letters, articles and other prose pieces. The most important of these from our point of view is a long essay entitled 'The Power of the Powerless' in which Havel analyses the character of communist regimes and suggests strategies for pursuing political change. With the fall of the communist regime in the 'Velvet Revolution' of 1990 Havel was immediately nominated for the presidency. A living symbol of unwavering opposition to the communist regime, Havel was propelled with considerable reluctance into the highest office of the land. From a life of internal exile and extreme hardship Havel, a modest and quietly spoken man, had become within a matter of weeks an internationally known figure and the embodiment of a people's desire for a better future.

Although, unlike Arendt, Friedrich and the other thinkers we have so far considered, Havel has not produced a major study of totalitarianism or totalitarian systems this is not to say that Havel's work on totalitarianism is insubstantial. The reality is that all of his work, his plays and articles, and even his letters, is in an important sense a contribution to the understanding of communism. Most of his best-known plays deal with life in communist society. They deal with what it means to be a part of the system, to conform to its logic (or illogic), to mirror its values and concerns. They deal with what keeps the system going, why people obey the rulers and how compliance is orchestrated. Reading Havel's plays it quickly becomes apparent that they give us something that no amount of academic explanation or description can give: they allow us to see what it means to exist within a culture. They show us what domination is, and what it means for the lives of ordinary people. Whereas an academic study gives us an impression of the form that a communist system takes, his work gives us an impression of its content. If they describe the skeleton, he gives us the flesh and blood. Although by comparison with writers such as Arendt and Friedrich Havel's contribution might appear sparse, not only is much of his output relevant to the issues we are addressing, issues about the nature of tyranny and domination, it confronts such issues in a direct and highly original way.

The starting-point of the essay 'The Power of the Powerless' is Havel's evident dissatisfaction with the totalitarian model as a description of the system in which he himself lived. In his view there was a wide disparity between the account that theorists of totalitarianism have given of communist systems and the reality that he saw before him.[3] The difficulty is that communist systems no longer appeared to him to be dictatorships at all, particularly not the sort of harsh tyrannies described by theorists of totalitarianism when describing the regimes of Hitler and Stalin. A dictatorship as Havel sees it is characterised by a number of different traits. Firstly, it is a political system in which a smaller group possesses and exercises a monopoly of power over a larger group, the population. This power is normally used to benefit the group either directly or indirectly. The group may have some end or vision of society in view, but this does not change the essential nature of a dictatorship which is that one group of people dictates what everyone else is allowed or expected to do. A further trait of dictatorships is that they normally represent a break with the past. They are often created as a result of a coup, revolution or conquest sweeping away the *ancien régime*. They often introduce radical changes to the institutions and structures of rule to cement the authority of the new regime. To live in a dictatorship is to be subjected therefore to something novel and original. Even if the new regime does not have any great plans for the reconstruction of society, it still represents a change from the society that existed. As Havel goes on to note:

> One of the essential aspects of this traditional or classical notion of dictatorship is the assumption that it is temporary, ephemeral, lacking historical roots. Its existence seems to be bound up with the lives of those who established it. It is usually local in extent and significance, and regardless of the ideology it utilises to grant itself legitimacy, its power derives ultimately from the numbers and the armed might of its soldiers and police. The principal threat to its existence is felt to be the possibility that someone better equipped in this sense might appear and overthrow it.[4]

Dictatorship is in this sense something open and physical. It is a visible presence in the lives of everyone living under it. There is something very straightforward about living in a dictatorship and everyone knows their position within the system. A person is either a ruler or one of the ruled; he or she is either victor or vanquished. This is political power without any embellishment or deception, because it is power exercised without concern to hide itself.

The problem in Havel's view is that this description of a dictatorship has very little relevance when it comes to looking at the communist system that existed in Czechoslovakia, or its neighbours. To begin with, Czechoslovakia and the other systems in Eastern and Central Europe were not geographically distinct in the way in which traditional dictatorships are. They were part of a vast power bloc run by one of the superpowers. Thus to be a ruler at the periphery of the system was quite different to being a dictator in the conventional sense of the term. Whereas the leader in a dictatorship is the one who normally makes all the important decisions, the one around whom power rotates, in these systems it was people in Moscow who held effective power. The job of the local leader was simply to implement those decisions and to keep a lid on potential discontent. The men who 'ruled' these countries were thus essentially barons rather than kings. Sovereignty over their own affairs was something they dreamed of, not something they possessed. Secondly, rule in these systems was backed by a vast military and police apparatus that could be and was called out at the merest hint of disobedience to the Moscow line. Accordingly there was little sense of that uncertainty and instability that characterises life in the 'classical' dictatorship. These were systems backed by the greatest weight of force any ruler could ever have enjoyed or endured. Stability and a singular lack of drama were the chief features of life in communist societies. Thirdly, unlike a dictatorship there was no lack of historical roots under-pinning the communist regimes. Communism in Eastern Europe was the product of a social movement, socialism, which in Havel's view had an 'undeniable historicity'. In other words, the systems did not emerge 'out of the blue', but were connected to the socialist and left movements of the nineteenth century. This gave these systems a sense of durability and permanence that dictatorships often lack. This durability was of course reinforced by the longevity of the system and the society that it spawned. By the 1980s communism had been around for a very long time and had become part of the fabric of daily life. Furthermore, with such limited opportunities for travel many people had no experience of what other systems were like or of how other people lived. Communism was all they knew. Whereas, therefore, dictatorships are characterised by 'an atmosphere of revolutionary excitement, heroism, dedication, and boisterous violence', such feelings had all but vanished from the communist bloc.[5] In place of the dangerous uncertainty of the dictatorship there evolved simply 'another form of the consumer and industrial society, with all the concomitant social, intellectual, and psychological prob-lems that that implies'.[6] These were flat, rather unexciting systems where people led a dull, routine sort of existence. Life in Eastern Europe was just as tedious and uneventful as it is in any other modern society, which of course was just the way the Soviet Union wanted it.

The most significant difference between traditional dictatorships including totalitarian regimes and the systems that existed in Eastern Europe which Havel terms 'post-totalitarian', is, however, the nature of the relationship between rulers and ruled. A dictatorship is characterised by an ongoing friction between the regime and the population. Dictators are people who have plans for society, they have measures that they want to implement to benefit themselves and their supporters. Hitler and Stalin, classical dictators on this view, possessed ideas or blueprints for future forms of society that they wished to see translated into reality. This ideology is then presented to the population as the truth, thereby relegating all competing conceptions of the good life to the status of falsehood. This attempt to fix a monopoly on the truth inevitably leads to friction between the regime and the population given the diversity of beliefs that people have about what is in their own interests and the interests of society. It is this disparity between what on the one hand the regime wants and what on the other hand any given individual wants that creates the necessity for the use of force, and hence which makes the regime truly a dictatorship. The use of force is thus the sign of dictatorship at work. It is a sign that the regime's plans and proposals meet with the disapproval of the people. In Eastern Europe, however, this friction had all but disappeared. Of course there were periodic crises such as the Hungarian Revolution in 1956 and the Prague Spring in 1968, but these were quickly dealt with, with the result that they had an unreal quality for the people who witnessed them. They were irruptions in the normal order of things, reminders of a form of existence that had long since been left behind.

For reasons outlined above the totalitarian model seemed unfitted to describe the sort of system that existed in Eastern Europe. The model seemed to describe not merely a different political system, but a different reality. It belonged to the age of ideologies, the age of bold and sweeping schemes of social reconstruction, the age of the masses. Yet in Havel's view we are deeply mistaken to regard these systems as in a sense less dominating, less tyrannical. Communist systems had changed over time, they had evolved or moved on. Although life was certainly different within these systems, the idea that this difference could be translated as meaning that domination had lessened is deeply misguided. What had occurred was an evolution in the practice of totalitarianism, not an evolution towards a more humane, more Western style of government. Change, in other words, did not mean improvement, it meant rationalisation: a honing and refining of an oppressive system of rule. Thus at a time when many in the West questioned the applicability of the totalitarian model to communist systems, Havel argued for a reappraisal of the totalitarian model precisely so that it could be made to fit the reality of life in the Communist Bloc. If the old model no longer applied, he argued, it was not because these systems had moved on past a point where the model was no longer relevant. Far from it: the model was highly relevant. The problem was that it had become antiquated and was no longer relevant to the form of domination to be found in communist systems. The model therefore had to be saved from the scrap-heap and given a major overhaul. This new revamped model Havel terms 'post-totalitarianism'.

The apparent acquiescence of people inhabiting 'mature' communist systems such as those in Eastern Europe has, as we have seen, been taken by some theorists as a sign of the success of the regime's 'war' on its own people. Carl Friedrich, we might recall, was so impressed by the ability of communist regimes to control and manipulate the socialisation process that he was prepared to concede that the relationship between the rulers and ruled in these systems could be said to be based on 'consent'. Since, he reasoned, the regime was able effectively to manufacture its own citizens, it was now impossible to talk about the domination of the ruled by the rulers. In Havel's view, however, this analysis is gravely mistaken. The conformity or consent of the population in these systems is merely apparent. The reality is simply that the way in which compliance is secured is no longer overt, that is based on the actual or threatened use of violence, but has become covert and hence invisible to the roving eye. The difficulty facing Havel was of course that if the domination was really invisible to the roving eye then how were we to tell that it existed at all? If people appear perfectly content with the situation in which they find themselves then how are we to know that they are being dominated? What are the signs that this consent has been produced by force and is not now freely given? It is this conundrum that Havel's work is in a sense dedicated to solving.

Havel attempts to explain how this new mode of domination works by moving to the level of the individual citizen living in a communist society. Instead of trying to discern the motivations and feelings of people from above, from as it were a survey of the landscape, he moves down to what might be termed the micro-level, the level at which ordinary people live their lives. In a highly effective piece of analysis Havel asks us to see the world from the point of view of a greengrocer who displays in his window a sign on which is written 'Workers of the World, Unite!'. On the face of it we could read the placing of the slogan in the window as a symbol of the person's acceptance of the system, of the fact that he regards the system as legitimate. Here, after all, is the clearest affirmation of loyalty to the regime and to the philosophy it extols. As Friedrich might have said, here is the evidence for the success of the communists' attempt to manufacture a new subject. Here is the New Man;

the man who embodies and embraces the norms of the new, progressive society. Here is the evidence that shows that the regime has won the war against its own people. On the other hand, as Hough might have claimed, here is evidence for supposing that the regime has succeeded in winning over the support of the people, that it has catered for the people's needs and hence gained their confidence. Havel, however, interprets the greengrocer's sign as meaning something quite different. For him the very fact that the greengrocer wants or needs to affirm his loyalty to the system is one that should arouse our suspicions. Why, we should be asking, do people feel the need or desire to affirm their loyalty to the system in such a way? Why should they want to confirm to all those around them their fealty to the values of the system? Havel has a point. Greengrocers living in Britain or France do not in general feel any sort of equivalent need. They do not display slogans saying 'Long Live Capitalism!' or 'We love the market order!' They do not feel the need to affirm their attachment to the norms and values upon which British and French society rests. Why is the situation different in communist systems? Why do people living in these societies feel they should affirm their commitment to the prevailing maxims?

Far from being a sign (as Friedrich might have it) of the success of the regime in manufacturing genuine consent, what this action shows is how far the daily existence of each person is permeated by fear. As Havel explains, what is written on the sign is completely irrelevant; it could be one of hundreds of similar slogans. The true meaning of the sign is not contained in the words, but in what the sign represents. The sign is essentially a subliminal message that Havel translates as meaning: 'I, the greengrocer XY, live here and I know what I must do, I behave in the manner expected of me. I can be depended upon and am beyond reproach. I am obedient and therefore I have the right to be left in peace.'[7] In other words, the sign is a talisman. It is an attempt to ward off difficulties and problems through an overt display of 'loyalty' to the system. In other words, rather than being a symbol of freely given consent, of genuine contentment with the *status quo*, it is a symbol of fear. The greengrocer puts the sign in the window because he thinks that by doing so he will appear loyal to those around him, to officials and, ultimately, to the police. Given that in these societies every public space is plastered with similar such slogans the grocer's display is a form of camouflage. It helps him slip quietly into the background of daily life, into the 'panorama' as Havel puts it, thereby confirming his acceptance of the system. It is an attempt to become part of the backdrop of society and thereby escape the stage upon which ugly human dramas take place.

In Havel's view what this example illustrates is the fundamentally novel way in which power is exercised in communist systems. In traditional dictatorships power is open and physical. Such regimes want to be seen to be powerful, they want to celebrate their power as a symbol of their own potency. Thus they have no compunction about openly terrorising elements of their own population, and chasing their enemies real or pretended. Dictators have traditionally measured their own strength by the amount of force they are able to command. The more jackbooted he-men they can mobilise the safer and more content they feel. In communist systems, on the other hand, power is insidious, hidden, 'subliminal'. It acts on the unconscious of all citizens, gnawing away at their sense of independence or autonomy. Power in these systems does not grow, at least immediately, out of the barrel of the gun, but through each citizen feeling the 'existential pressure' to conform. The difference between communist systems and traditional dictatorships, including totalitarian systems, is thus the role that ideology comes to play. Because of the sheer longevity of the former, because of the certainty of power that the regime enjoys, the ideology is no longer something that opposes the individual as it might formally have been. It is the bedrock of society. Everything within society is justified by reference to the ideology, everything is judged in terms of the standards and values it lays down. The ideology is the truth. It is also sovereign. The difficulty confronting people in Eastern Europe was that they all knew that the ideology was a pack of lies, albeit intricately woven. The communists claimed that they had come to power by the will of the people, whereas everyone knew that it was the Soviets who put them there. They claimed to be improving everyone's living standards when everyone knew that the Soviets were repatriating the productive base to help their own ailing economy. Everyone knew that the system was ridiculously inefficient even though they were told it was the incarnation of rationality and progress. Everyone implicitly knows that all of this is lies, but since there are no available avenues for the expression of real opinions people are unable to challenge it. Each person is therefore confronted with the same choice. They can, like the greengrocer, choose to 'live the lie'. They can choose, that is, to conform with the norms and rules of the system and otherwise live as if they were perfectly content with the *status quo*. Living within the lie thus involves a tacit agreement between citizen and regime. Each person agrees to do everything that is expected of the loyal, obedient citizen: they will turn up to workplace meetings; they will take part in elections, and not grumble too much when there is nothing to buy in the shops. In other words, they will agree to perform the rituals, comically explored in Havel's plays *The Garden Party* and *The Memorandum*, that are so much a part of life in a communist society. In return they will be able to enjoy a reasonably normal life. They will, that is, be able to apply for and eventually receive a flat, have access to health care facilities, have their children educated, and so on. In short, they will be able to go about their daily business relatively unimpeded by the regime; but only so long as that slogan remains in the window, the rituals are observed and the grumbles do not become too loud. Choosing, on the other hand, to 'live within the truth' is in effect to rip up this agreement and thus to announce oneself as an enemy of the regime. It is to deny the propaganda and the lies of the regime and in a sense to live in the real world. However, the price for rediscovering one's sense of identity, one's freedom to think and say what one actually feels, is as Havel was to find out a heavy one. In a system whose legitimacy derives entirely from the regime's claim to possess the truth, the existence of people who might want to examine or even challenge fundamental nostrums is one that cannot be tolerated. A choice to live within the truth thus necessarily involves not merely giving up any career prospects, and any privileges or advantages that a person might have enjoyed. It necessarily involves giving up physical if not mental freedom. As the example of Havel illustrates, liberating the mind from the shackles of propaganda and falsehood coincides with giving up the freedom to move, to speak, to write what one wants.

It is this theme of the choice between lives that forms the subject matter of a number of Havel's plays. In the semi-autobiographical *Audience*, for example, we see directly the nature of the choice described above.[8] The play concerns a young man, evidently independent of spirit, who has been sent to work in a brewery. The play begins with the man being ushered into the boss's office for a chat about the nature of the work he will be expected to do. The boss, helping himself to a handily placed crate of beer, offers a drink to the young man and attempts to engage in some friendly conversation about his interests and habits. The boss wants to find out a little bit about his new employee, to enter into a position of trust with him, to make him feel at home. However, as this evidently uncomfortable encounter unfolds and the boss gets drunker it becomes evident that the real reason for the conversation is that the boss has been told by 'them' (i.e. the authorities) to find out as much as he can about the young man. It is at this point obvious that the latter is some sort of dissident and has been sent to the brewery as a punishment for his independence of mind. Yet what also becomes apparent is that despite the boss's apparent position of strength it is he, para-doxically, who is in the weaker position. The boss after all has been told to collect as much information on the man as possible. As the boss himself admits, if he collects nothing of any substance it will be he who will stand to lose, not the young man. At the moment he has a cushy job, as much beer as he can drink, a warm office, responsi-bility, and so on. Yet were he to fail in his task all of this would be in danger of being taken away. The young man on the other hand seems to have nothing to lose. Whatever status or position he once had has already been taken away from him which is why he finds himself in the brewery. There is little more that the state can do to him to make him conform. If they treat him worse that might provoke a rumpus. It might if he is sufficiently well known, as of course Havel was, cause demonstrations, petitions, international approbation and the like. The boss therefore ends up pleading with the young man. He offers him a better job, warmer surroundings, other perks and privileges to get the man to throw out at least a few titbits of information to please 'them'. It is at this point that the choice we have been talking about becomes clear. If the young man decides to help the boss then the latter will be saved the indignity of failure. He will keep his position, his perks and privileges, and the sleepy normality of the brewery will be undisturbed. Furthermore, the young man's position will be greatly improved. He will have a warm office, a better job, as much beer as he can drink, and so on. He will also of course be helping those around him, most immediately his boss, the man he must try to get along with. It is clear that if the boss is content, then his life will be much easier. He will even, as the boss admits, be able to get on with the forbidden 'work' that probably caused him to be brought to the brewery in the first place. After a short pause the young man returns to the office. However, the nervous diffidence that was evident before he went out has been replaced by a new-found confidence. To the boss's delight the young man sits down and joins the latter in a drink. A reconciliation has evidently been effected. The pressure to live the lie has finally told.

Private View, a similarly autobiographical piece, explores the same territory. Here the young man is invited to the home of two friends, a married couple, whom he obviously has not seen or been in contact with for some time. The couple appear ingratiatingly successful. The husband has a good job that enables him to travel abroad regularly and to obtain goods not otherwise available. He dresses well and buys the latest pop records, which he insists on playing loudly to the evident discomfort of his guest. The wife is an excellent cook and prepares exotic canapés in the latest culinary style. Their flat is expensively if garishly furnished, and, as they are at constant pains to emphasise, they enjoy a fabulous sex life. All of which apparently contrasts with the style of life of the young man. He, according to the couple, has a bad job, a tiny apartment, few goods, and his sex life is non-existent. Unsurprisingly the young man appears utterly uncomfortable in such surroundings, particularly as the couple are forever offering him advice on how to become more like them, the very model of a successful and happy family. Unable to take any more of their crowing self-eulogising the young man eventually gets up to leave. However, as he does so the attitude of the couple changes completely. The wife bursts into tears and dashes off into the kitchen accusing the young man of 'betrayal'. As the husband explains, he is their 'best friend'. All this effort that they have put into their lives was, so the husband claims, done for him. It was done to impress him, to make him feel that the people around him cared about their lives. By turning his back on them the young man is therefore placing in doubt the values they thought he shared. The couple conformed with what they believed to be the ideal, they had done what had been expected of them, and now everything was in doubt. As the husband makes clear, if he walks out the young man will destroy the bonds and expectations that they share; he will make their lives meaningless. Again, therefore, the young man faces the 'existential pressure' to conform discussed earlier. If he walks out, he not only confirms his own status as an 'outsider', as someone who has set his face against the system of values, he destroys the couple's own sense of worth and satisfaction, the satisfaction that derives from their having attained the model of the good life. If, on the other hand, he stays he will be admitted to the 'inside'. His own life will be easier because all he has to do is conform with an already constructed ideal of how to live. He will, moreover, make the couple and, by extension, all those who conform to society's norms feel better, because they will have confirmed the validity of their own assumptions about what constitutes a happy and fulfilled life. Again, the choice is heavily loaded in favour of staying inside, going with the flow, following the herd. After a short pause the young man announces 'I'm back'. Suddenly the atmosphere changes, the frostiness of the husband disappears, and the wife wipes away her tears. The young man happily accepts a drink, the music is turned up, and the party which only moments earlier had looked like being a complete disaster gets into full swing. Again, reconciliation appears to have been achieved and 'wholeness' restored.

Whilst both plays clearly demonstrate the nature of what Havel has called 'existential pressure', it is interesting to note the different context or setting of the plays, and the different message that each of them contains. *Audience* is clearly about the nature of communist systems in a way in which *Private View* is not. To begin with in *Audience* it is clear that we are actually in a communist system. The boss, we learn, is really a brew master, a craftsman, rather than a businessman, or one trained in how to run an industrial enterprise. He has been sent to the brewery not it seems for any particularly good reason, not because he necessarily possesses the skills to run it, but because 'they' want him there. His sense of frustration and alienation about his situation is perhaps evident in his heavy drinking and generally morose air. The young man, the subject of the play, has been sent to the brewery as some sort of punishment for his activities and as a way of keeping him out of harm's way. This of course was the classic tactic of communist regimes when confronted by the obdurate or the disobedient. Rather than jail them or punish them physically, something that may well raise the hackles of other dissidents and possibly foreign opinion, the regime used simply to strip dissidents of their posts and privileges and return them to the level of the lowest proletarian. Thus the play is clearly about the victims of the communist system, and the dilemmas and difficulties that they face. *Private View* is in an important sense quite different. In this play all the action takes place between friends in a private flat and there are few clues to tell us that the action is taking place in a communist or post-totalitarian regime. The situation is entirely natural in the sense that it could be taking place in any society. There is no reference to any regime or system, to 'them' or anyone else. Moreover the pressure to conform which the young man is under is a pressure to conform with norms and values familiar to many people living in modern society. The values the couple are attempting to foist upon the young man are not after all derived from communist ideology; far from it. They are the values of a consumer society. The couple are not trying to conform with communist or socialist stereotypes, but with those derived from consumer society. In what sense, therefore, is the existential pressure to conform felt by the young man any different from the kind of pressure felt by people in all modern societies? To put it the other way round, is not the penalty for the young man's non-conformity exactly the same as that for people living in capitalist societies, i.e. being ostracised, cold-shouldered, being made to feel inadequate, and so on?

The perhaps rather surprising answer to that question is that in Havel's view there is indeed a similarity between the pressures faced by people living in advanced communist systems and those living in 'consumer societies'. As he makes clear in 'The Power of the Powerless', there is something fundamentally similar about the sort of pressures faced by individuals in both forms of society. In his view, for example, the unwillingness of people to challenge or think critically about the nature of consumption and the virtue of immersing ourselves in the latest fads and fashions mirrors closely the unwillingness of people in post-totalitarian society to reflect upon the lies propagated by the regime. Like Marcuse, Havel is sharply critical of what he sees as the abdication of our capacity to think about what he terms 'the higher values'. We have, he thinks, given up the search for a better, more human world for what he terms the 'trivialising temptations of modern existence'.[9] Instead of thinking about who we are and where our societies are going, we have settled down to an indolent life of meaningless consumption. We have in effect bought 'the lie' operating in capitalist societies that more means better.

The question immediately raised by such observations is, what is the difference between these societies if the stability of both rests on 'lies'? Why do we do not simply talk about the mode of domination prevalent in *modern* societies and thus regard – as Marcuse does – communist and capitalist systems as mere variants on a theme? Although Havel is prepared to admit that there may well be certain similarities between the way people live in the two forms of society, he is not prepared to let that similarity undermine the fact that there is a crucial difference between them. In essence this is a difference between being able and not being able to choose whether to surrender one's identity to an ideology. What makes a Western society different from a communist system is that it is perfectly open for a person living in the former to reject the expectations and values propagated by the establishment, the powers that be. Although most people are in fact content to go along with the *status quo*, to reaffirm the value of consumption, to live what Havel believes to be sadly impoverished lives, they are always free to reject it. No one is forcing people to go to the supermarket, to follow the latest fashion, to purchase the latest gadget. Indeed, if people feel strongly about these matters they can always try to persuade other people to reject these values. They can stand for parliament; they can print a newspaper; or they can get on a milk crate and stand at Hyde Park Corner appealing to people's better instincts, their 'higher values'. Although, in other words, there is pain attached to rejecting the values dominant in a consumer society, although there is the fear of ostracism or ridicule in choosing an alternative way of life, there is rarely any fear of punishment, imprisonment or exile. Havel is not therefore convinced as Marcuse is that people have no choice but to obey the values propagated by the system. In Havel's view people are capable of seeing the position they are in, they can think rationally about the political systems and the imperatives that underpin them. Furthermore, they are perfectly able as many in the West are to live their lives according to a quite different set of goals precisely because they are not faced with the prospect of losing everything and everyone they hold dear. This choice in favour of a different life is one that is realistically and practically not open to people living in communist systems. They are trapped because the system holds not merely all the aces, but all the cards. Few people in this sense choose to be dissidents, because that choice is so one-sided. They are usually chosen by the regime because they are unable to find a way of carrying on living the lie.

The difference between living in a capitalist system and a posttotalitarian one is thus that in the former you are not required to live a lie. If you follow the prevailing norms and live according to the values and beliefs, that is your choice and something that you have chosen for yourself. Such a life might well be 'trivial and frivolous', but at least it is one that people choose for themselves. Post-totalitarian systems are quite different. We are not talking here about a loosely assembled set of values that people can choose either to hold or reject. We are talking about an ideology, an elaborately constructed world view that gives answers to every conceivable question. Moreover it is a world view that is palpably false. The account of reality contained within it does not correspond to reality, to what is 'out there', to history, to the facts. Thus adopting the ideology is akin to 'living the lie', to abdicating one's sense of responsibility and autonomy for the sake of preserving those few elements of existence that make life tolerable. As Havel comments there is in everyone 'some willingness to merge with the anonymous crowd and to flow comfortably along down the river of pseudo-life.'[10] Yet, as he continues, the willingness to go with the flow has far greater danger in post-totalitarian societies than consumer ones, for in the former this act of conformity amounts to 'a challenge to the very notion of identity itself'. In conforming with the ideology people are in essence giving up the right to decide for themselves how to run their lives, what beliefs they should hold on any matter, how they should respond to any situation. It is therefore an act representing the abdication of the self. What a person is doing in 'agreeing' to conform is agreeing not to be himself or herself, but to be someone else, a 'person' chosen by the regime. The novelty of the system is that this dilemma is the same for everyone, because *everyone* is trapped, not just the ordinary relatively defenceless citizen. As Havel explains:

> Differing positions in the hierarchy merely establish differing degrees of involvement: the greengrocer is involved only to a minor extent, but he also has very little power. The prime minister, naturally, has greater power, but in return he is far more deeply involved. Both, however, are unfree, each merely in a somewhat different way. The real accomplice in this involvement, therefore, is not another person, but the system itself.[11]

It is the ideology's role as a mechanism of compliance that therefore differentiates post-totalitarian from other forms of political system, including traditional forms of dictatorship. In the latter the regime is opposed to the individual. It is as if the two wills were directly opposed to each other with only the availability of force allowing the will of the regime to gain the upper hand. In a post-totalitarian society opposition and conflict has all but disappeared. As Havel explains the line dividing the rulers and ruled is not drawn according to social class, as it is in dictatorships. It is a line that 'runs *de facto* through each person, for everyone in his or her own way is both victim and supporter of the system.'[12] As Havel continues:

> What we understand by the system is not, therefore, a social order imposed by one group upon another, but rather something which permeates the entire society and is a factor in shaping it, something which may seem impossible to grasp or define (for it is in the nature of a mere principle), but which is expressed by the entire society as an important feature of its life.[13]

How by way of concluding this section can we sum up Havel's account of post-totalitarianism? What are its chief features and how does he believe it differs from more traditional forms of dictatorship, including totalitarian systems? For Havel what characterises most forms of dictatorship is the presence of tangible conflict between the rulers and the ruled, between the regime and the population subject to its rule. Most dictatorships are established as the result of a seizure of power by a group or party representing only a small element of the population. Unless the old rulers were extremely unpopular, it will be difficult for the new regime to establish genuine legitimacy in the eyes of the population. Secondly, dictatorships are systems in which by definition the rulers dictate to the ruled. Most such systems are set up by people who think they understand what is in the best interests of society and rarely, therefore, do they feel the need to consult the people about their plans for society. This unwillingness to enter into communication with society thus further adds to the problem of establishing legitimacy for what the regime is trying to do. Without any mechanism for seeking the approval of their policies the only way the regime can implement its programme and thus keep the system from collapsing is to resort to the threat of force, or, in extreme circumstances, to the actual use of force. This of course further highlights the regime's lack of legitimacy and the distance between it and the population.

In Havel's view what distinguishes post-totalitarian systems from dictatorships is that this elemental conflict between the regime and its subjects is hidden from all but the most inquiring eye. These are societies that to the casual observer appear stable and relatively peaceful. There is rarely any open display of force, the tanks do not rumble through the streets (often), and life has an air of sullen normality familiar in modern industrialised systems. These are societies that do not look as if the people lived in permanent fear of their lives. However, as quickly becomes apparent, this calm should not be taken as a sign of genuine acquiescence. It is, rather, the product of fear and of the fact that people have been forced to 'consent' to the regime. They force themselves to regard the regime as 'legitimate', 'normal', and 'peaceful', whilst at the same time knowing the true nature of the power that lies behind the deceit. The success of these systems is thus due to the fact that they are able to involve everyone in the ritual of legitimation. Everyone in this society is faced with a Faustian choice. They can, as Havel puts it, live within the lie. This involves pretending to believe in the ideology. It is to act out the role of the model citizen, to vote in the meaningless elections, to turn up to the workplace meetings to discuss the thoughts and writings of some appalling court ideologist, to cheer the latest statistics announcing another huge step forward on the road to socialism. In other words, it is to agree to surrender one's identity and independence in favour of a role manufactured by the regime. It is to give up being oneself. In return for this abdication of their right to think people are allowed to go about their daily business relatively unimpeded by the direct actions of the regime. They can apply for jobs, housing, have their children educated, enjoy what leisure facilities may be available, and join all the other citizens in the queues for whatever might be available in the shops. In short, they can lead what passes in such a society for a 'normal' life.

Living within the truth, on the other hand, is to reject the role so carefully created by the regime for the sake of remaining true to oneself. However, living with the truth and rejecting the closely woven fabric of lies that passes for the official ideology is a choice in favour of becoming an enemy of society with all the radical consequences that that choice implies. As Havel's own experience graphically testifies, to live within the truth is automatically to qualify as a 'dissident' and thus as an outsider who must be sealed off, like a medieval leper, from the rest of society. People may therefore choose to live within the truth, but they know that the price of that freedom will probably be internal exile or a prison cell.

The point Havel is making, therefore, is that the choice confronting each individual is really no choice at all and that is why the system is able to keep itself in being. Most people, and not only those living in dictatorships, do not have the energy or the confidence of their own convictions to mount what is inevitably seen as an assault on the very foundations of the society they inhabit. Life in a communist society with all its attendant ills is complex and difficult enough as it is without people bringing upon themselves, and of course their family and friends, all the heartache, discomfort and despair that follows from the decision to assert their own autonomy. The system is kept in being therefore as long as people feel that the advantages to be accrued from living the lie outweigh those of living in the truth. However, as Havel makes clear, this relationship is not a static one. Individuals do not lose the capacity to judge for themselves what is in their own best interests. People living the lie remain people; it is just that they do not *behave* like real individuals because they have abdicated their right to behave like people. When it is no longer clear that it is advantageous for people to go on lying to themselves and to everyone else, then truth is likely to assert itself. As soon as people begin to feel that it is no longer worth sacrificing their person-hood and integrity, they will begin to turn against the system. When doubts enter the heads of enough people about continuing the charade then the consensus that sustains these systems is ripped apart and revealed for what of course it is: a forced quiescence.

*   *

As this brief account shows, Havel gives us an account of totalitarianism that is every bit as systematic and original as the contributions of the other theorists we have been considering, even though unlike many of them he has never written a major work on the subject. The fact that Havel was a victim of the system he describes gives his writings particular piquancy and relevance, adding considerably to the impact of his work. What we still need to establish, however, is how valuable his account is as a basis for a more general theory of totalitarianism. Is his analysis only relevant to the systems he describes, that is, to the communist regimes of Eastern Europe? Or, could it be applied to other contexts, perhaps to non-communist regimes?

Before moving directly to these questions, it might, to begin with, be worth discussing how Havel's work fits in with, or modifies the work of the theorists we have already considered. After all, as we have seen, Havel is concerned not with totalitarian systems, which he considers to be variants of the traditional dictatorship, but with *post*-totalitarian systems. What needs to be established therefore is what relevance Havel's work has to our inquiry. Why, in other words, do we need to concern ourselves with the writings of someone who does not appear to be directly interested in totalitarian systems at all?

The reason for looking at Havel's work is because it provides a possible solution to one of the most pressing difficulties that theorists of totalitarianism have had to deal with, which is how to continue justifying using the term in a context where consent to a regime appears to be freely given; where, to put it another way, a political system appears to be legitimate. As we have seen in previous chapters, the concept of totalitarianism was originally formulated to describe systems in which rule was based on terror. The argument of theorists such as Hannah Arendt was that what made regimes such as those of the Nazis and communists different was precisely that they were *not* interested in obtaining the consent of the ruled. Indeed, if we follow Arendt, they were not interested in establishing a normal or settled relationship with the people subject to their rule. What they wanted, rather, was to destroy the very basis of each person's subjectivity so as better to dominate them. Terror was thus a vital component in this system because without it conventional relations of ruler and ruled would re-establish themselves and bring to an end the sense of flux and uncertainty that is the true hallmark of the revolutionary regime. In her view, therefore, the moment a regime ceased to terrorise its citizens was the moment when totalitarian rule came to an end and more familiar patterns of dictatorship came to establish themselves. However, other theorists such as Carl Friedrich were much less certain about the matter than she was. As we have seen, he insisted on regarding the Soviet Union and all other communist systems as totalitarian even though the consensus amongst commentators appeared to be that terror was no longer a factor in explaining how the system managed to sustain itself. The problem these theorists faced was in attempting to explain why these systems should still be regarded as totalitarian when it seemed plain to many commentators that they enjoyed at least a certain degree of legitimacy. What many of them concluded was that because such regimes were able to control the process of socialisation they were able in effect to manufacture their own citizens. If, it was argued, a regime holds a monopoly on what a person is able to learn at school, see on television, read in the newspapers and so on, is that not akin to a control over that person's thoughts and beliefs? Given, furthermore, that control over this process amounts to a form of domination, are we not then justified in continuing to maintain that these systems are totalitarian? All that had changed, they therefore argued, was the way in which domination was achieved. These systems were still totalitarian, but the basis upon which people were dominated had changed from something overt and physical to being covert and insidious.

The difficulty with this argument is that theorists like Friedrich were then forced to admit that these systems had in a sense become legitimate, that they rested on the consent of the people. If it really was true that the communists were able quite literally to create citizens who would unblinkingly regard the values and beliefs fostered by the regime as their own, then in a sense these systems could no longer be regarded as dictatorial in the ordinary meaning of the word. People who believe that the orders and commands they are given are legitimate do not, after all, require to be forced to obey those commands. They will carry them out willingly. Those, for example, who have become convinced Nazis do not need to be coerced into giving the Hitler salute and shouting 'Sieg Heil!'. They will do it because they want to do it. It was this dilemma about how to render accurately this evolution in the practice of totalitarianism that lay behind the coining of various labels such as 'mature totalitarianism', 'popular totalitarianism', 'totalitarianism with a human face', to describe contemporary communist systems. Many commentators and writers on communist politics were not, however, impressed by these attempts to square an ever-enlarging circle, and thus by the 1970s many of them had concluded that the concept had outlived whatever utility it might once have had. As they reasoned, a system could not both dominate its subjects and be a perfect democracy at the same time. Either communist systems were totalitarian or they were not.

The importance of Havel's contribution is that it provides a potential solution to the dilemmas faced by those like Friedrich who continued to view communist systems as a variety of despotism. If Havel is correct the trap the theorists of totalitarianism fell into was to view the absence of overt conflict between the people and the regime as a sign of the development of genuine consensus and hence of the legitimacy of the system. These theorists were making the mistake of believing the claims of those commentators who argued that this stability was due to the development of some tacit contract.

In the view of theorists like Hough the reason communist systems
had stabilised and achieved support amongst the population was
because the relationship between the regime and the people had
altered in a fundamental way. Instead of attempting to force people
to believe in communism through indoctrination and intimidation
the regime had adopted a more conciliatory approach, part of which
involved ensuring a continuous rise in the standard of living,
guarantees of work, access to health care, housing, holidays and so
on. As part of this 'destalinization' the regime also put its system of
justice on a more regular footing thereby removing the fear of
arbitrary arrest, a potent weapon in the armoury of the police in
Stalin's time. In return the people would promise, like the good
Lockian citizens they were supposed to have become, not to attempt
rebellion or revolution, and to support the regime's attempts to
construct an 'All People's State'. The principal difference between
the theorists of totalitarianism and what we might call the tacit
contract theorists such as Hough was about the manner in which
social consensus came about. There was very little doubt that such a
consensus existed. However, whilst Hough and others believed this
contract to be the product of a highly sublimated process of negotia-
tion between regime and people, those who supported the
totalitarian thesis regarded the existence of consensus merely as
evidence for the success of the communists' programme to
brainwash and indoctrinate those unfortunate enough to live under
them. In other words they argued that the people went along with the
regime because they were unable to consider any other course of
action. The disagreement was about how this social consensus was
arrived at, not about the fact that such a consensus existed.

The significance of Havel's analysis is that it challenges both sets of
assumptions. In his view a consensus does exist in such societies and
stability is able to be achieved, but not for the reasons given by either
group of theorists. The tacit contract theorists are wrong because
they assume that consent to the regime is freely given; that the people
consciously choose not to rebel because they can see the advantages
and rewards that accrue from compliance. As Havel convincingly
argues, this analysis simply mistakes compliance for voluntary
agreement. In his view, people living in such systems put up with
their rulers because if they show any signs of resisting the regime will
at the very least make their lives significantly less comfortable than
might otherwise have been the case. People living in these systems

FEAR

know that to rebel is to make their lives and the lives of all those with whom they are connected extremely difficult, and, unsurprisingly, few people are prepared to break out of the vicious circle. People are thus effectively browbeaten into compliance by fear of the consequences that would come from not doing so. This is not a contract, therefore, it is a Faustian pact, and the essence of such a pact is that unlike a valid contract it is made under duress. In other words it is something people enter into because it is the only realistic course of action open to them. The bargain entered into here is thus similar to the offer to save a drowning person for a thousand pounds. He or she will of course accept the contract, but most of us would at least hesitate before saying that it was entered into voluntarily.

On the other hand the argument of totalitarian school theorists such as Friedrich that the presence of consensus and stability is a sign of the success of the regime's attempt to brainwash people to think critically about the predicament in which they find themselves is also mistaken if we follow Havel's argument. To begin with such an account makes it enormously difficult to account for one of the familiar features of communist systems which is the persistent emergence of dissidence. If the process of socialisation is so thorough and far reaching how is it, we need to ask, that certain people are able to escape the process and think critically about their situation? What is it about these particular people that makes them so special? As Havel powerfully argues, the phenomenon of dissidence can only really be made sense of once we accept the idea that people in these systems are still capable of thinking for themselves, of weighing up the pros and cons of continuing to obey, and of understanding the nature of the predicament in which they find themselves. What Havel argues is that we must not look at dissidents as fantastic aberrations from the norm, but as people who have decided that they simply cannot go on lying to themselves and to others. One of the messages that comes across very strongly in Havel's work is that everyone living in these societies is in a sense a potential dissident. This is because everyone possesses the means of discriminating between truth and falsity, between right and wrong. Everyone has the capacity to see the nature of the situation and to act upon it. People do not lose these capacities in communist systems or in any other type of tyranny, and to suggest that they do is tantamount, in Havel's view, to writing off a section of humanity. What prevents people from acting is the knowledge that were they to do so they would instantly make themselves and those close to them pariahs. The regime survives, then, by making self-aware people believe that they have everything to lose and very little to win by not continuing to go along with the status quo. For most people the price of regaining self-respect and the freedom to think for themselves is simply too high to be worth paying. It is precisely this fear of losing the albeit shoddy comforts and services available to the obedient citizen, of losing the sense of stability and certainty afforded by compliance, that prevents the system breaking down.

Part of the strength of Havel's argument is thus that unlike the argument of the totalitarian school it does not require us to make a great leap of imagination to make his analysis plausible. He is not claiming, as they are, that an entire population can be brainwashed or indoctrinated with beliefs that they would not otherwise hold. He is not asking us to believe that it is possible to hold sway over the lives of millions of people at the same time. He makes no such demands on our imaginations, because what he argues is that the people living in these regimes are just ordinary people with the same concerns, fears, hopes and expectations as ourselves. They are, in other words, people capable of thinking critically, of weighing up alternative courses of action, of calculating the likely costs and benefits of obeying the authorities. Far from writing off the capacity of individuals to think about the nature of the situation in which they find themselves, Havel bases his entire argument on it. All he is asking is that we attempt to put ourselves in their position, to understand the difficulties they face. What he ends up arguing is that the reason for the continuing stability of these systems, the reason consensus appears to prevail, is because ordinary people have become convinced that they are powerless to change the situation they are in and that consequently they have to obey the regime. His point is thus that we do not need to explain people's actions by pointing to the success of attempts to indoctrinate them, because as he shows, to comply with the regime is the response of rational individuals when confronted with overwhelming odds. This is the action of highly self-conscious individuals, not of those who have been rendered unable to think for themselves. People living in totalitarian states are only doing what the citizens of tyrannies have been doing for thousands of years: hoping for the best whilst planning for the worst.

The significance of Havel's contribution is thus that it appears to provide a potential solution to the difficulties faced by those who regard the concept of totalitarianism as still relevant for describing communist systems but who remain unconvinced by the analysis of 'mature totalitarianism' given by theorists such as Friedrich. The great strength of Havel's analysis is that he is not asking us to believe that what has occurred is a fundamental alteration in the nature of people themselves. He is not suggesting that indoctrination and brainwashing have produced an infinitely manipulable New Man. What he is suggesting is that it is the relationship between regime and rulers that has changed. Instead of this relationship being one based on the immediate threat of force, it is now far more subtle, far better hidden. We therefore have to dig beneath the surface to see how power operates and to see how people are dominated. Havel has therefore retained the essence of the theory of totalitarianism, but adapted it to account for changed conditions. Terror and fear are, he argues, still the basic constituents oiling the wheels of the system; they have just moved beneath the surface of daily life. Havel's argument is compelling for the same reason that Orwell's account of domination in *Nineteen Eighty-Four* is compelling. Winston Smith, Julia, and the other characters Orwell describes are not after all unthinking subjects of Big Brother, but self-aware individuals who see all too clearly the nature of the dilemmas they face. We can therefore identify with these characters precisely because they are like us. They are ordinary people faced by the extraordinary demands of living in a system where every public utterance can be used against them. Indeed the nature of the dilemma faced by Winston is almost exactly the same as that faced by the subject of the post-totalitarian state Havel describes. He has a choice of sorts: he can be true to himself, he can 'live the truth', but at the same time he knows that the penalty for choosing the truth is to be cast out, to lose everything he has including quite possibly his life. Or, he can continue to 'live the lie' with the necessary consequence that he must put on a public mask and thereby adopt a new subjectivity to survive. This is the dilemma faced by Winston and this is the dilemma faced by the post-totalitarian subject: act the role or give up what passes in these states for normality. The question that still needs to be asked, however, is how valid is this explanation of the nature of domination in post-totalitarian states? Is it really true to say that everyone, leaders included, have to confront and come to terms with the Faustian Pact?

There is no doubt that the strength of Havel's explanation is its plausibility. Yet there are difficulties. It has to be remembered that what Havel is telling us is that in post-totalitarian states it is *everyone* who is faced by the same dilemma: whether to live the truth or carry on living the lie. The reason Havel feels confident about making this conclusion is that he feels it is simply inconceivable that anybody should be able to believe the lies upon which the power of the state is based. Everyone knows that these states were created by the Soviet forces at the end of the Second World War. Everyone knows that were it not for the lurking presence of these troops communism would collapse. Everyone knows that these are not really socialist systems but a yet more degenerate version of the 'Workers' State' existing in the Soviet Union. In other words it is simply beyond the bounds of imagination for anyone not to understand the nature of the situation they are in. Even those who take no interest in politics at least understand that what exists is the product of deceit and fraud, and hence that the normality of everyday life is merely apparent.

Despite the cogency of this account there are a number of issues that need to be discussed to assess its validity. To begin with, Havel seems to be assuming that it is impossible for anyone to support or at least willingly obey a regime that systematically lies to its people or whose claim to legitimacy is more mythic than real. Yet it is difficult to see why this should necessarily be the case. This position appears entirely to discount the fact that these regimes exercised a monopoly over all educational institutions, over all forms of public communication, and over most if not all sources of information such as libraries and archives. In other words it discounts the fact that we are discussing regimes in which what counted as being true was to an unprecedented degree determined by the state. Havel tells us that everyone living in these systems knows that the entire edifice is built on lies but it is difficult to see why this has to be the case. If the only source of information is that provided by the state then how, we might ask, will people know when they are being lied to? Of course Havel is right to argue that a very great number of people did know that they were being lied to. Those who lived in freer times, and those like Havel himself who had access to alternative sources of information in the form of *samizdat* or contacts with the West were able to cling to an alternative version of reality. It is also difficult to believe that some sort of folk collective memory did not survive the years of communist rule. It is probably beyond doubt, for example, that the vast majority of Czechs knew, despite the efforts of the regime to hide the fact, that the creation of communism in their state came about through the efforts of the Soviets not of the Czechs themselves. Yet the point remains that not everyone had access to the sources or necessarily the desire to seek out those facts which would reveal the true extent of the regime's mendacity. As Havel himself argues, when the onus rests on simply getting on with life without thinking too deeply about the nature of the system there must be a strong temptation for people just to accept the 'official' version of reality. Is this type of passive quiescence with the regime, this uncritical, almost fatalistic consent still 'living the lie'? Is it accurate to say that these people are still faced by the Faustian Pact Havel describes? Maybe; but there is room for doubt.

Perhaps more serious is Havel's reluctance to admit that this monopoly on the socialisation process might have had some effect on the formation of values and beliefs of those subject to it. Havel argues, for example, that one of the principal lies propagated by the regime is that what they are attempting to do is build 'socialism'. He feels people understand that this must be a lie because the policies of the regime are so at odds with what socialism really means and with the values held by socialists. How, he asks, can people mistake the activities of the Communist Party with real socialism? How could they be fooled when it is so patently obvious that the only beneficiaries of this form of pseudo-socialism are the Soviets? Clearly for Havel it is inconceivable that there might be any sympathisers or fellow travellers. In fact it is clear from his account that, paradoxical though it may seem, he is quite unwilling to harbour the possibility that in these communist systems there might be any communists. The difficulty is that what might be clear to Havel and to others who dispute the authenticity of 'actually existing socialism' might not be so clear to those whose only education in the ideals and values of socialism has been at the hands of the socialist state itself. We do not have to go all the way down the road to Friedrich's position to admit that the effort to indoctrinate might have had some impact on people's thoughts. If people have been told from the earliest possible age that the system in which they live is socialist, that for example, it is perfectly consonant with socialist ideals to have one party ruling over society, but also, say, to have access to free health care, leisure facilities, education, and so on, why would they necessarily disagree? Why would their idea of socialism have to contradict that of the regime? Given the extreme measures that were taken to ensure that people did associate socialism with these systems, is it really so absurd to imagine that some people might actually have regarded them as being socialist? If they did so, is it equally absurd to suggest that some socialists might not have regarded these systems as legitimate?

The drawback with Havel's account is that there is no room for admitting the existence of the person who, say, swallowed the regime's promises of a bright and glorious future and who was prepared to put up with its manifest imperfections for the sake of reaping the benefits to come. There is no room either for the cynical fellow traveller who believes that lies and prevarications may be needed to secure power for the immediate future. He cannot admit that anyone might have had any reason at all for regarding the actions of the regime as in any sense justifiable or legitimate. I am reminded in this connection of a conversation I had with a young East German woman shortly after the reunification of Germany. Expecting her to be full of hope and expectancy for the future and full of regret for what had occurred in the past, I was surprised when she told me how disappointed she was by how events had turned out. Although she knew the East German leadership was utterly corrupt and that all sorts of unsavoury practices were rife in the state, not least the victimisation of dissidents, she was convinced of the basic justice and humanity of the communist system that had just been dismantled. For her the fall of the Berlin Wall was something to be lamented not celebrated. Something had been lost, and very little appeared to have been gained. The interesting question from the point of view of this discussion is where, given that she had lived in a system very similar to the one that existed in Czechoslovakia, she would fit in to Havel's analysis. Was she 'living the lie' or 'living the truth', the only two options that Havel allows? Clearly it cannot have been the truth she was living because she was affirming her support for the system and, as we know, in Havel's view supporting the system is incompatible with living the truth. His whole point is that it is effectively impossible to support the regime given that people retain the capacity to know when they are being lied to. Can we then say that she was living the lie, the only other explanation that Havel offers us? Hardly. The discussion I had with her was held well after the East German state had disappeared. Furthermore, it was in the privacy of my own home. Thus there was no reason for her to go on lying to herself and to those to whom she talked. There was nothing at stake; there was nothing for her to lose. Why then should she want to continue to lie when there is nothing left to lie for? The fact is that neither of the two options fit for the simple reason that the person I was talking to was a convinced communist who believed that for all its problems and inhumanities the system that existed in East Germany was basically just and that it catered for the needs of the East German population. Moreover, the people she knew shared a sense of solidarity, of togetherness that in her perception is signally absent in West German society. It is not important for our purposes where her communism came from, i.e. whether it can be put down to 'indoctrination' or her own 'voluntary' assumption of communist values. What is significant for our purposes is to note that she did not experience the traumas of the Faustian Pact. She did not have to decide whether to carry on living the lie because for her there was no lie confronting her in the manner described by Havel. There was an awareness that the actions and policies of the regime were unsatisfactory to say the least. Yet for her, rightly or wrongly, there was a distinction to be made between the actions of the regime and the philosophy underpinning the state; the former could not be equated with the latter. Although she was disappointed by the regime, she retained a hope in the state. Thus for her the obligation to obey the state was one that was willingly assumed. It was not forced upon her by her own perceived sense of powerlessness.

What an example like this shows is that Havel's assumption that it is in effect impossible for a person to regard a post-totalitarian state as legitimate is one that has to be greeted with at least a certain degree of scepticism. The difficulty stems from his assertion that given knowledge of the origins and nature of the states in question no one in their right mind could conceivably maintain that they were legitimate or that they were interested in building socialism. For him these states are so clearly the product of the Soviet Union's *realpolitik* that any attempt to dress them up in more attractive clothing is doomed to failure. What he is saying therefore is that the only rational or reasonable response to these regimes is to regard them as illegitimate. What he tends to underestimate, however, is the impact of the process of socialisation on the populations concerned. He asserts that the lies are there for everyone to see, but given the extent of the regime's control over most sources of information it is difficult to imagine how everyone would be able to see with his clarity of vision. What he also discounts is that although much of what these regimes did was thoroughly obnoxious, they did nevertheless attempt to implement a certain version of socialism, albeit impoverished. It is not inconceivable that those who regarded themselves as socialist might regard the efforts of the regime as actually justifying the lies and deceit propagated by the state, perverse though such a position may well seem. What he tends to ignore therefore is that people might be unwilling or unable to perceive what he regards as the 'real' character of the state, or alternatively that they might identify with the regime for the values it represents. Thus in a sense Havel falls into the same trap as the other theorists we have been considering. Like them he seeks what we might term a monocausal explanation for the appearance of 'total domination'. He wants one solution to the question of why it is that people obey the state. That his account is more plausible than many of those that we have considered does not alter the fact that he is only providing one explanation for why people appear to consent to a regime. Surely we need a form of explanation that is able to take account of a variety of possible responses to any given regime, i.e. that is able to take account of the diversity of ways in which people respond to any given situation.

When it comes to considering the suitability of Havel's analysis for a more general model of totalitarianism there is, however, much more evident difficulty in that what he is describing is not so much a political system as a political sub-system. As Havel himself makes clear, it is unimaginable that a post-totalitarian system could emerge in a state that had not been conquered, annexed or in some other fashion fallen under the influence of another. The hopelessness and sense of despondency that he identifies as a key aspect of life in these societies is the direct product of the realisation that this society is not the master of its own affairs. It is the mentality of those who have lost everything and await their fate at the hands of some distant, yet hopefully benign master. It is precisely this absence of power that accounts for the ritualistic quality of life in a post-totalitarian system. People know that their actions will not make the slightest difference, because these actions have been denied consequence or effect. Life is thus in essence a process of going through the motions. Think again of the greengrocer's act. He puts the sign in the window not because it will have any tangible effect on the world, but because it is imperative that he shows his willingness to carry on behaving in the way expected of him; and of course this is the reaction of everyone in this system, even the rulers, *especially* the rulers. Nothing matters because everything has been taken care of by 'them', i.e. Moscow. Politics and public life have thus been reduced to empty farce precisely because politics as the taking of decisions affecting the life of the community is elsewhere, outside the 'system' itself. Given this analysis it is difficult to imagine how Havel's account might be applied to systems that have not been reduced to the status of satellites. In all other systems the relationship of rulers and ruled, elite and people does apply, and thus on his terms all other systems are 'political' in the sense of having the power to make decisions concerning the life of the community. This is not a criticism of Havel. It is simply to point out the difficulty of applying his analysis to other communist systems such as the Soviet Union or China and to other types of regime such as fascist states or the Islamic republics. In essence what Havel has given us is not so much a readily applicable model, but rather a pungent and highly original account of Central and Eastern Europe under communist rule.

Notes

1 Marcuse's analysis was an interesting exception. Whilst he endorsed the view that industrial socities were in the process of 'converging', he of course argued that they were at the same time becoming more totalitarian, not less. See his *Soviet Marxism* (London, 1958) and of course *One Dimensional Man*.

2 See Herbert Spiro's entry on 'Totalitarianism' in the *Encyclopaedia of the Social Sciences*, second edition, pp. 106–13.

3 Václav Havel, 'The Power of the Powerless', in Václav Havel *et al.*, *The Power of the Powerless*, edited by John Keane (London, 1985).

4 *Ibid.*, p. 24.

5 *Ibid.*, p. 26.

6 *Ibid.*, p. 27.

7 *Ibid.*, p. 28.

8 The transcripts for these plays were taken from the BBC television broadcast of 6 January 1990.

9 'Power of the Powerless', p. 38.

10 *Ibid.*

11 *Ibid.*, p. 37.

12 *Ibid.*

13 *Ibid.*

Conclusion:
Totalitarianism in perspective

Having had the chance to examine some of the best-known accounts of totalitarianism, it is now time to return to the questions we posed in the introduction. What is totalitarianism, and how does it differ from other kinds of autocracy or dictatorship? What are the characteristics of a totalitarian system? What is at the root of totalitarianism? Does totalitarianism have a future?

From the work we have been examining it is, to begin with, difficult to make out any sign of a consensus about what the essential constituents of a totalitarian regime or system are. Indeed so apparently lacking is such an agreement that it is possible for one theorist, Herbert Marcuse, to describe as totalitarian a political system, namely that of the United States, which most of the other theorists we have been considering would regard as being an example of a democracy not a dictatorship. Even if we discount the findings of Marcuse, which many of those who employ the concept urge that we should, there still appears to be a signal absence of agreement among the others about what totalitarianism is. Hayek believed totalitarianism to be essentially an extension of collectivism, that is of the belief in the desirability in state intervention to remedy social injustices. For Arendt totalitarianism is the product of mass society and the breakdown of an authentic political life. Far from being a manifestation of the desire for order in social and economic life, as Hayek argues, it is the product of a desire to dominate and ultimately to destroy. For this reason, for Arendt the totalitarian state is marked by chronic shapelessness and lack of authority. Friedrich and Brzezinski, on the other hand, believe that totalitarianism is the product of radicalism, of 'totalising ideology'. They argue, *contra* Arendt, that the totalitarian ideal is not terror and the camps, but uniformity, consensus and stability. Totalitarians seek adulation, not destruction. Marcuse disagrees with all of them in arguing that it is the most democratic not the most despotic states that are totalitarian, for it is here that we witness the greatest extent of control over the subject. Finally, Havel distinguishes between totalitarian and post-totalitarian regimes arguing that the latter is in essence a traditional form of dictatorship, whereas it is the latter that is really novel. In his view it is not overt terror nor the establishment of a manufactured consensus that is the real novelty of modern tyranny, but the ability of regimes to convince people of the necessity to 'live the lie'. In short, there seem to be as many formulations of totalitarianism as there are theorists using the concept. All of which tends to support Benjamin Barber's view that 'the concept is used by different writers in a confusing multiplicity of often incompatible meanings which render its application idiosyncratic and arbitrary'.[1] Are we, as Frederic Fleron argued in the 1960s, faced with a concept that is little more than, as he puts it, a 'boo word' to be employed whenever we want to describe 'boo regimes'?[2] Is there no core to the concept, no agreement on what characterises totalitarianism?

Reflecting on the work we have been examining it is apparent that, firstly, most theorists of totalitarianism agree that what distinguishes totalitarian form of rule from other forms of dictatorship is the commitment of a ruling elite to fashioning an entirely new form of society. Marcuse is the major exception on this point. He of course argues that it not the desire to construct a new society that leads to totalitarianism, but the necessity of defending existing society from revolutionaries like himself. However, even his account of totalitarianism blends back into the analysis given by the others when it comes to examining the nature of domination within these systems. For the other theorists totalitarianism is more often the product of the drive to create a form of perfect society, a utopia in which the dissonance and difficulties of everyday life will be over-come. The elite want to build what we might term a post-political community, a community that is, where the subject has become so completely identified with the collective that the possibility for dispute and antagonism has effectively been removed. What is com-mon to totalitarian movements is thus the demand to demolish the old order, the old practices, institutions and structures and to replace them with an entirely new society more in keeping with the real needs of humanity or some other target group such as the Aryan race or the proletariat. Totalitarianism is thus borne above all of radicalism, a discontent with the present that is translated into a longing for the new. Part of the difference between totalitarian regimes and other forms of tyranny is thus that they possess an ostensibly 'positive' programme for social change. Totalitarian regimes are never content with simply allowing things to go on as they are; they are never happy, as tyrants often are, with simply reaping the immediate benefits of power together with increased wealth or prestige. They have a project they wish to pursue, and they measure their own success or failure in terms of the distance they must travel to reach their goal. However, what the implementation of this programme requires is not merely the construction of new institutions and structures. It requires the creation of a new subject. Totalitarian movements have a particular model of human behaviour, a particular subjectivity that they want everyone to adopt. Communists and Nazis may differ about what the form of this new subjectivity is. There may be significant differences between, in other words, the New Soviet Man and the National Socialist *Übermensch*; but what they both call for is uniformity of behaviour. In essence they want everyone to think and behave in the same way, to conform to an idealised model of human life. It is this desire at the heart of the totalitarian project that explains the emphasis in these systems on the monopolisation of the education process, on the regulation of all aspects of family life, and on the control of all sources of information. In these systems there is no room for private life. Indeed there is no room even for private thoughts. Totalitarian regimes are never happy merely with securing obedience or compliance: simply carrying out the commands of the authorities is never enough to guarantee a person's safety as it would be in most other forms of dictatorship. What the regime demands is a change in the entire outlook on life, the opinions, beliefs, values and aspirations of ordinary people. The corollary of such a demand is thus that individuals must give up their autonomy, their independence. They must conform rigidly and absolutely with the role defined by the regime. Freedom as the capacity of individuals to set their own goals is entirely anathema to the totalitarian outlook. It is in essence a threat to the order and regimentation of life that they require.

Although most theorists agree therefore that totalitarianism is caused by the attempt to implement a radical or utopian programme for the construction of a new society there is significant disagreement

about the nature of the system created to pursue this project.
Essentially this disagreement is about whether such regimes are able
to gain total control over the subject population, whether they can
achieve 'total domination'. On the one hand there are those who
regard this attempt to dominate the people as largely successful.
These theorists such as Friedrich and Brzezinski, Marcuse and
arguably Arendt write in terms of what we might call a 'strong
model' of totalitarianism, a model that emphasises the strength and
potency of the regime. Others such as Havel, Kolakowski, Orwell,
Popper, and possibly Hayek, are more sceptical. They and others put
forward a 'weak model' that stresses the difficulty of gaining complete control over people's actions and thoughts.

For theorists of the strong model the capacity of the regime to
mobilise its citizens to participate in the myriad organisations and
events that characterise such systems must be taken as evidence that
the regime has been successful in undermining the independence and
autonomy of each individual. As Friedrich and Brzezinski make
clear, the systematic organisation of all aspects of social existence

> constitutes an effort to conduct a nation-wide process of
> brainwashing which only a very few succeed in completely avoiding. It
> is on these propaganda processes, as well as on the educational
> training scheme that the regime depends for the achievement of the
> total ideological integration of its people. It is these instruments of
> mental moulding that are used by the administration to reproduce a
> generation of convinced followers thinking and acting in disciplined
> unison.[3]

The fact that well-established totalitarian dictatorships often appear
to be quite stable systems of rule should not therefore be taken as a
sign that people have willingly accepted the regime and its ideology.
Neither should it be taken simply as evidence of the regime's ability
to keep dissent and opposition away from the public eye so as to keep
unsullied the picture of harmony and unanimity that it likes to paint.
On the contrary, the apparent stability, even legitimacy of
totalitarian systems should be taken as stemming from the success of
their policy of brainwashing their citizens to the point where they are
no longer capable of thinking and acting for themselves. As Maurice
Cranston in his article defending this interpretation makes clear,

> the very pressure of repression ... is a measure of failure in a
> totalitarian system: it is only when all the people have been made to

want what they have . . . that the difference between a totalitarian and a despotic regime is fully manifest. In other words, the most totalitarian system is the one where the penetration of the regime into the soul of the individual is complete.[4]

Because of the pressures placed upon them, totalitarian subjects are unable to think or act for themselves. In these systems the subject is virtually an extension of the regime, a 'transmission belt' functioning merely as part of a greater whole. It is the leader or in certain cases the elite who possesses autonomy, and who decides what people are able to think or do. Here is the novelty of totalitarianism. It is as Cranston infers, the first tyranny to be able to dispense with tyrannical methods. In these systems, therefore, the regime does not merely claim to possess total control over the population, it succeeds in achieving this control. In short, it actually breaks down the barrier between individual and system, subject and leader. Again, as Karl Dietrich Bracher makes clear:

> The regime quite openly and insistently demands the complete politicization of every aspect of life; its success in realizing this dimension of total control, involving simultaneously a reorientation of values, is a measure of the regime's capacity to reach its aim of fusing totally state and society, party and people, individual and collectivity into the ideal of total unity.[5]

The novelty of totalitarianism according to theorists of the strong model is that it moves beyond being a mere dictatorship to the point where it becomes a mirror of the most democratic, most harmonious systems of rule. This is because totalitarian systems are able to overcome the single most important obstacle that the dictatorship faces in its war of survival, i.e. the autonomous individual. The friction and enmity that characterises most dictatorships is absent in the true totalitarian system because here the regime is able to construct a model citizen. Not only does it possess a monopoly on the socialisation process, but on all those sources of information upon which individuals rely for their view of reality. Just as the world becomes something to be infinitely manipulated in the hands of the regime, so too does the person subject to totalitarian rule. Totalitarianism is thus the mirror of democracy. It is the inverse of a world where people order their affairs according to their own needs and desires. Totalitarianism works by making people think they are free where in reality they are mere pawns in the regime's schemes. It works by constructing the image of a society run from the 'bottom up' whereas in reality it is a system run from the 'top down'. Totalitarianism is, as Arendt puts it, the ultimate 'world of appearances' where nothing is as it seems. It is the world in which the appearance of complete freedom coincides with the reality of the complete domination of every individual.

This assumption that a regime can successfully gain control over the minds and actions of those living under it, that it can shape and mould human life in whatever way it desires is one challenged, albeit implicitly, by theorists of the weak model. For those such as Havel and Kolakowski there will always remain barriers to the achievement of what the latter terms 'a fireproof totalitarian system' of the sort described by theorists employing the strong model. Such barriers are, he explains, not merely logistical. They are not, that is, simply a reflection of the difficulty of organising the lives of so many different people at the same time or of controlling, in the fashion of Big Brother, knowledge of the past. They are, in Kolakowski's view, a reflection of the impossibility of undermining or transforming essential aspects of human existence. As he comments, 'much in the make-up of human beings resists the pressures of totalitarian control. Family life, emotional and sexual relationships, individual and collective memory, art and literature escape to a certain extent the impact of the system'.[6] He adds elsewhere that even where conformity has apparently been achieved, the process of 'socialisation' remains shallow and hence can rapidly break down under the impact of political shocks.[7] Far from being able to maintain the perfectly transparent domination described above, totalitarian regimes thus of necessity constantly fail in their attempts to eliminate scepticism, dissent and opposition. Michael Walzer echoing this view remarks, 'except in the matter of murder, it (i.e. totalitarianism) isn't noticeably successful. It doesn't produce a new man and a new woman; it doesn't produce a new language; it can't sustain loyalties. The thrust toward totality is so extravagant a version of wilfulness that it is doomed to failure'.[8]

Reflecting these doubts about the degree of control able to be exercised by a regime over the people living under it, Kolakowski makes clear that for him the term 'totalitarianism' does not represent a form of dictatorship in which total control has successfully been achieved. As he puts it, 'when we talk about totalitarian regimes we do not have in mind systems that have reached perfection, but rather those that are driven by a never ending effort to reach it, to swallow all channels of communication and to eradicate all spontaneously emerging life forms'.[9] It is precisely this gap between the promise and the reality of totalitarian rule that theorists such as Kolakowski and Havel believe is to blame for the terror that pervades such systems, even if that terror has crept beneath the surface of everyday life. As we saw in the last chapter, for Havel the novelty of totalitarianism is that it makes terror humdrum, part of the normal life of each individual. The appearance of consensus and stability is thus not a sign of the success of the regime in transforming the character of the population. It is simply a sign of its convincing people that it pays to perform the rituals expected of them. Terror in these systems is thus not open and overt for the reason that it does not need to be. Much more effective is the slow yet relentless build-up of pressure on the individual to make him or her conform. This is not the overcoming of terror, therefore, but its transformation into something routine or normal. This is the terror experienced when people know that they are completely defenceless against the state. It is the terror that comes from knowing that at any moment everything might be lost, house, job, privileges, family. It is the terror, as Havel puts it, of the powerless, of those who know that they must play the game because there is no other option open to them. Such a form of terror might be less spectacular and better hidden than the apocalyptic nightmare described by Arendt; but terror it remains. Far from representing some entirely new form of despotism totalitarian systems are just like every other tyranny that has ever existed: they crave absolute power over their subjects and yet find the road to the attainment of that power blocked by the realities of human life. What is distinctive about totalitarian regimes, however, is their total unwillingness to recognise any such limits or barriers to the achievement of total power. The regime thus carries on attempting to achieve the impossible, holding back reality like Canute holding back the waves, shedding the blood of all those who stand in its way.

The difference between the strong and the weak models of totalitarianism should thus be clear. For theorists of the weak model totalitarianism is a system of rule in which a regime attempts to pursue a vision of social life whose realisation would consist in the complete subordination of each individual and by extension a complete transformation in the very character of human existence. It is this confrontation between the ambition of the elite and realities of human life that makes terror and coercion necessary. The regime cannot realise its vision of utopia, yet it is prepared to sacrifice everything and everyone to carry on trying. Terror is in this sense a necessary characteristic of totalitarianism, for abandoning this war on the people would be tantamount to abandoning the *raison d'être* of totalitarian rule, namely the construction of a perfect society.

Theorists of the strong version of the totalitarian model believe, on the other hand, that such systems do succeed in creating a new form of life. They point to the diminishing use of terror in 'mature' totalitarian systems such as the Soviet Union after the death of Stalin as evidence of the regime's success in constructing what in effect amounts to a new people. That success is the product of the regime's ability to call upon more refined technologies of surveillance and repression, and of its having established a monopoly on all agencies of socialisation from the educational system down to the family unit. By being able in effect to withhold those ingredients that make possible the emergence of an autonomous and independent subject the need for direct forms of coercion disappears. In a world created and sustained by the regime the whole idea of opposition appears quite irrational. Since there is no need or scope for the display of any form of behaviour other than that officially sanctioned by the ideology, the population simply descends into a somnambulant conformity, unwilling and unable even to imagine how life might otherwise be like. The strong model of totalitarianism thus mirrors to a large extent the image of society that totalitarian dictators themselves like to portray. It is an image above all of uniformity and regimentation, of a society united by one idea led by one man. It is the image of crowds of smiling Mao-jacketed people waving Little Red Books; of row upon row of collectivised farmers sitting atop their gleaming new tractors; of the rallies, the parades, the trance-like adulation induced by the 'hypnotic' power of the leader. It is the image, in other words, of a people prostrated before an all-powerful puppet-master.

Having identified two different and largely incompatible models of totalitarianism the question that needs to be faced is which one is preferable? Which of the models, the strong or the weak, gets closest to giving us a workable definition of totalitarianism?

Approaching this question in a negative way there certainly

appear far greater pitfalls and difficulties with the strong model than with the weak. The theorists of the strong model are, after all, asking us to believe considerably more than are those of the latter, not least that it is possible to brainwash virtually an entire nation. How legitimate is the idea of a regime wielding total power over a defenceless population? Indeed, does such an account of domination actually make sense?

There seems, firstly, to be a conceptual difficulty with this account of domination which is how we are to know that people have been brainwashed. How do we know that they are under the 'total control' of someone else? What evidence can we call upon which would show that people possess the values and beliefs they do because at some point in the past they were forced to do so? It is of course no use asking people themselves. People who have been brainwashed do not after all readily admit that they have been brainwashed or that they are under the 'total control' of some hidden agent. If we ask a Moony, or some other person we strongly suspect of having suffered intense indoctrination, whether they have been brainwashed it is very likely they will answer that they have not. People do not generally take kindly to the suggestion that their heads have been filled with ideas and assumptions that under ordinary circumstances they would have no time for. What therefore can we look for as evidence?

It seems perfectly reasonable to point out, as defenders of this account do, that totalitarian regimes attempt to brainwash those subject to their rule or to indoctrinate them with the fundamentals of a given ideology. Why else, we can ask, do they attach so much importance to establishing a monopoly over the agencies of socialisation such as education and the media? Why else do they attack the freedom of speech and the autonomy of newspapers, publishing houses and the like? Why do they insist on people joining workplace discussions on the thoughts of some philosopher or ideologist? All of this would be completely meaningless unless it were understood as being for the purpose of inculcating certain beliefs and values, and by extension fostering respect and love for the regime or leader. However, it is one thing to point out that a regime is attempting to brainwash its population but quite another to show that those efforts have been successful. As, for example, the swift collapse of communism in Eastern Europe shows, the fact that people have been exposed to years of lying and propaganda does not mean that they have to believe what they are told or that they will necessarily show any sympathy for those values the regime is attempting to foist on them. As Havel argues, because people act as if they were followers of a given ideology should not automatically be taken to mean that they really *are* followers of the ideology. They may pretend to be so to avoid the punishment that follows from disobedience or a lack of enthusiasm. Alternatively they may wish to show they possess the faith to reap the rewards that accrue from demonstrations of loyalty. On the other hand, we can reverse the picture and ask why we should necessarily assume that those who believe in the ideology do so because of the actions of the regime in attempting to *make* them do so? Many millions of people, after all, voted for Hitler *before* he assumed power and was able to begin attempting to indoctrinate them. How, we may ask, do these people fit into the analysis? That someone is a Nazi (or whatever) does not surely give us the necessary evidence to assume that they had been forced to adopt their beliefs. Why can we not simply assume that they have become a Nazi because they find attractive or compelling the ideas of the Nazis? Are we to assume that it is *impossible* for a person to find extreme or radical ideologies such as Nazism or communism appealing? If so, we have a great deal of explaining to do. We would have to begin by explaining, for example, how it is that radical or revolutionary movements ever manage to get off the ground, for even the most unspeakable movements need believers and even the most tyrannical and heartless regimes need officials before the machinery of indoctrination or brainwashing can be wheeled into place.

As even this brief discussion indicates there are serious difficulties with the assumption at the heart of the strong model of totalitarianism, i.e. that the success of totalitarian movements and regimes can be ascribed to their ability to brainwash large numbers of people and thereby control their thoughts and actions. The difficulty is essentially in showing that this explanation is the right one. It is in persuading us that only brainwashing could have produced the sort of societies we wish to discuss. The inescapable fact is that the account of domination given by theorists of the strong model is circular. There is no standard available either for proving or indeed disproving their findings. There is no way in which we can establish whether it is right or wrong. It explains everything, which is effectively the same as saying that it tells us nothing.[10] The model is in essence a form of cultural and moral critique. What theorists employing it are saying is that they do not believe people willingly become, say, Nazis or communists because the values and ideals of such movements are so distasteful that it is impossible to see how anyone in their right minds could want to be associated with them. In other words, what they are saying is that people have to be brainwashed in order to get them to behave in the ways Nazis and communists want them to behave. If people were left to themselves, if they were not indoctrinated, they would never become Nazis or communists and hence the regime would founder for lack of support. Whilst it is easy to sympathise with this argument, precisely because with the benefit of hindsight we can see how destructive such ideologies can be, this view does not help us understand how ideologies such as Nazism and communism came to prominence because there is no room within the account for what we might term the idea of the 'honest supporter', i.e. the person who genuinely believes in a given ideology, or more loosely, a given set of values or beliefs.

Although it might be said that the strong model conforms with the popular image of totalitarianism, that is of a 'top-down' system with the leader dominating a thoroughly 'atomised' society held in thrall by the 'spell' of ideology, there are, as should now be clear, good reasons for rejecting it. The first and most obvious reason is that no system has ever come close to achieving the sort of control over people described by theorists of the strong model. As historians of Nazi Germany and Soviet Russia frequently remind us, neither Hitler nor Stalin achieved 'total control' nor anything like it. Indeed the more we learn of these systems, the more inaccurate such an analysis appears. However, the model is not merely inaccurate as a description of certain regimes or systems, but flawed as an account of a possible form of domination. It does not begin to explain how power operates or what domination means. The idea of 'total domination' is in this sense the 'fool's gold' of totalitarianism studies. It looks like the solution to the problem of how to distinguish totalitarian systems from other forms of tyranny, but in reality it hides more than it reveals. As has just been argued, to say of a person that they have been 'totally dominated' or that leaders possess 'total power' over a given population is really to say very little. It is the *substitute* for an explanation of how power is exercised, how domination is achieved; not an explanation itself.

What then of the weak model of totalitarianism? Do we necessarily want to endorse the findings of Havel, Kolakowski, Popper and indeed Orwell? Or are there difficulties with this model as well? If there are, should we not simply scrap the totalitarian model altogether as an unwanted relic of the Cold War as indeed some critics have suggested?

Perhaps the key idea that comes across in the work of such theorists is that totalitarianism is not so much the product of any specific ideology as of a specific *desire*. This is the desire to impose or reinforce a 'correct' view of the world, a view of what is and what must be. Totalitarianism as they see it is born of certainty, of the knowledge a movement, a party or a group has that it has access to the truth and hence that all other versions of reality are deficient. Totalitarianism is thus born from the desire to impose this version of the truth on a given population. It is this act of imposition that accounts for the character of totalitarian rule. Totalitarianism is a sort of evangelism taken to its logical extreme; it is the desire to have everyone everywhere recognise the same truth. This is the real source of the energy of the groups and movements that emerge to defend it. They think they have access to the secret of human happiness and they want to 'share' this secret with everyone else. Thus what is important is not that these movements share the *same* vision of perfection, only that they possess *a* vision. It is for this reason that totalitarian movements are relentlessly intolerant of other groups and views. They simply cannot tolerate the existence of other movements proclaiming other truths and other conceptions of how social life should be ordered. It is also for this reason that when they come to power intolerance is regarded as a virtue and a guide to state policy. Totalitarian governments are not therefore just content with banning other groups and movements; they hunt them down and attempt to eliminate the possibility of their emergence. It is also for this reason that totalitarian states are loathe to recognise the distinction between the public and the private realms of human activity, between an area of legitimate social concern and the space for private thought and action. Individuals cannot be trusted to arrive at the truth by themselves, and so like Winston Smith they must constantly be cajoled and persuaded to abandon their privacy and join the herd. Totalitarianism thus represents the denial of individual autonomy and hence the denial of politics, of a realm of moral and ethical contestation. Totalitarian systems make politics superfluous because the general recognition of the right to ask questions, to pose difficulties and to challenge orthodoxies has been denied. Since all the answers to all the questions people might want to ask are to be found in the ideology, in the sacred texts, or in the words of the leader or some other prophet, discussion, debate, and deliberation are superfluous. Politics therefore comes to an end and the public realm is reduced to serving as a space for ritual adulation and the confirmation of fealty to the system. Whatever space exists for the deliberation of public policy or for the examination of issues of public concern is abolished. Private life thus becomes public life.

When these theorists discuss totalitarianism they are not therefore talking about the effects of power, but rather the specific practices of a regime. It is irrelevant on this view how successful the regime is at dominating its subjects or how many numbers of people it manages to incarcerate or control. The crucial consideration is what the regime does. Does it, for example, hunt down people who might disagree with it? Does it ban newspapers, journals, films or television documentaries that might be critical of the regime? Does it organise education and training to promote the Truth? Is the regime in any meaningful sense accountable to the people? Does it allow demonstrations, petitions or the formation of organisations hostile to the government line? Do people enjoy rights, or is the system of justice arbitrary and under the thumb of the state? Can people enjoy the privacy of their own home? Can they join private associations? Do private associations exist? These and other questions like them are what is relevant in determining whether a given regime or system can be considered totalitarian. What is not relevant is whether the regime appears to enjoy total domination or total control over the people subject to it. Indeed, as we have noted theorists of the weak model do not as a rule believe that regimes are capable of controlling absolutely all those or even any of those who exist under them. What is important is the *practice* of rule, what a regime does to keep itself in power. Whether a regime appears to enjoy the support of those living under it is in their view a red herring if at the same time there are people locked away in Gulags and concentration camps, if all criticism has been outlawed, if there is no accountability and if the education system has been turned into a conveyor belt for churning out cadres to serve the Movement or Party. In this sense judging whether a system is totalitarian is no different from judging whether, say, a system is democratic. What we are looking at is the way in which power is organised, the nature of the institutions and structures of the state, the character of the relationship between the state and the population, and above all what the state *does*.

The merit of this weaker model is that it moves away from one of the central difficulties with the studies we have examined, which is the concern with proving the increased potency of the totalitarian state, its power to make people comply. At the heart of the strong model is the claim that what makes a system totalitarian is essentially the capacity to make people consent to the regime, the power to manufacture legitimacy through socialisation and brainwashing. Thus the debate about whether a system is totalitarian tends to centre on the ability of the theorist to show that whatever consensus or stability exists is due to the efforts of the regime to induce support from the population. It is this approach that leads to the self-defeating claims of the defenders of the strong model that totalitarianism is coterminous with the achievement of 'total domination'. It is this claim that finally leads to the sterile not to say fruitless debate concerning exactly when total domination or total power was achieved; or indeed when it passed into some other form of practice. It is this claim therefore that made the totalitarian model so easy for historians and other commentators to knock down, for showing that at any given moment power or domination was less than 'total' was tantamount to refuting the totalitarian thesis. The merit of looking, on the other hand, at the practices of the regime as opposed to the effect which rule has on the population is that the whole issue of consent and coercion is rendered secondary. The central issue becomes the manner in which regimes exercise power, not whether that power is total. In this sense the weak model presents us with a model of a possible form of domination. It describes a political system that might exist. The question remains, have there been any totalitarian states? Can the weak model actually be applied to systems that have existed or that still exist?

To begin with, this reformulation of the totalitarian model appears to overcome two of the major objections to applying the concept to Nazi Germany and Stalin's Russia. The first objection is that the ideologies of these regimes were so different that it is meaningless to talk in terms of their being in any sense similar political systems. Whilst Nazi ideology – if such a hotchpotch of prejudices and partialities can be regarded as an ideology – is certainly radical in the sense of calling for drastic changes to the fabric of society and to the institutions and structures of the state, it is an essentially reactionary doctrine. In other words, the radicalism of the state was directed towards maintaining elitist social relations and in building an Aryan super-state cleansed of inferior races and peoples. Communism on the other hand is clearly revolutionary. Communists call for a change to the fundamental structure of the social and economic system, not just the formal structures of the state. They seek to overhaul social life completely in order to abolish alienation, hierarchy and subordination. Moreover they believe that they have a solution to the ills confronting the whole of humanity, not just one race. How, it was asked, could both systems be the same when the type of society called for by the two movements is so different? Furthermore, is this not clearly an attempt to discredit revolutionary or socialist ideologies by lumping them together with the ideology of fascists and Nazis?

As our discussion has shown, this attempt to find a 'totalitarian ideology' common to all those regimes described as totalitarian is indeed a major weakness of some accounts of totalitarianism. It is undoubtedly the case, as critics suggest, that there is remarkably little in common between communist and Nazi ideology and indeed little in common between the types of society they would like to build or see develop. There is a world of difference after all between Marx's vision in *The German Ideology* of a society in which each individual is allowed and encouraged to develop his talents and capacities to the maximum extent and the vision of *Mein Kampf*. One is a vision of phoenix-like rebirth of humanity from the drudgeries of everyday life. The other is a bleak vision of competition and struggle between the races. However, what we are discussing is not visions of future society, but the realities of the political systems built by the respective movements. The merit of the weak model is that it ignores the undoubted differences in values and beliefs between movements and concentrates on the methods and characteristics of rule. Considered solely on these terms, that is, with what regimes do, there is undoubtedly a basic similarity between the Nazi and communist regimes.

The second objection made against the totalitarian model by historians of the Nazi and Stalinist periods is that the system of rule it portrays is 'monolithic'. It portrays, in other words, a political system in which power moves from the leader down through the political apparatus to the people. It sees power moving in one direction only, i.e. from the top of the system to the bottom. The image of the totalitarian system is thus the image of the omnipotent prophet-like figure of the leader manipulating all those below, including the other members of the political elite. Much work has been done to show how inadequate this understanding of both Nazi Germany and Stalin's Russia is. Commentators on the Nazi period have, for example, stressed the importance of other institutions within the hierarchy such as the SS, the Army and the *Gauleiters*. Indeed, some have gone so far as to suggest that Nazi Germany resembled a 'polyocracy', that is, a system with multiple centres of power and hence with confused and overlapping chains of command creating not order and omnipotence as the totalitarian model insists, but confusion and chaos.[11] Other commentators interested in the history of 'everyday life' in Nazi Germany have stressed how little power the regime often had over ordinary people. As is evident from the records of the secret police the Nazi regime was constantly concerned about the effect their policies were having on public opinion, going to the extent of changing tack if they appeared too unpopular, or keeping secret those programmes they knew would meet with disapproval. They were also concerned about the large numbers of people who in various ways were a thorn in the side of the regime. The presence of all manner of groups from the 'Swing Youth' and the 'Edelweiss Pirates' to the White Rose opposition movement was a constant and painful reminder to the Nazis of how limited their power was.[12] Once again the conclusion is drawn that the image of a regime exercising anything like unconstrained power over society is quite misleading and only hampers efforts to reveal the true nature of the relationship between regime and people.

Critics of the totalitarian model when applied to the Soviet system are just as scathing. Again research appears to show the existence of competition amongst elites within the Soviet hierarchy, and how the power of the leader was diluted by the fief-like structure of the Soviet apparatus. Like Hitler Stalin was not, therefore, an omnipotent leader, but had to operate within the constraints imposed by the system, constraints imposed as much in this case by the size and diversity of the country, as by other centres of authority. Although the study of everyday life in Stalin's Russia is not as developed as it is for Germany, not least because of the Soviet police's comparative lack of rigour or concern with collecting information concerning public opinion, indications are that the Soviet regime faced similar difficulties in attempting to control the actions, never mind the thoughts and opinions, of ordinary people. On the other hand, it is also becoming clear that as with the Third Reich Western theorists of the totalitarian school have seriously underestimated the degree of support for the regime, preferring instead to read into displays of loyalty signs of the success of indoctrination. Once again, therefore, the totalitarian model is held up as inadequate for coming to terms with the complexity of the Soviet system.[13]

As we have already noted these criticisms are more than justified when applied to the strong model. We agreed that the image of a leader wielding absolute power not merely over a defenceless people but over a prostrated political apparatus is one that fails to get close to the reality of the situation in either Nazi Germany or the Soviet Union. Furthermore, we went beyond these criticisms to argue that the model was not merely historically inaccurate, but internally flawed as an account of domination because it does not give us the means to distinguish between situations in which domination is real and when it is merely apparent. However, our claim is that these objections do not have the same impact when made against a weaker model of the sort we have been discussing. To begin with, the model does not present the relationship between the people and the regime as one based on the *achievement* of total power. Indeed theorists such as Havel and Kolakowski argue that it is inconceivable to imagine a regime ever attaining total power due to various factors, not the least of which is the difficulty of controlling individual experience and behaviour. What they are interested in is the *desire to achieve* total power, not its final realisation. Thus for them the hallmark of the totalitarian regime is that it *attempts* to gain control over people without ever succeeding. Neither do such theorists stress the centrality of the leader within the hierarchy as do defenders of the strong model. Indeed the whole issue of the relations within the regime, relations between the various offices and branches of the state is regarded as being of secondary importance, and they have a point. Just as there are different ways of organising democratic states (for example on unitary or federal lines), so there are different ways of organising totalitarian states. What is important according to this account is not the nature of the institutions and structures comprising the regime, but the nature of the regime itself. With this consideration in mind it is difficult to argue that the practices of Nazi Germany were greatly different to the practices of the Soviet Union, particularly under Stalin. They both attempted to outlaw opposition and dissent; they both attempted to instil in their respective populations approved values and norms; they both monopolised the media; they both made the system of justice an extension of the will of the state, if not of the leader; they both regulated the field of artistic and literary production to an unprecedented degree. Put in these terms, that is, concentrating on the nature of rule, the way in which rule is exercised, it becomes difficult to deny the applicability of the weak model. Can we really be so impressed, after all, by the undoubted differences between these systems that we are going to allow this to obliterate the obvious similarities between them?

When it comes to assessing other periods of communist rule in the Soviet Union and indeed other communist systems there seems little reason to suggest that the weak model of totalitarian rule is any more inappropriate. Despite the growing stability and apparent legitimacy of the Soviet Union after the death of Stalin, we have every reason, as Kolakowski and numerous others long argued, to be sceptical about the claim that this stability was based either on the successful brainwashing of millions of 'defenceless citizens' *or* on the emergence of a genuine social contract bestowing the approval of the masses on the regime. The fact remains that at no point in its development did the Soviet state allow the people to have a say in whether they wanted to be ruled by the Communist Party. Single candidate elections were the norm until the dissolution of the Soviet state and all candidates were either nominated directly by the Party or had to be approved by them. There remained strict censorship of the press and of all other media; the schools and colleges retained their primary role as importers of the communist way of life; dissidents were still hounded, victimised and often jailed. A vast police state was maintained in order to intimidate people into complying with whatever they were told to do. People were prevented from travelling freely even within the confines of their own country. Do we really want to say that a shift of a fundamental nature took place after Stalin's death? There are strong reasons to suggest that we should not. Life might not have been quite so fraught with danger for the average Soviet citizen, and there might not have been quite the numbers of people in fear of their lives as there were under Stalin. However, it is difficult to deny that many of the characteristics of that period remained in evidence. Given that the situation in the other communist countries was and remains, if anything, even more unpleasant than it was in the Soviet Union, we can without a great deal of hesitation regard the communist systems that existed and still exist in countries such as North Korea, Ethiopia, Albania, East Germany, Vietnam, and Rumania as essentially totalitarian in character.

More difficult is the question of judging whether states such as the Islamic republics can be considered in the same terms. The problem here is that we are discussing states in which the governing 'ideology', namely the Muslim religion, is clearly not one that has been imposed on the people, but is rather the indigenous faith of the vast majority of the population. There appears therefore to be little parallel between these states and many of the systems we have been discussing in which it is all too obvious that values and norms are being forced upon at best an antipathetic audience. Furthermore, those sympathetic with Islamic states would want to point out that, for example, the Iranian republic was created by what was arguably a popular revolution rather than by *coup d'état*. They would also point to the establishment of people's councils and other such institutions as evidence of the regime's commitment to involving ordinary people in the processes of government. For sympathetic commentators the emergence of such republics represents a return to an authentically Islamic way of life thereby satisfying the needs of what are essentially Muslim populations. These states are in a sense restoring the nation to its proper state of affairs after the meddling of colonial powers and petty dictators such as the Shah.

There is no doubt considerable truth in these suggestions. It is indeed difficult to contradict the basic premise that far from imposing an ideology on an unwilling audience these regimes propound norms and values that are adhered to by most of the people. Yet it is difficult to ignore the fact that in an important sense the practices of these states mirror those of the states we have been discussing. Although it appears safe to say that these regimes are legitimate in the sense of being recognised by most people as having a right to rule, the manner in which dissidents and critics are treated by the regime parallels closely the practices of totalitarian states. The reality is that opponents, dissidents and even ordinary people who have for some reason flouted a particular law face the same threats and dangers that opponents did in communist states and in Nazi Germany. Public execution is, by all accounts, commonplace, as is the exiling or jailing of those with suspect views. Furthermore the monopolistic element associated with totalitarian rule is present here as well. Every possible agency of socialisation is closely controlled as is the press, the television and every other organ of opinion. More generally, an atmosphere of intolerance pervades society making the lives of those who may not be convinced of the benefits of Islam, for example the many women who took advantage of the greater liberty of former times to express themselves, develop careers and wear Western clothes, to feel oppressed. Of course we do not hear much about such people for exactly the same reasons as we did not hear much about the opinions of Germans living under the Nazis or those living under the communists. When the penalty for challenging norms and values is so high we should not be surprised that people choose to conform. As Havel argues, the appearance of stability and consensus may hide as much as it reveals about relations between state and society. To be clear, we are not saying that Islam is a totalitarian ideology or even that it is has despotic tendencies contained within it. What we are saying is that a system can be totalitarian or despotic even when as in the Islamic states the vast majority of people hold the values and norms being propagated by the state as legitimate or 'true'. That a large number of people support the murderous policies of a given regime does not surely change the nature of those murderous policies. It simply makes it easier for a regime to carry on performing them. It is after all much easier for people to perform crimes if it appears that they meet with general approval. However, the fact that a crime is committed and witnessed *en masse* does not in general make it any less of a crime.

Does this discussion not show, however, that the totalitarian model being discussed here is little more than the projection of liberal values on to the rest of the world? Are we not merely holding up 'our' comfortable, Western world view as inherently superior to all others? Are we not in danger of ideological imperialism, writing off different systems and regimes because they do not conform to some Platonic idea of liberal-democracy? This is of course a criticism that has often been made and one that has a certain validity given the use to which the concept was put during the Cold War. Nevertheless it seems as pointless to write off the concept of totalitarianism as it is write off the concept of democracy. We are not claiming that any particular set of values or any ideology is necessarily superior to any others. Nor are we saying that any values are necessarily more likely to lead to totalitarianism than any other. After all even liberals, those who arguably should be most sceptical about claims to have found the Truth or the perfect society, are capable of intolerance and hence of instituting the type of practices we have been describing as totalitarian. We only have to remind ourselves that McCarthyism, a totalitarian 'movement' par excellence, arose in the United States. As Arendt justifiably warns, all ideologies have the potential to become weapons in the hands of the intolerant because all ideologies hold up their view of the world, their account of human nature or needs, as superior to all others. Our concern is not with values, but with the practices of governments, with what regimes do to and with their people. Frederic Fleron is therefore quite right in arguing that the term 'totalitarian' is a 'boo' word to describe 'boo' regimes; but it is difficult to see why for example we cannot criticise the term 'dictatorship' on the same grounds given that most of us would not like to live in such a system and pity those who do. There is no escaping, in other words, the connection between the words we use to describe particular systems and the emotions we have about them. It is a fact of life that the word 'democracy' is a 'hooray' word because most of us appreciate living in democracies; but should we abandon use of the word because it is charged with this type of meaning? Should we attempt to eliminate or at least avoid all those words that have such connotations? It is right to point out that we are treading on the toes of those who see all political systems, all values, all ways of living as equally valid. It is correct to say that in calling systems totalitarian we in effect condemn them. However, what is curious is that at the end of a century in which states have made it official policy to burn people in ovens, to condemn whole races and peoples to death, to rob and loot on a mass scale we should be worried that in the process of describing regimes we find ourselves judging them at the same time.

*

To sum up this chapter, we have found that despite significant differences between the way in which theorists have defined and applied the concept of totalitarianism it is possible to discern the outline of two conflicting models of totalitarian rule. The first model, which we labelled the 'strong', stresses that the innovation or 'novelty' of totalitarian rule rests in the achievement of total domination or total control by a regime over a given population. Unlike conventional or traditional dictatorships totalitarian systems are thus largely stable systems in which the regime enjoys the apparent consent of the people. However, this consent is merely illusory, resting as it does on the continual brainwashing of the people and the monopolisation of all sources of information or education. Thus although the perfected totalitarian system appears legitimate it rests on the continuous domination of all those subject to its rule. The success of these regimes thus rests on harnessing modern techniques of control and surveillance to manufacture an obedient citizen whose values and beliefs mirror those of the ruling elite. Having outlined the strong model we then argued that the model suffers from a significant weakness which is that the account of domination contained within the model is circular. In arguing that the emergence of consent in these systems is the product of the regime's attempts to brainwash the population the model adopts a form of explanation that, whilst immune against refutation, is at the same time impossible to verify.

The weak model, on the other hand, concentrates on the practices of rule rather than its effects. It stresses the actions of the regime, what the regime does as opposed to the degree of control it is able to wield. Similarity between ideologies is considered less important than similarity in actions and practices. All totalitarian regimes make as it were a 'total claim' on those subject to them; they all demand a particular mode of behaviour from their citizens, and a uniformity of beliefs, values and norms. Whether this amounts to the enforcement of an ideology, in other words a clearly mapped out ideal of behaviour and outlook, is less important than the evident commitment to undermining the autonomy or freedom of action of the individual. It is this claim that lies behind the importance of establishing a monopoly on the process of socialisation and the media for the dissemination of opinion. It is also this desire for control that lies behind the clamping down of all opposition and all dissidence, actual or potential. Totalitarian regimes crave omnipotence and the recognition of their infallibility. Thus any views contrary to their own must be controlled or quashed. The emphasis in the weak model is thus on the practice of rule, rather than the formal operation of power or the nature of specific ideologies. What is stressed is the existence of a gap between the ambition to achieve uniformity and the reality of discordance and pluralism. It is this gap that accounts for the use of force in such systems. Totalitarian dictators cannot tolerate the existence of those with different values and beliefs, different ideas and ambitions, and thus they resort to coercion to keep their hopes of uniformity alive. The continuing resort to repression is not therefore the sign of a failed totalitarianism, as Cranston and others claim. It is, rather, the *sine qua non* of totalitarian rule just as it is for any form of dictatorship.

Notes

1 Benjamin R. Barber, 'Conceptual Foundations of Totalitarianism', in *Totalitarianism in Perspective: Three Views*, edited by Carl J. Friedrich (London, 1969), pp. 3–39.

2 Fleron, 'Soviet Area Studies', p. 339.

3 *Totalitarian Dictatorship and Autocracy*, p. 145.

4 Maurice Cranston, 'Should we Cease to Speak of Totalitarianism?', *Survey*, 23, no. 3 (1977–78), p. 18.

5 Karl Dietrich Bracher, 'The Disputed Concept of Totalitarianism. Experience and Actuality', in *Totalitarianism Reconsidered*, edited by Ernest A. Menze (Port Washington, NY, 1981), p. 30.

6 Leszek Kolakowski and George Urban, 'The Devil in History: A Conversation', *Encounter*, 56, no. 1 (January 1981), p. 13.

7 Leszek Kolakowski, 'On Total Control and its Contradictions. The Power of Information', *Encounter*, 73, no. 2 (July/August 1989), p. 71.

8 Michael Walzer, 'On "Failed Totalitarianism"', in *1984 Revisited. Totalitarianism in Our Century*, edited by Irving Howe (New York, 1983), p. 133. For similar criticisms of the idea of totalitarianism as the realisation of 'total power' see, for example, John Keane's introduction to his edited volume *Civil Society and the State. New European Perspectives* (London, 1988). See also the article "Totalitarianism Revisited' by Jacques Rupnik in the same volume, and Robert Orr's 'Reflections on Totalitarianism, Leading to Reflections on Two Ways of Theorizing', *Political Studies*, 21 (1973), pp. 487–8.

9 Leszek Kolakowski, 'Totalitarianism and the Virtue of the Lie, in *1984 Revisited*, edited by Irving Howe, p. 133.

10 A similar conclusion is reached by, among others, T. H. Rigby who argues that the idea that we can meaningfully describe a given population as 'brainwashed' mirrors Marcuse's 'repressive tolerance' thesis, and as such 'is similarly vulnerable to charges of circular argument and unverifiability'. ' "Totalitarianism" and Change in Communist Systems', *Comparative Politics*, 4 (1972), p. 436. See also the criticisms of Robert Tucker in his article 'Does Big Brother Really Exist?', in *1984 Revisited*, edited by Irving Howe, pp. 92–4.

11 A good starting-point for these debates and observations is Ian Kershaw's *The Nazi Dictatorship. Problems and Perspectives of Inter-*

pretation (London, 1985). For more discussion see Jeremy Noakes, 'The Nazi Party and the Third Reich: The Myth and Reality of the One-Party State', in *Government, Party and People in Nazi Germany*, edited by Jeremy Noakes (Exeter, 1980), and Reinhard Mann, *Protest und Kontrolle im Dritten Reich* (New York, 1987). See also the interesting set of essays in Gerhard Hirschfeld and Lothar Kettenacker (eds), *The 'Führer State': Myth and Reality* (Stuttgart, 1981), particularly the essays by Tim Mason and Hans Mommsen.

12   There is now a very sizeable literature on public opinion in the Third Reich. Amongst the most useful studies are those by Ian Kershaw, see especially his *Popular Opinion and Dissent in the Third Reich. Bavaria 1933–1945* (Oxford, 1983), and the essays 'Popular Opinion in the Third Reich', in *Government, Party and People in Nazi Germany*, edited by Jeremy Noakes, and 'How Effective was Nazi Propaganda', in *Nazi Propaganda*, edited by D. Welch (London, 1983). See also the informative study by Detlev Peukert, *Inside Nazi Germany. Conformity, Opposition and Rascism in Everyday Life* (London, 1989), and the collection of essays in *Life in the Third Reich*, edited by Richard Bessel (Oxford, 1987).

13   For accounts of the Stalinist system that directly challenge the monolithic imagery of the totalitarian model see in particular Graeme Gill, *Stalinism* (London, 1990), and Gabor Rittersporn, 'Rethinking Stalinism', *Russian History*, 11, no. 4 (Winter 1984). For discussion on public opinion in the Soviet Union under Stalin see Rittersporn's article 'Soviet Politics in the 1930s: Rehabilitating Society', *Studies in Comparative Communism*, 14, no. 2 (Summer 1986). See also a special edition of *The Russian Review*, 45, no. 4 (1986) which contains a number of essays by those both hostile to and supportive of attempts to 'rehabilitate' Stalinist society, in particular those by Sheila Fitzpatrick, Stephen Cohen and Alfred Meyer. Fitzpatrick has written a number of studies examining the role of public opinion in the Soviet Union. Among the most useful are: 'Culture and Politics under Stalin: A Reappraisal', *Slavic Review*, 35, no. 2 (1976), 'Stalin and the Making of a New Elite, 1928–1939', *Slavic Review*, 38, no. 3 (1979), and 'The Russian Revolution and Social Stability: A Re-Examination of the Question of Social Support for the Soviet Regime in the 1920s and 1930s', *Politics and Society*, 13, no. 2 (1984).

Bibliography

Addison, Paul, *The Road to 1945. British Politics and the Second World War* (London, 1975).

Adler, Les K., and Thomas G. Peterson, 'Red Fascism; the Merger of Nazi Germany and Soviet Russia in the American Image of Totalitarianism, 1930s-1950s', *American Historical Review*, 75 (1970).

Adorno, Theodor W., and Max Horkheimer, *Dialectic of Enlightenment*, second edition, translated by John Cumming (London, 1986).

Allen, William S., 'Totalitarianism. The Concept and the Reality', in *Totalitarianism Reconsidered*, edited by Ernest A. Menze (London, 1981).

Arato, Andrew, 'The Budapest School and Actually Existing Socialism', *Theory and Society*, 16 (1987).

Arendt, Hannah, 'Totalitarian Terror', *Review of Politics*, 11 (1949).

——, 'Understanding and Politics', *Partisan Review*, 20 (1953).

——, 'Authority in the Twentieth Century', *Review of Politics*, 18 (1956).

——, *The Human Condition* (London, 1958).

——, 'Totalitarian Imperialism: Reflections on the Hungarian Revolution', *Journal of Politics*, 20 (1958).

——, 'The Cold War and the West', *Partisan Review*, 29 (1962).

——, *Eichmann in Jerusalem. A Report on the Banality of Evil*, revised and enlarged edition (Harmondsworth, 1965).

——, *On Revolution*, second edition (Harmondsworth, 1965).

——, *Men in Dark Times* (London, 1968).

——, *Crises of the Republic* (London, 1972).

——, *Between Past and Future. Eight Exercises in Political Thought*, enlarged edition (Harmondsworth, 1977).

——, *The Origins of Totalitarianism* (London, 1986).

Ayçoberry, Pierre, *The Nazi Question. An Essay on the Interpretations of National Socialism (1922–1975)*, translated by Robert Hurley (London, 1981).

Barber, Benjamin R., 'Conceptual Foundations of Totalitarianism', in

Totalitarianism in Perspective: Three Views, edited by Carl J. Friedrich (London, 1969).

Barber, Benjamin and Herbert J. Spiro, 'Counter-Ideological Uses of "Totalitarianism"', *Politics and Society*, 1 (1970).

Barry, Norman P., 'Is There a Road to Serfdom?', *Government and Opposition*, 19 (1984).

Bell, Daniel, *The Coming of Post-Industrial Society* (New York, 1973).

Bernstein, Richard J., 'Negativity: Theme and Variations', in *Marcuse. Critical Theory and the Promise of Utopia*, edited by R. Pippen, A. Feenberg and C. P. Webel (London, 1988).

Besançon, Alain, and George Urban, 'Language and Power in Soviet Society', *Encounter*, 68, no. 5 (May 1989).

Bessel, Richard (ed.), *Life in the Third Reich* (Oxford, 1987).

Bracher, Karl-Dietrich, 'The Disputed Concept of Totalitarianism. Experience and Actuality', in *Totalitarianism Reconsidered*, edited by Ernest A. Menze (London, 1981).

Broszat, Martin, *The Hitler State*, translated by J. W. Hiden (London 1981).

Brown, Archie, 'Political Power and the Soviet State: Western and Soviet Perspectives', in *The State in Socialist Society*, edited by Neil Harding (London, 1984).

Bunce, Valerie, and John M. Echols III, 'From Soviet Studies to Comparative Politics: The Unfinished Revolution', *Soviet Studies*, 31 (1979).

Burrowes, Robert, 'The Revised Standard Edition', *World Politics*, 21, no. 2 (January 1969).

Canovan, Margaret, *The Political Thought of Hannah Arendt* (London, 1974).

Cohen, Stephen F., *Rethinking the Soviet Experience: Politics and History Since 1917* (New York, 1975).

——, 'Bolshevism and Stalinism', in *Stalinism. Essays in Historical Interpretation*, edited by Robert C. Tucker (New York, 1977).

——, 'Stalin's Terror as Social History', *The Russian Review*, 45, no. 4 (1986).

Connerton, Paul, *The Tragedy of Enlightenment. An Essay on the Frankfurt School* (Cambridge, 1980).

Cranston, Maurice, 'Should We Cease to Speak of Totalitarianism?', *Survey*, 23, no. 3 (Summer 1977–78).

Crick, Bernard, 'On Rereading The Origins of Totalitarianism', *Social Research*, no. 44 (1977).

Curtis, Michael, 'Retreat from Totalitarianism', in *Totalitarianism in Perspective: Three Views*, edited by Carl J. Friedrich (London, 1969).

Dukes, Paul, and John W. Hiden, 'Towards an Historical Comparison of Nazi Germany and Soviet Russia in the 1930s', *New Zealand Slavonic Journal*, no. 1 (1979).

Eley, Geoff, 'History with the Politics Left Out – Again?', *The Russian*

Review, 45, no. 4 (1986).

Fainsod, M., How Russia is Ruled (Oxford, 1963).

Fehér, Ferenc, 'The Dictatorship over Needs', Telos, no. 35 (Spring 1978).

——, Agnes Heller, and György Márkus, The Dictatorship over Needs. An Analysis of Soviet Societies (Oxford, 1986).

Fitzpatrick, Sheila, 'Culture and Politics under Stalin: A Reappraisal', Slavic Review, 35, no. 2 (1976).

——, 'Stalin and the Making of a New Elite, 1928–1939', Slavic Review, 38, no. 3 (1979).

——, 'The Russian Revolution and Social Stability: A Re-Examination of the Question of Social Support for the Soviet Regime in the 1920s and 1930s', Politics and Society, 13, no. 2 (1984).

——, 'New Perspectives on Stalinism', The Russian Review, 45, no. 4 (1986).

Fleron, Frederic J., 'Soviet Area Studies and the Social Sciences: Some Methodological Problems in Communist Studies', Soviet Studies, 19 (1968).

Friedrich, Carl J., The New Image of the Common Man (Boston, Mass., 1950).

——, Constitutional Government and Democracy. Theory and Practice in Europe and America, revised edition (New York, 1950).

——, 'The Unique Character of Totalitarian Societies', in Totalitarianism. Proceedings of a Conference Held at the American Academy of Arts and Sciences, 1953, edited by Carl J. Friedrich (Cambridge, Mass., 1954).

——, 'The Problem of Totalitarianism – An Introduction', in Totalitarianism. Proceedings of a Conference Held at the American Academy of Arts and Sciences, 1953, edited by Carl J. Friedrich (Cambridge, Mass., 1954).

——, 'Political Philosophy and the Science of Politics', in Approaches to the Study of Politics, edited by R. A. Young (London, 1958).

——, 'Political Leadership and the Problem of Charismatic Power', Journal of Politics, 23 (1961).

——, Man and His Government (New York, 1963).

——, 'Totalitarianism: Recent Trends', Problems of Communism, 17, no. 3 (1967).

——, An Introduction to Political Theory (New York, 1967).

——, 'The Evolving Theory and Practice of Totalitarianism', in Totalitarianism in Perspective: Three Views, edited by Carl J. Friedrich (London, 1969).

——, 'The Theory of Political Leadership and the Issue of Totalitarianism', in Political Leadership in Eastern Europe and the Soviet Union, edited by B. R. Farrell (Chicago, 1970).

——, 'In Defence of a Concept', in Political Opposition in One-Party States, edited by Leonard Schapiro (London, 1972).

——, *Tradition and Authority* (London, 1972).

——, and Zbigniew Brzezinski, *Totalitarian Dictatorship and Autocracy* (London, 1954). (The second expanded edition revised by Friedrich was published in Cambridge, Mass., 1965).

Fry, John, *Marcuse. Dilemma and Liberation, A Critical Analysis* (Stockholm, 1974).

Fukuyama, Francis, *The End of History and the Last Man* (London, 1992).

Gill, Graeme, *Stalinism* (London, 1990).

Gleason, Abbott, ' "Totalitarianism" in 1984', *Russian Review*, 43 (1984).

Greiffenhagen, Martin, 'The Concept of Totalitarianism in Political Theory', in *Totalitarianism Reconsidered*, edited by Ernest A. Menze (London, 1981).

Gross, Jan T., 'A Note on the Nature of Soviet Totalitarianism', *Soviet Studies*, 34 (1982).

Hardach, Karl, *The Political Economy of Germany in the Twentieth Century* (London, 1980).

Havel, Václav, 'The Power of the Powerless', in Václav Havel *et al., The Power of the Powerless*, edited by John Keane (London, 1985).

——, *Disturbing the Peace*, translated by Paul Wilson (London, 1990).

Hayek, F. A., *The Road to Serfdom* (London, 1986) (first published in 1944).

——, *The Constitution of Liberty* (London, 1960).

——, *The Fatal Conceit. The Errors of Socialism*, edited by W. W. Bartley III (London, 1988).

Held, David, *Introduction to Critical Theory* (London, 1980).

Heller, Agnes, 'An Imaginary Preface to the 1984 Edition of Hannah Arendt's The Origins of Totalitarianism', in *Western Left, Eastern Left. Totalitarianism, Freedom and Democracy*, edited by Ferenc Fehér and Agnes Heller (Cambridge, 1987).

Hennessy, Peter, *Never Again. Britain 1945–51* (London, 1993).

Hiden, John and John Farquarson, *Explaining Hitler's Germany. Historians and the Third Reich* (London, 1983).

Hirschfeld, Gerhard and Lothar Kettenacker (eds), *The 'Führer State': Myth and Reality. Studies on the Structure and Politics of the Third Reich* (Stuttgart, 1981).

Hitler, A., *Mein Kampf*, edited by D. C. Watt (London, 1969).

Hough, J. F. and M. Fainsod, *How the Soviet Union is Governed* (Cambridge, Mass., 1979).

Jay, Martin, *The Dialectical Imagination. A History of the Frankfurt School and the Institute for Social Research* (London, 1973).

Kassof, Allen, 'The Administered Society: Totalitarianism Without Terror', in *Communist Studies and the Social Sciences: Essays on Methodology and Empirical Theory* (Chicago, 1969).

Kateb, George, *Hannah Arendt. Politics, Conscience, Evil* (Oxford, 1983).

Keane, John, 'Introduction', in *Civil Society and the State. New European Perspectives*, edited by John Keane (London, 1988).

Kellner, Douglas, 'Schoolman on Marcuse', *New German Critique*, no. 26 (Spring/Summer 1982).

——, *Herbert Marcuse and the Crisis of Marxism* (London, 1984).

——, 'Herbert Marcuse's Reconstruction of Marxism', in *Marcuse. Critical Theory and the Promise of Utopia*, edited by R. Pippen, A. Feenberg and C. P. Webel (London, 1988).

Kershaw, Ian, *Popular Opinion and Dissent in the Third Reich. Bavaria 1933–1945* (Oxford, 1983).

——, 'How Effective was Nazi Propaganda?', in *Nazi Propaganda*, edited by D. Welch (London, 1983).

——, *The Nazi Dictatorship. Problems and Perspectives of Interpretation* (London, 1985).

Kirkpatrick, Jeane and George Urban, 'American Foreign Policy in a Cold Climate. A Long Conversation', *Encounter*, 61, no. 3 (November 1983).

Kitchen, Martin, *Fascism* (London, 1976).

Kleinberger, Ahron F., 'Is "Totalitarian Education" a Significant Conceptual Framework for Comparative Research?', *Compare*, 11, no. 2 (1981).

Koestler, Arthur, *Darkness at Noon* (London, 1985).

Kolakowski, Leszek, *Marxism and Beyond* (London, 1971).

——, *Main Currents of Marxism*, 3 vols. (Oxford, 1978).

——, 'Totalitarianism and the Virtue of the Lie', in *1984 Revisited. Totalitarianism in Our Century*, edited by Irving Howe (New York, 1983).

——, 'On Total Control and its Contradictions. The Power of Information', *Encounter*, 73, no. 2 (July/August 1989).

——, and George Urban, 'The Devil in History: A Conversation', *Encounter*, 56, no. 1 (January 1981).

Kontos, Alkis, 'Through a Glass Darkly, Ontology and False Needs', *The Canadian Journal of Political and Social Theory*, 3, no. 1 (Winter 1979).

Krancberg, Sigmund, '1984 – The Totalitarian Model Revisited', *Studies in Soviet Thought*, 29, no. 1 (January 1985).

Lacquer, Walter, 'Is There Now, or Has There Ever Been Such a Thing as Totalitarianism?', *Commentary*, 80, no. 4 (October 1985).

Lenin, V. I., *The State and Revolution* (Moscow, 1977).

Lewin, Moshe, 'The Social Background to Stalinism', in *Stalinism. Essays in Historical Interpretation*, edited by Robert C. Tucker (New York, 1977).

Lowenthal, Richard, 'Beyond Totalitarianism?', in *1984 Revisited. Totalitarianism in Our Century*, edited by Irving Howe (New York, 1983).

MacIntyre, Alastair, *Marcuse* (London, 1970).

Mann, Reinhard, *Protest und Kontrolle in Dritten Reich. National-Sozialistische Herrschaft im Alltag Einer Rheinischen Grusstadt* (New

York, 1987).

Marcuse, Herbert, *Reason and Revolution. Hegel and the Rise of Social Theory*, second edition (London, 1955).

——, *Soviet Marxism. A Critical Analysis* (London, 1958).

——, *Eros and Civilization. A Philosophical Enquiry into Freud* (Boston, Mass., 1966).

——, *One Dimensional Man. The Ideology of Industrial Society* (London, 1968) [Sphere Books edition].

——, *An Essay on Liberation* (London, 1969).

——, *Five Lectures. Psychoanalysis, Politics and Utopia* (London, 1970).

——, *Counterrevolution and Revolt* (London, 1972).

——, 'Some Social Implications of Modern Technology', in *The Essential Frankfurt School Reader*, edited by Andrew Arato and Eike Gebhardt (Oxford, 1978).

Marwick, Arthur, *Britain in the Century of Total Wars: War, Peace and Social Change, 1900–1967* (London, 1968).

Marx, K., *The German Ideology* (London, 1974).

Mattick, Paul, *Critique of Marcuse. One Dimensional Man in Class Society* (London, 1972).

Millward, Alan, *War, Economy and Society, 1939–45* (London, 1977).

Morgenthau, Hans J., 'Hannah Arendt on Totalitarianism and Democracy', *Social Research*, 44 (Spring 1977).

Nelson, John S., 'Politics and Truth: Arendt's Problematic', *American Journal of Political Science*, 22 (1978).

Noakes, Jeremy (ed.), *Government, Party and People in Nazi Germany* (Exeter, 1980).

Nove, Alec, *An Economic History of the USSR*, second edition (London, 1989).

——, *The Economics of Feasible Socialism* (London, 1983).

O'Brien, Patrick J., 'On the Adequacy of the Concept of Totalitarianism', *Studies in Comparative Communism*, 3, no. 1 (January 1970).

O'Sullivan, Noel K., 'Politics, Totalitarianism and Freedom. The Political Thought of Hannah Arendt', *Political Studies*, 21 (June 1973).

Offe, Claus, 'Technology and One Dimensionality: A Version of the Technocracy Thesis', translated by A. Feenberg, in *Marcuse. Critical Theory and the Promise of Utopia*, edited by R. Pippen, A. Feenberg and C. P. Webel (London, 1988).

Orr, Robert, 'Reflections on Totalitarianism, Leading to Reflections on Two Ways of Theorizing', *Political Studies*, 21, no. 4 (1973).

Orwell, George, *Nineteen Eighty-Four* (London, 1977).

Peukert, Detlev J. K., *Inside Nazi Germany. Conformity, Opposition and Rascism in Everyday Life* (London, 1989).

Pirsch, Hans, 'Wiederbelebung der Totalitarismusdoktrin', *IPW Berichte*, no. 2 (February 1983).

Popper, Karl, *The Open Society and its Enemies*, fifth edition, 2 vols. (London, 1966).

Reichmann, Henry, 'Reconsidering "Stalinism"', *Theory and Society*, 17 (1988).

Rigby, T. H., '"Totalitarianism" and Change in Communist Systems', *Comparative Politics*, 4 (1972).

Rittersporn, Gabor T., 'Rethinking Stalinism', *Russian History*, 11, no. 4 (Winter 1984).

——, 'Soviet Politics in the 1930s: Rehabilitating Society', *Studies in Comparative Communism*, 14, no. 2 (Summer 1986).

Rupnik, Jacques, 'Totalitarianism Revisited', in *Civil Society and the State, New European Perspectives*, edited by John Keane (London, 1988).

Sauer, Wolfgang, 'National Socialism: Totalitarianism or Fascism?', *American Historical Review*, 43, no. 2 (December 1967).

Schapiro, Leonard, 'Reflections on the Changing Role of the Party in the Totalitarian Polity', *Studies in Comparative Communism*, 2, no. 2 (April 1969).

——, 'The Concept of Totalitarianism', *Survey*, no. 73 (1969).

——, 'Totalitarianism in the Doghouse', *Government and Opposition*, 6 (1971).

——, *Totalitarianism* (London, 1972).

——, 'Totalitarianism in Foreign Policy', in *The Soviet Union in World Politics*, edited by Kurt London (London, 1980).

Schoenbaum, David, *Hitler's Social Revolution. Class and Status in Nazi Germany 1933–1939* (London, 1967).

Schoolman, Morton, *The Imaginary Witness. The Critical Theory of Herbert Marcuse* (New York, 1980).

Serge, Victor, *Memoirs of a Revolutionary*, translated by Peter Sedgewick (London, 1984).

Seton-Watson, Hugh, 'On Totalitarianism', *Government and Opposition*, 2 (1966–67).

Shreir, Sally, 'Marxist Totalitarianism: Inheritance or Heresy?', *Salisbury Review*, 3, no. 4 (July 1985).

Spiro, Herbert J., 'Totalitarianism', in *The Encyclopaedia of the Social Sciences*, second editon (New York, 1968).

Tarschys, Daniel, 'The Soviet Political System: Three Models', *European Journal of Political Research*, 5 (1977).

Terrill, Ross, 'Problems in Applying the Theory of Totalitarianism to the USSR', *Politics. The Journal of the Australasian Political Studies Association*, 3, no. 1 (May 1968).

Therborn, Göran, 'The Frankfurt School', *New Left Review*, no. 63 (September/October 1970).

Tormey, Simon, 'Presuppositions of Theories of Totalitarianism: A Critical Examination', unpublished Ph.D. thesis (University College, Swansea,

1991).

Trotsky, Leon, *The Revolution Betrayed. What is the Soviet Union and Where is it Going?*, fifth edition, translated by Max Eastman (New York, 1972).

Tucker, Robert C., 'Does Big Brother Really Exist?', in *1984 Revisited. Totalitarianism in Our Century*, edited by Irving Howe (New York, 1983).

Walzer, Michael, 'On "Failed Totalitarianism"', in *1984 Revisited. Totalitarianism in Our Century*, edited by Irving Howe (New York, 1983).

Welch, William, 'Totalitarianism: The Standard Critique Revisited', *Rocky Mountain Social Science Journal*, 10, no. 2 (April 1973).

Wellmer, Albrecht, 'Reason, Utopia, and the Dialectic of Enlightenment', in *Habermas and Modernity*, edited by Richard J. Bernstein (Cambridge, 1985).

White, Stephen, 'Political Science as Ideology: The Study of Soviet Politics', in *W. J. M. M. Political Questions. Essays in Honour of W. J. M. MacKenzie*, edited by B. Chapman and A. Potter (Manchester, 1974).

——, 'Communist Systems and the "Iron Law of Pluralism"', *British Journal of Political Science*, 8 (1978).

Whitfield, Stephen J., *Into the Dark: Hannah Arendt and Totalitarianism* (Philadelphia, 1980).

Wolfe, Bertram D., *Communist Totalitarianism – Keys to the Soviet System* (London, 1956).

Index

Numbers in italics indicate main page references.